Praise for David Kuo's *Tempting Faith*

"The very fact that it took David Kuo's book *Tempting Faith: An Inside Story of Political Seduction* to put President Bush's faith-based initiative back into the news proves that the author's thesis is right. . . . Exposés of hypocrisy are the mother's milk of Washington journalism. Yet the most useful thing that could flow from Kuo's revelations would not be a splashy exchange of charges and countercharges but rather a quiet reappraisal by rank-and-file evangelicals of their approach to politics. . . . When Kuo says there's something wrong with 'taking Jesus and reducing him to some precinct captain, to some get-out-the-vote guy,' he sounds a trumpet that makes you want to follow him into the battle."
—E. J. Dionne, *The Washington Post*

"We hope this explosive new book causes many church members to realize they have been exploited for politics."
—*The Charleston Gazette*

"Early Monday morning, a tell-all book from a former Bush White House official hit Washington like a small explosion, generating at least a Color Orange political threat level."
—Amy Sullivan, *The New Republic*

"Should be required reading for evangelical conservatives."
—*The Wall Street Journal*

"Kuo's new book *Tempting Faith: An Inside Story of Political Seduction* has some current and former White House operatives busily rewriting history. . . . Kuo offers a damning indictment, both of those religious leaders so willing to be used and those who used them."

—*National Catholic Reporter*

"As former White House staffer David Kuo points out in his new book *Tempting Faith,* the dirtiest Republican trick of all is their pretense to care about evangelical Christians and their issues when in fact they have contempt for them."

—*The Nation*

"Explosive."

—*The Christian Science Monitor*

"An acute warning of the dangers that evangelicals pose to democracy."

—*The New Republic,* cover story

"Trouble comes when we mix church with state, which is far different from mixing religion with politics. And according to David Kuo, this is where the Republican Party has gone astray."

—*Pittsburgh Tribune-Review*

"Though *Tempting Faith* (Free Press) is a story about the Bush presidency, it is even more a story about Mr. Kuo. As much as it is a story about politics, it is also a story about faith. . . . Mr. Kuo is forthright about his own love of Jesus, and he never questions the president's. But he does recognize the temptation this poses for evangelicals like himself—of substituting for Jesus, whom 'you can't see,' someone else identified with him and ready at hand."

—*The New York Times*

"The great merit of the Kuo account is that it shows how even the prospect of government money had a strangely corrupting effect on many Christian Right leaders. He further shows how the original agenda of the Bush administration kept getting pushed aside in favor of other political priorities. The evangelicals were being used, he argues, and then dumped once their usefulness was assured."

—*The Detroit News*

"Kuo's narrative sheds disturbing light on the insularity of partisan politics and the dangers of ideological enclaves. . . . Kuo is right to warn Christians about the dangerous lures of politics . . . perchance Kuo's book and the controversy it stirs will help turn Christians away from the temptation to place their primary confidence in politics as God's path to cultural restoration."

—*Christianity Today*

"David Kuo's *Tempting Faith: An Inside Story of Political Seduction* is the rare political tell-all that is actually better than its prerelease quotes suggest. . . . Kuo comes off as a sincere believer . . . a jilted lover. But not a spiteful one."

—*The Christian Century*

"If you are an evangelical Christian, you need to put this book at the top of your reading list . . . [an] extraordinary book."

—*Tucson Citizen*

ALSO BY DAVID KUO

Dot.Bomb:
My Days and Nights at an Internet Goliath

TEMPTING
FAITH

An Inside Story of Political Seduction

David Kuo

FREE PRESS
New York   London   Toronto   Sydney

FREE PRESS
A Division of Simon & Schuster, Inc.
1230 Avenue of the Americas
New York, NY 10020

First Free Press trade paperback edition October 2007

FREE PRESS and colophon are trademarks of Simon & Schuster, Inc.

For information about special discounts for bulk purchases,
please contact Simon & Schuster Special Sales at
1-800-456-6798 or business@simonandschuster.com.

Manufactured in the United States of America

10   9   8   7   6   5   4   3   2   1

The Library of Congress has catalogued the hardcover edition as follows:
Kuo, David
Tempting faith: an inside story of political seduction / David Kuo.
p.   cm.
Includes index.
1. Kuo, J. David, 1968–.   2. Church and state—United States.   3. Christianity and
politics—United States.   4. Religious right—United States.   5. Christian
conservatism—United States.   6. Presidents—United States—Staff.   7. United
States—Politics and government—2001–.   I. Title.
BR516 .K86   2006
973.931092[B]—dc22   2006046810
ISBN-13: 978-0-7432-8712-8
ISBN-10:   0-7432-8712-6
ISBN-13: 978-0-7432-8713-5 (pbk)
ISBN-10:   0-7432-8713-4 (pbk)

This book is dedicated to Laura, Rachel, Olivia, and Aidan

And as with everything, it is for Kim

If individuals live only seventy years, then a state, or a nation, or a civilisation, which may last for a thousand years, is more important than an individual. But if Christianity is true, then the individual is not only more important, but incomparably more important, for he is everlasting and the life of a state or a civilisation, compared with his, is only a moment.

—C. S. LEWIS, *Mere Christianity*

CONTENTS

PROLOGUE

I shouldn't be alive right now. Early Palm Sunday morning in 2003 I had a seizure, causing my whole body to go rigid and, in the process, my right foot to slam down on the accelerator and me to black out while driving my SUV down a winding parkway in Washington, D.C. By God's mercy, and my wife's quick reflexes, the crash didn't kill us.

A few hours later I was diagnosed with a very bad brain tumor that the doctors said would soon do the job. Kim mobilized about 3.35 percent of the country in prayer. By the next day the tumor appeared to be more benign than malignant. Ten days later, the doctors took out everything tumor-related they could find—and pronounced me not cured. I would have to be regularly monitored for the rest of my life. No one could tell me just how long that might be.

Hearing the words "brain tumor" in proximity to the words "you have a" clarifies things. Parking tickets, the size (or lack thereof) of my biceps, and even what others might think of me no longer concern me much. My wife, my daughters, how I treat others, and how I live before God concern me greatly.

That's why I decided to write this book.

Ever since my college years, I have been in the middle of the contentious world where conservative Christian faith and politics collide. It wasn't one I initially sought out. But it became my world and I fought its fights alongside men who would become dear friends, and with one president. I have thrown golf clubs with Ralph Reed and speared fish with John Ashcroft. I have eaten epic meals with Bill Bennett. George W. Bush whipped me silly in a private running race. From 1989 until I joined the Bush White House in 2001, I longed for the day the right political leaders would arrive, govern morally, eloquently profess their Christian faith, and return America to greatness. Most of our problems could be solved politically, I believed.

Now I know better. I have seen what happens when well-meaning Christians are seduced into thinking deliverance can come from the Oval Office, a Supreme Court chamber, or the floor of the United States Congress. They are easily manipulated by politicians who use them for their votes, seduced by trinkets of power, and tempted to turn a mission field (politics) into a battle-field, leaving the impression Jesus' main goal was advancing a particular policy agenda. I know: I've seen it, I've done it, I've lived it, and I've learned from it.

I met Jesus in high school, and for me there is no life without him. I became a conservative in college, and soon fused the two. When I arrived in Washington in 1990, it just so happened that the newest movement of religious conservative political activism was emerging.

In Chesapeake, Virginia, there was a brand-new organization called the Christian Coalition. Across town, the Family Research Council was eighteen months old. During my time in Washington these groups would go from "wanting a seat at the table" to sitting at the head of that table as the single most important political constituency in America since the height of the labor movement in the 1950s.

I grew up, politically, as the movement matured. We all mourned President George H. W. Bush's loss to a certain Arkansas governor. We celebrated the "Republican Revolution." We mourned Bob Dole's loss to that same man from Arkansas. We wildly celebrated George W. Bush's election, because we knew he was one of us.

In the process, however, we were all tempted to lose our priorities. Our faith's mandate was clear: God was to be first, our families were to be second, and our work was to be third. I regularly got the order wrong, putting politics first and second and relegating God and family to the third spot. Many of us did.

That includes many of us in George W. Bush's White House. There I saw the healthy clash between faith and politics resolved as faith submitted itself to a political throne. I watched as George W. Bush's "compassionate conservatism" that promised to "restore hope for all Americans" was repeatedly stiff-armed by his own White House staff, and then preened to look good for the religiously inclined and for "nontraditional" (black and Hispanic) Republican voters. I heard the mocking of religious conservative leaders by that staff. I learned that votes were "god" even if getting them meant blaspheming God.

Throughout nearly twenty years in politics, I have seen the tender seduction of well-meaning Christian leaders and their followers by politicians parched for votes but apathetic about these Christians' faith. On one hand this shouldn't be surprising: politicians are all about courting (or seducing) voters so that they can win. On the other hand, Christian leaders are supposed to be putting Jesus above and before all things, enabling them to recognize and resist this seductive power. Instead, it looks like they believe a political agenda is the most important thing.

Has this trading Jesus for politics worked? There are a lot of Christians among the Republicans who have controlled Congress for the last twelve years. The president is a sincere Christian. But our political dreams have hardly come true. Teen pregnancy has hardly ceased. Divorces are as common as ever. More people than ever are eschewing marriage in favor of cohabitation. Abortion is as prevalent as ever. Pornography is everywhere. Gambling is, too.

But the spiritual consequences of this dance are enormous.

When I talk to neighbors or strangers and tell them that I try my best to follow Jesus, many look at me queerly. I've come to learn that their first thoughts about me are political ones—they figure I don't care about the environment, I support the war in Iraq, I oppose abortion, I am ambivalent about the poor, I want public schools to evangelize students, and I must hate gays and lesbians. That is what they associate with my faith. And this isn't just a Washington thing. I've heard it everywhere. Moreover, in the heat of many political moments, I have been what they feared. I have been far more partisan than Christian. I hated Bill Clinton, yet he is a Christian just like me. I took sides on issues that don't have much to do with my faith. Above all, I let the passions of politics distract me from what matters in life. By some "severe mercy," however, God has given me the chance to step back and take a look at it all.

This book recounts my story as a way to explain how Jesus, who said he came to "give life and give it in full," became most heavily associated with a political agenda he certainly never embraced. It also suggests a different path. On the verge of the next presidential election, Christians have a unique opportunity to turn all of this around and potentially achieve what we have been looking for all along. Here's a hint: think fasting.

TEMPTING
FAITH

CHAPTER ONE

God, Politics, and Fishing

I've never known life without God, politics, or fishing. Eventually I would fuse them all.

First came fishing. A mile down the road from our house just north of New York City was a little lake. Hot, humid summer days were spent on a bridge with my father, emaciated earthworms, and an old saltwater reel and pole. Those days were always fishless—but full. A son loves fishing with his father.

Over time I ventured there alone, discovering holes under a fence that opened up a world that felt like home. To the objective eye it wasn't much: several hundred yards of rocky shoreline, tall weeds, and scrawny trees. For me, though, there was comfort behind the fence and in front of the water. The fence kept out the world and the water held fathomless possibilities.

Fishing was a repeated act of trust. I trusted that there were fish where I was throwing lures and I trusted that I would have the sense to tug at the right time when a fish took the offering. I trusted that the thing at the end of the line was a prized large-mouth bass and not some stinky carp or catfish. My trust was rewarded often enough that I believed this cycle would never end. That, I suppose, is similar to faith, and may explain why Jesus loved fishermen so much.

Growing up, I knew Jesus was the Son of God. I just wasn't quite sure what that meant. A picture of him, blond and doe-eyed with long robes and holding a little lamb, hung in my parents' bedroom. I remember lying on their bed one afternoon when I was little, looking up at him. He seemed sweet. He was pretty. That's all I thought about him for the longest time. My mother, a liberal Baptist, talked about him some, but mostly she sang about him. She sang about him when preparing dinner or washing dishes or doing most anything else. She had a high, beautiful voice. The verses got lost in the singing but not the choruses. I still occasionally find myself doing dishes and humming "How great thou art."

My mother's voice was also slightly haunting and sad. She had good reasons—the Great Depression, World War II, her father's early death. If I had gone through all of that, I might have ditched God altogether. But my mother chose God, again and again. And though there was great sadness to her faith, there was a great richness, too. She knew what suffering was like and knew God was refuge, fortress, sustainer, and comforter.

My father, however, seemed passively hostile to faith. He was born in China in 1922 and grew up there. His mother's feet were bound, his father had a concubine, and he was given opium as medicine. Of course there wasn't really much of a youth. At sixteen he ran away from his home in the middle of the night before the Japanese overran his hometown near Shanghai. For the next eleven years he fought. First there were the Japanese on the Burma Road, in one of the more horrendous theaters of fighting of the war he would know. This was the land of the bridge over the river Kwai and the "forgotten army." Then there were the communists in the north. These were the years that held his life's horrible hidden stories.

To me, as a child, he felt so tough and so strong and so huge that he didn't seem to need God. Of course, he may have questioned whether God even existed. Or his pain may have been so great that he had little place for the Prince of Peace. I didn't know. He didn't talk about it.

Then again, perhaps he just disliked our little United Methodist Church, as did my two older sisters. It had a stereotypically awful Sunday school replete with felt cutouts of famous biblical scenes. Moses was green, David was blue, Goliath was purple, and Jesus was brown. The services were worse, but then again I was a kid. The pastor, large and red-faced in billowing robes, scared me. Years later, when someone said God smiled, I laughed. God frowned.

But there was another side to my childhood faith. There was Mom reading me the Psalms in the evenings. She showed me stories of daring and adventure: a boy taking on a giant with a stone; a man thrown into a den of hungry lions, only to befriend them; three friends thrown into a furnace of fire, yet untouched by the flames. Church was dull but God wasn't.

Throughout my childhood—until high school at least—I never heard words like "saved" or "accept Jesus" or "salvation." There was just God and Jesus, somehow one and somehow different.

Then there was politics. Mine came mostly by osmosis. I remember at the age of five charging through the screen door, breathless from my twenty-third game of baseball with neighborhood friends, in desperate need of water. For weeks on end, it seemed to me, the rest of the family had been gathered around our small black-and-white television set watching something riveting. I paused and saw my first-ever congressional hearing. It made no conscious impression; nor did any of the news about this thing called Watergate.

Far more powerful was my mother's own past political activism. In college, in California, she felt God calling her to serve the poor. She studied nursing at Emory University. She hated it. She told us about the discrimination against blacks by whites, the ghetto housing with no running water or electricity, and the regular denial of medical care to even critically ill black patients. Then there were the stories about her summer living in rural southeast Georgia on an interracial Christian commune. It was a farming collective where men and women of different races lived together to prove that such things were possible. There were shotgun blasts in the middle of the night, cross burnings, and racial hatred of the nastiest kind. She left the South and pledged never to return.

Out of these stories I picked up two inviolable truths. Good people fight against poverty. Bad people live in the South. The first lesson has never left me. With regard to the second, it took me years to see that my mother left Georgia with a certain bigotry of her own.

I consolidated all these teachings in my first political letter. It was fall 1976 and I was eight:

> *Dear President Ford,*
> *I hope you don't lose to Jimmy Carter. He is a peanut farmer from Georgia and he is stupid. You are the President of the United States and you were an Eagle Scout. I know you can beat him.*
>
> *Love,*
> *David Kuo*

Ford lost, but I survived and lived to have my revenge with Ronald Reagan in 1980. At the age of twelve, I adored his military buildup. While my mother and sisters all marched together for the nuclear freeze, my father and I made models of fighter jets and bombers, and that was enough for me to support Reagan, at least in the manner of a twelve-year-old. Reagan's social service cuts and seeming indifference to the poor did trouble me, however. So by 1984, when I was still two years shy of voting age, I volunteered for Gary Hart's presidential campaign and genuinely thought Walter Mondale had a shot at becoming president. I was my mother's son, after all.

At no point in my youth did politics impact God, or vice versa. Politics seemed to be about the practical—keeping America safe, stopping crime, rescuing the needy—and God seemed to be about the spiritual: love, heaven, felt cutouts. They were complementary, not intertwined; the secure bookends of my childhood.

My sense of God changed in high school. Jeff Brown was the proximate cause.

Jeff was in his mid-twenties, thin and mostly nondescript. His brown hair, pale white skin, thin nose, and mustache were standard issue, as was his height, weight, and build. He was nice, moderately funny, moderately serious, and moderately smart. He came from Wisconsin, a perfectly nice state. He wasn't charismatic in an inspiring kind of way. Neither did he possess the kind of indomitable force of will that draws people to a person. He wasn't William Wilberforce. Still, there was something enthralling about him. The Bible says that after Moses had glimpsed just a shadow of God's back, he was radiant and needed to shield his face for days. Jeff had a kind of dim version of that glow. "Dim" might sound derogatory, but in comparison to the other minister in the church, to most of the congregation, to my high school teachers, and to virtually every other grown-up I knew, that dull glow seemed like otherworldly radiance.

He came to our church to start a "youth group." I had never heard of such a thing before but I gave it a shot. The first night he gathered us all together, told us we would do all sorts of fun stuff, and handed us a questionnaire. Most of the questions were pretty basic: "What are your favorite subjects in school?" "What music do you listen to?" "What do you like doing in your free time?" Then there was number 10.

"Question 10. Let's say, God forbid, you were killed in a car crash going home tonight and you ended up at heaven's gate. God asks you why he should let you in. What do you say? (P.S. Drive safely!)"

"Die and go to heaven?" a fellow teenager, named, coincidentally, Christian, mumbled. "Don't we all go to heaven?"

Another girl exclaimed, "Oh! I remember the answer to this one." She turned to our brand-new youth pastor and said, "Is it that thing you said the other day about accepting Jesus or something weird like that?"

Our youth pastor smiled and said, "Yeah, something weird like that."

I laughed. How silly. How do you accept someone? I knew all about accepting. My father was a college professor. Colleges accepted people. People don't "accept" people. Besides, what does accepting Jesus have to do with heaven?

Everyone knew the answer to the heaven question. If I died and had to stand at the pearly gates explaining why I deserved to be admitted, I would have to tell God I had lived a fairly decent life and leave it at that. I wasn't worried. At seventeen I hadn't killed anyone or pillaged any cities. Sure, I bought that *Playboy* with Madonna in it. But those hairy armpits were punishment enough. I feared Jeff might be nuts.

It says something about either the gentleness or the ineptitude of our church that I knew nothing about Jesus' role in Christianity by the time I was seventeen. Of course, it might have been my own theological density. I had been through a confirmation class when I was twelve or thirteen. I even remembered parts of the Nicene Creed, the theological foundation of virtually every Christian denomination since the fourth century: "We believe in one Lord, Jesus Christ, the only son of God, eternally begotten of the Father, God from God, Light from Light, true God from true God, begotten, not made, of one being with the Father." Still, the whole accepting thing seemed simply weird.

Over the following months our group went horseback riding, hung out at Jeff's house with his wife, Jodie, and talked about the Bible. We also memorized the order of New Testament books, with the help of nifty mnemonic devices like "God Eats Popcorn" to remember that Galatians precedes Ephesians, which precedes Philippians.

Jeff let us ask questions about anything. Nothing was off-limits. During one entire meeting, for instance, he let me present my case that Michael Jackson might actually be the Archangel Michael in human form. An article in *People* seriously speculated about his potential divinity. I could see it. It was 1985 and Jackson, still black and odd only insofar as he hung out with Elizabeth Taylor and a chimpanzee named Bubbles, reigned over the pop music world. I thought my case was sound—Michael sang well, his dancing was otherworldly, he seemed to possess an untainted innocence, and children were drawn to him. I didn't convince anyone. No one even laughed. I still suspect Jeff prepped them.

One night, in the summer between my junior and senior years, I got a call from Christian. He was normally a quiet kid who didn't laugh much, but that night he was giddy. "I prayed for Jesus to enter my heart and I feel different, changed, alive." I was happy for him. For the first time, I could also basically understand why someone would want to do that. God existed before there was time and existed outside of the universe that he had created. He was the playwright. But we were the actors, who tried to live out a different life from the one he had desired. Our script was about us. That is why Jesus came—to pay the price we could not pay to get us back on God's script. Jesus was the unknowable and unreachable God in knowable human form. He wasn't just a great man or a great prophet. He was God. Yet, somehow, he was man. To know Jesus meant to know the true nature of God. Jesus had all the answers. And he had taken every wrong thing I had ever done and would ever do onto himself, dying on a cross only to live again three days later. Who wouldn't want to tap into that kind of power? I told Christian I was thrilled for his new life. But I ended the call quickly. Christian had Jesus. I had tickets to go see Tina Turner with my girlfriend.

We dove into the soulful exuberance of that blond wig–wearing leggy Buddhist. Driving home I was feeling very mature. I had the mobility of wheels, instant access to New York City, a cute girlfriend, and only life in front of me. Though it was August in New York, the air had cooled after a night of intense thunderstorms. Leaves and small branches were strewn across the parkway as we drove north to our homes. Even more evidence of the storms was visible when I dropped off my girlfriend. There were so many leaves on her front lawn that night that, in the darkness, it looked like fall. I drove around town, past my elementary, middle, and high schools, reveling in the night, windows down, sweet air, loud music. It was good. I got home, opened the windows in my room, and went to sleep.

At seven in the morning the phone rang. It was Jeff.

"David, Christian was killed in a car crash last night. He was driving and the car must have hydroplaned. He went head-on into a tree and was killed instantly."

It happened on a road I had driven the night before.

I didn't say another word for quite a while. Jeff said some stuff but I didn't hear any of it. How could my laughing friend Christian, who had just accepted Jesus, be dead? Death only happened on TV or to old people. How could he be gone? We had conversations to complete. I needed to know about his Jesus experience.

Was it real? What was it like? And we had life to live. It never occurred to me that he might be in heaven and that he might be a whole lot happier there than he was here.

Over the following days I discovered death. There was the sickly sweet smell of a funeral home, the disturbingly shiny casket, and the frantic numbness. I felt nothing, so all I could do was to watch others. Some mourned and grieved with such desolation that it seemed the world had ended. It was a grief with pain but no balm. When God or Jesus was mentioned, some spat at the names with their words or glances. On the other hand, there were some, like Jeff, who were crushed but not destroyed. His eyes were red and his pain was clear but it was as if he were moored to something that kept him from sinking.

When it was all over, I went fishing. As I did, I kept coming back to the contrast—desolation versus grieving with hope. Of course, now I realize that people grieve in many different ways. Still, the difference in someone like Jeff was undeniable. It seemed to me that if "accepting Jesus" mattered, it had to show itself as something more than words that purportedly delivered someone to heaven. If this faith thing was real it had to show up as real at the most unexpectedly difficult times—the times when your true nature is revealed unedited; when you stub your toe badly and want to scream great expletives, when someone cuts you off in traffic and flips you the bird, when horror visits. In Jeff I saw that difference. It made me want to be like him, and I knew the best part of him was Jesus.

One day, after more time with Jeff, I went home and ended up sitting in the bathroom. The bathroom had the only door in the house that locked and I didn't want anyone seeing what I was about to do. I told Jesus that I wanted him in my life and I wanted my life to be about him. I said that I couldn't make it without him. I needed his sacrifice and life to take me back to God. I waited for the smile to cross my face. I waited for tears or tingles or emotion.

I didn't feel anything. I tried it again. Did I do something wrong? Was it real? Was I good with God?

I went about the rest of the day and then tried again before sleep. I still didn't feel anything. The next morning, the same thing. Still there was nothing. I kept this up for several days before telling Jeff about my experience. He was thrilled and excited for me and told me not to worry, I was now officially a Christian. I had been born again.

Christian faith wasn't about emotion, he said. It wasn't devoid of emotion but it wasn't based on it. Faith shouldn't ebb and flow based on how happy or sad or grumpy or sneezy we are. Faith in Jesus is rooted in something deeper. Then he pointed me to Jesus' parable about the man who built his house on a rock versus the man who built his house on sand. A storm came and the man housed on the rock remained firm. The guy with his house on the sand was blown away into nothingness. Building on rock was harder than building on sand because it took more time, required more work—motion was the sand, faith was the rock. In the end, though, it would be worth the work because when storms like Christian's death arrived, I wouldn't get swept away. I liked that.

Perhaps because I wasn't a suddenly reformed drug addict or a repentant marauder, my life didn't change all that much. If pressed, I would say that my temper became more muted. I ceased screaming every time the New York Mets lost a baseball game. (I just fumed.) The temptations to do the "wrong thing" were every bit as strong as before: My girlfriend didn't suddenly become less attractive. I still desperately wanted to move farther around the sexual bases. My room didn't suddenly become spotless and I didn't go out and serve the poor or sell all my possessions.

But God had grown. The God of my early youth had existed effortlessly but ethereally, more real than the Tooth Fairy, not quite as concrete as Santa Claus. Now, as high school was concluding, God had a face. God was Jesus and Jesus was God and while they were theologically one, Jesus made God approachable. God was infinite. Jesus was palpable. My occasional Bible reading focused much more on the Gospels and Paul's letters to the various churches than on the Psalms.

In the process I discovered that Jesus moved me. When I read his invitation, "Come to me all you who are weary and weighed down and I will give you rest. For my yoke is easy and my burden is light," it made me long, deeply long, for something I couldn't identify, a kind of supreme peace infinitely more intense than anything I had found behind the fence of my lake. I began to wonder if I had missed something in that picture of the doe-eyed Jesus carrying the lamb. Maybe those soft eyes belied the strong hands of a shepherd who'd rescued many lost lambs and given them perfect comfort and peace—lambs like me.

I knew I had missed the most powerful part of that picture. While recuperating from life-threatening wounds during World War II, my father ended up in a hospital where a distant aunt was a doctor. As he recuperated, they went on walks together. He learned she was a Christian, and from time to time she took him to her small Episcopal church. Jesus made little sense to him. Jesus was totally foreign and he wanted nothing to do with him. Over time, though, Jesus intrigued him. He asked his aunt why she was a "foreign religion believer." She never gave a direct answer. Perhaps it was because she knew my father—the fastest way to get him interested in something was to pique his curiosity.

He began to think about this Jesus he had discovered. It occurred to him at the time that Jesus was the most selfless and unselfish man ever. My father liked that. Before leaving China on the eve of the communist takeover, he saw the silk-screened picture of Jesus holding a lamb. He began to walk away from it but couldn't. He emptied his pockets to buy it. Years later, after being baptized a Christian, he had it framed and gave it to my mother.

Throughout this, my political interest never faltered, never altered. I was still a liberal Democrat. In the fall of 1986 I ended up going to Tufts University to study law and international relations and politics. I was against the death penalty. I was in favor of programs that helped the poor. I supported international human rights and the United Nations. Upon my arrival in Boston I signed up for classes, joined the crew team, and volunteered for Joe Kennedy's first campaign for Congress.

I kept my politics at an ambivalent distance from my faith. It wasn't a wall of separation. It just hadn't dawned on me that my powerful relationship with God and my intense interest in politics could be merged into a single force. To the degree I did think of the two together I simply thought about whether the things I sought through politics lined up with the things I knew of Jesus. That made everything fairly easy. I was confident he liked my positions. But I never thought of invoking that endorsement to support my orientation. That seemed disrespectful.

My minister was no longer Jeff Brown. Now that I had moved to Tufts, it was an older man who worked with Christian groups at Harvard and MIT. Kevin was the walrus. He had a friendly face with emerging jowls and a big mustache and a friendly belly. In many ways he was the anti-Jeff. Kevin was brilliant and learned. He could have answered every one of those questions we asked when Christian had been killed. He would probably have cross-referenced those answers with dozens of books, articles, and sermons. He didn't have quite the same Jeff-like glow. But there was a profound kindness and gentleness to him. When he picked up on my intellectual hunger for Jesus he fed me books like G. K. Chesterton's *Orthodoxy*, which I found initially thrilling and eventually impenetrable, and numerous works by the late Oxford theologian C. S. Lewis. And when he learned about my interest in politics, he introduced me to Chuck Colson.

One winter day during my sophomore year, Kevin told me Colson was going to speak at Brown University on Christian involvement in the political arena. I eagerly went. I knew very little about Colson, save that he had been Nixon's hatchet man, famously saying he would walk over his grandmother to get the president reelected. He had actually done far worse. He authored Nixon's famous "Enemies List" of all the president's political opponents. He led a dirty tricks campaign against George McGovern, Nixon's opponent in 1972. He leaked information on Daniel Ellsberg's psychiatric care, in hopes of discrediting the man who himself had leaked Pentagon information on how poorly the Vietnam War was going. Colson was eventually sent to prison for his crimes, but not before accepting Jesus and being born again.

His conversion gave political cartoonists months of fodder. But when released, Colson didn't retreat. After several years of quiet theological study, he founded a ministry for prisoners called Prison Fellowship. Still a right-wing Republican, he had seen the wasted lives of prison. He began advocating for better conditions for all prisoners and for white-collar criminals to be forced to give something back to society with their skills. At its heart, though, Prison Fellowship sought to bring Jesus into prisons through Bible studies. By early 1987 Colson had become one of the most influential voices in the evangelical world.

We sat on old wooden chairs in a cavernous hall with thick, old windows and an exposed beam ceiling. Great, pensive portraits of dead white men adorned the walls. It was the kind of room that felt like it would be cold no matter what the temperature was. Colson, who looked like the human equivalent of a very tanned sharpei, with symmetrical wrinkles and folds of skin around his face, was returning to Brown for the first time since a 1973 speech he had given there from his lofty perch as President Nixon's general counsel. As he reached the lectern he joked that when he worked for the White House, Brown had hailed him as a conquering hero; now that he represented God, only Brown's small Christian fellowship had invited him.

Colson wasn't preaching and he wasn't delivering a rousing political message. He spoke as an academic trying to make his case to an intellectually suspicious audience. His thesis was simple. Never before in American life had the public square been so stripped of Judeo-Christian influence and so actively hostile to Christians. He wasn't arguing, he explained, for a power grab, but simply for the reclamation of the first freedom of American life, the right of religious people of all faiths to influence the political process. America faced a burgeoning cultural war. What was now at stake was the loss of religious freedom itself, and the erosion of the Judeo-Christian ethic so essential to democracy.

He traced the descent of this tradition through the Supreme Court decision banning school prayer, the campus popularity of "relativistic" French writers Albert Camus and Jean-Paul Sartre, the 1960s ethic of "do your own thing," and the resultant "spiral of easy sex and hard drugs."

"Religion in American culture has lost its cutting edge," Colson said that night. "It has become part of 'the scene.' Eighty-one percent of American adults say they are Christian, yet in terms of moral values our society today is really decadent. We have simply accommodated the culture. Whenever the church does this, it loses its vitality." Christians were supposed to be different. They were supposed to be vibrant and alive. They were supposed to be living fully in the world but were also to be different from the world and the world's standards. But that wasn't happening. The truth was actually quite the opposite. Christians were exactly the same as the world. Christians divorced at the same rate as non-Christians, they had premarital sex at the same rate, they had just as many abortions, they hoarded their money without giving sacrificially to the poor, and always wanted more.

What America needs, Colson said, "is a restoration of religious values in public life. The shockwaves that threaten the very foundations of our culture today emanate from society's failure to understand man's need for God and Christians' failure to accurately present Christ's message of the Kingdom of God." I wrote it all down, as furiously as I could scribble. I even wrote down another quick point he made: Much of what needed to be done was actually beyond the reach of politics. Reformation, after all, wasn't the work of government. I just wouldn't remember it for years.

Mixing religion and politics wasn't unconstitutional; it was the basis of American civilization. The Declaration of Independence, the Ten Commandments on the wall of the Supreme Court, the prayers that open and close House and Senate sessions, the Constitution itself—these are all religion and they are all politics and they are all fundamentally American.

It wasn't easy, he said, and it wasn't going to get any easier. "I don't know of any presidential candidate who has taken what I believe to be a correct position on the role of religion and politics."

My head was spinning faster than my scribbling pen. I was inspired. I was dazzled. I could help solve the greatest problems in America just by being a Christian—a *real* Christian. If I followed Jesus, helped others follow Jesus, and did it all publicly, I would be fighting back against the secularizing forces that were sweeping

God into the corner. This wasn't just a personal fight, it was a patriotic one as well. America was at stake. America's religious liberty was America's first liberty. If that is lost, *we* are lost.

I left Brown University that night inspired that I could save America religiously and politically. God now infused my politics even if politics didn't yet infuse my God.

I went back to Tufts and in the following weeks found every Colson book I could. Our library didn't own any copies of anything he had written, despite the fact that he had sold millions of books. So I ordered and devoured them: *Born Again, Loving God,* and *Against the Night.* They were stories about God, about faith, and about how Christian values have been lost. The more I read, the more inspired I became. Then I read his account of William Wilberforce in *Kingdoms in Conflict.*

Wilberforce, a wealthy member of Parliament in the late 1700s in Great Britain, had had a dramatic conversion to Christ. After almost perishing when his carriage nearly slid off the side of a mountain, he turned to God. Ready to renounce politics to pursue God, he was instead convinced by John Newton, a former brutal slave trader turned Christian, to use politics for God. Wilberforce worked for popular education, religious liberty, and parliamentary reform. He devoted his life to abolishing slavery. In 1788 Wilberforce introduced his first antislavery bill with a three-and-a-half-hour speech. He concluded, "Sir, when we think of eternity and the future consequence of all human conduct, what is there in this life that shall make any man contradict the dictates of his conscience, the principles of justice and the law of God?" For the next thirty years he fought against slavery. He finally saw the slave trade abolished, on the very night that he died.

Wilberforce was a model for how religion could influence government for moral reform. I seized upon that model. International human rights, the abolition of the death penalty, relief for the poor, aid for Africa, an end to apartheid—these all struck me as the great and purposeful moral issues of the day. These, I knew, were the sorts of moral issues that Wilberforce would have championed. That's what drove me deeper into Democratic politics.

That summer I worked for a Democratic polling firm and the

next summer, in 1988, I worked on Michael Dukakis's presidential campaign. It was abundantly clear to me that if I were to follow everything I had learned about my Christian duty to society I would have to work even harder on the issues I cared about so passionately. Who could doubt that Jesus supported me? I sure couldn't. And I didn't really interact with anyone who disputed me. Then again, I was going to school in Boston, not Austin.

Yes, elsewhere in America, many others would have disputed my priorities. For if slavery had been the moral issue for Christians in the nineteenth century, abortion was the same for many late-twentieth-century Christians. The *Roe v. Wade* Supreme Court decision in 1973 had mobilized Christian political activism more than any other single event. It wasn't just conservative Christians who were stunned. Not too long after the decision, Jesse Jackson wrote, "What happens to the mind of a person, and the moral fabric of a nation, that accepts the aborting of the life of a baby without a pang of conscience? What kind of a person and what kind of a society will we have 20 years hence if life can be taken so casually? It is that question, the question of our attitude, our value system, and our mind-set with regard to the nature and worth of life itself that is the central question confronting mankind. Failure to answer that question affirmatively may leave us with a hell right here on earth." Congress seriously considered and nearly passed a Human Life Amendment. Abortion became the litmus test for politically inclined Christians in examining the moral conscience of anyone running for office.

In 1989, the spring semester of my junior year, the Supreme Court was preparing to hear arguments in a case innocuously known as *William L. Webster v. Reproductive Health Services.* In 1986, the Missouri legislature had placed a number of restrictions on abortions. A law was passed stating that "[t]he life of each human being begins at conception." Public employees and public facilities were not to be used in performing or assisting abortions unnecessary to save the mother's life; counseling in favor of abortions was prohibited; and physicians were to perform viability tests upon women in their twentieth (or more) week of pregnancy.

For the first time since 1973 the legally guaranteed right to abortion was in serious jeopardy. Celebrities, Democratic political leaders, and abortion rights advocates championed the right to choose. Religious leaders, Republican political leaders, and pro-life advocates championed the rights of the unborn. Both sides fought for the moral ground. One side saw itself representing the rights of mothers, the other, the rights of the unborn children.

I had never thought much about abortion until my girlfriend had one.

In the midst of the *Webster* debate, my girlfriend became pregnant. She wasn't gung ho for Jesus, as I was. And when she was around, I was far more gung ho for her than for Jesus. I knew that premarital sex was a Christian no-no. But it didn't seem to me to be a big no-no. Murder and rape and adultery and genocide and torture were big issues. Sex? It seemed far less significant. Jesus was no match for my hormones.

Neither of us really wanted to become parents. When she discovered she was pregnant, it didn't occur to us that perhaps that choice had already been made. Instead, our fears were wholly selfish. We didn't want to be exposed. I didn't want my Christian friends to know I was having sex. She didn't want to tell her friends for fear that someone would have loose lips. Neither of us wanted to tell our parents. My sisters told me stories about how my father had been chaste throughout World War II, never sleeping with the woman who was his fiancée, even refusing to sleep in the same bed with her, preferring instead to sleep in a chair one night when they were forced to share a room. How could I tell him about a pregnancy? My girlfriend's parents owned a successful business in the Northwest and were very respected in the community. This sort of thing didn't fit well with that image.

Though the abortion debate swirled around us, we hadn't paid too much attention to it. I might have called myself pro-life and she might have called herself pro-choice but then again it might have been the other way around. As we flipped through the yellow pages to find a clinic we were dizzy with disgust and longing for relief. Much of the disgust was with us. Why had we been so stupid and not been more careful? It was unfair. The relief we longed for was the promise that a small procedure would just make the whole problem disappear. A few hundred bucks and all would be done. We didn't allow ourselves to ask any serious questions: Is "it" an "it" or a "he" or a "she"? Is this murder? Would our short-term relief become long-term regret? We asked ourselves these questions privately but didn't allow ourselves to ask them of each other. As much as we might be wrestling with the issue, we were going down the abortion route and didn't want ourselves to be dissuaded. It felt as if getting rid of the pregnancy quickly would make the abortion less of a problem, much as removing a tumor is easier if discovered sooner rather than later.

We chose a clinic on a prestigious street in Boston. It made it feel safer, more respectable. The thick, dark wooden doors had brass lettering. A nurse assured us that this procedure was normal, safe, and relatively painless. It was a morally neutral occurrence, she said, nothing to feel guilty about. We were so early in the pregnancy that we weren't aborting a child, just a bunch of tissue. The thing inside my girlfriend could feel no pain, had no brain, had no real distinguishing features that would make it human.

We both tried to act very grown-up, which meant some combination of asking questions, looking the nurse in the eyes, and being serious but not being emotional. We played the scriptless parts as best we could.

After it was over, my girlfriend lay in a room with eight tables partially enclosed with screens set next to them. Seven other women lay quietly, pretending the others weren't there. The room felt full of unspoken sorrow and unacknowledged shame. But perhaps that was just us. We walked back down the fancy street and took the subway back to school. We regretted it. We were relieved. I knew what we'd done. I had no idea what we'd done. We stayed together for a while. Then we went our separate ways.

I couldn't talk to anyone about it. So it just sat there. As the summer of 1989 began I tried to put the questions behind me as I started a long-planned internship for Senator Edward Kennedy. I loved him. I was a few degrees away from obsessive about his family. Most things about John Kennedy's martyr story I committed to memory. Camelot wasn't a legend, it was a goal. Even more than John Kennedy, I loved Robert Kennedy. Before I learned about Wilberforce, Bobby had been my main political idol, a man of privilege who fought ruthlessly for dreams that included helping the poor, righting racial wrongs, and pursuing justice around the world. And even with Wilberforce now in the picture, I believed the Kennedys had a lot in common with him.

The internship only strengthened that belief. I was in Ted Kennedy's office when China's Tiananmen Square crackdown began and ended up talking frantically with Lufthansa Airlines in our attempt to get some students out of China. A few weeks later I was able to go to the Kennedy compound in Hyannis Port and see some of the Tiananmen student leaders as they met with the senator. If he wasn't practicing Christian statesmanship, I didn't know who was.

A few weeks later, though, the Supreme Court upheld key parts of *Webster*. I still didn't know how I felt about abortion. I made the naïve mistake of asking one of the senator's more senior staffers whether Kennedy was pro-life or pro-choice. She snapped back, "Pro-choice, *of course!* Aren't you??" I assured her I was.

Over time I discovered it was easier to think and debate than it was to feel. I didn't know what to feel. Every time I saw a baby, was I supposed to feel sad that it wasn't mine or happy that it wasn't mine? When Christmas came should I be happy I was still the youngest in my family, or should I be mourning that? And what of Jesus? How could I have betrayed him so horribly? What kind of faith was mine?

So instead of feeling, I researched. I learned an unborn baby's heart begins beating by day 22. By eight weeks every organ in its body, save the lungs, is fully formed and functioning. Wouldn't these facts have changed our minds? Perhaps. But I doubted it. No amount of information could have dissuaded us from our passion to protect ourselves and our reputations. But still, I reasoned at the time, for others it might make a difference. The one thing I knew was that our pain and our experience gave me the chance to do a good thing.

So in the wake of my abortion experience, I became a pro-life activist. I helped establish Tufts's only pro-life group. I sponsored debates between pro-life and pro-choice student leaders, and invited pro-life advocates to campus. I pointed to the million and a half unborn children who were aborted every year. I asked people whether one of them might have had the answer to cancer or written the next great novel or been someone's soulmate.

Just like William Wilberforce, I became an advocate for the ultimately forgotten, in this case the unborn. In the process I joined the religious conservative movement, though I didn't realize it.

CHAPTER TWO

Odd Fellows

Three months before graduation, Kevin gave me one last Christian/political gift. He arranged for me to go to the National Prayer Breakfast in Washington, D.C., along with 150 other student leaders from across the country.

The National Prayer Breakfast began in 1952, growing out of off-the-record prayer meetings held in both houses of Congress. Though not officially sanctioned or funded by any branch of government, over time the annual prayer breakfast became one of the most overtly religious government occurrences. The president and vice president always attend and offer remarks, as do members of their Cabinet and members of Congress. Hundreds of other government officials from Capitol Hill, the White House, and various federal agencies attend, as does a significant chunk of the Washington diplomatic community. Every February the gathering fills Washington's largest ballroom with more than three thousand people.

The breakfast isn't explicitly Christian, but it isn't entirely ecumenical either. Technically it is nonreligious but pro-Jesus. To people (including me at first) who had never heard such lingo before, it didn't make a lot of sense. To the mysterious—some thought secretive—group behind the prayer breakfast known simply as the Fellowship, it was basic theology.

The Fellowship has been called the most powerful group in Washington that nobody knows. It is part of a larger religious-political world of Christian groups that infuse God into government not for political ends, but for spiritual ones. Theologically conservative Christian organizations sponsor "missionaries" in

D.C. in hopes of ministering to Christian leaders and showing Christ to nonbelievers in power. These groups tend to work almost exclusively with Republicans, principally because the groups have been more welcomed by conservatives than by liberals.

The Fellowship was different. It worked intimately with people from both parties and those with no party at all. In part this was because they believed religion and politics divided people but Jesus could unite people. To Christians, Jesus is the incarnate God. To Jews and Muslims, Jesus is a prophet. The Dalai Lama believes that Jesus was one of the highest possible deities. Hindus respect Jesus as well. So the Fellowship focuses on Jesus the man, and not Jesus the Christ. Their work is to introduce people to Jesus. Only God's Holy Spirit, as the Bible says, can reveal to a person that Jesus is also the Son of God. To that end, the Fellowship prints books that are selectively distributed to "friends." *Jesus Christ: The Life and Teachings of Jesus* contains the four Gospels and the Acts of the Apostles. They are presented as "Jesus' only authorized biographies."

As I would learn, the Fellowship's reach into governments around the world is almost impossible to overstate or even grasp. Friends of the Fellowship help run prayer breakfasts and Bible study groups for leaders in countries ranging from Uganda to Uzbekistan, Italy to India. Even the Dalai Lama likes the Fellowship. At its ten-acre compound overlooking the Potomac, known as "The Cedars," the Fellowship has hosted people as diverse as Yasser Arafat and Mother Teresa. The group secretly worked with the government during the Cold War by opening up its compound for confidential meetings, and served as a secret emissary between Egypt and Israel during the Camp David talks.

The Fellowship owns a townhouse on Capitol Hill where members of Congress have lived. Their principal occupation is facilitating Capitol Hill prayer groups. Taking place behind closed doors, with no one allowed except congressmen and senators (apart from the group's reclusive leader Doug Coe, who just sits and listens), the prayer meetings bring Democrats and Republicans together in the name of Jesus. Conservative Christians mingle with politically conservative Jews. Liberals mingle with conservatives. As hard as it is to believe, the Fellowship isn't pushing a particular political agenda. "Only Jesus" is their motto. The Fellowship would play a huge role in my life. I would even end up having to renew my wedding vows at The Cedars after the minister signed the wrong marriage certificate.

The evening after the prayer breakfast I received my last college lesson on God and politics. Doug Coe walked up to the lectern and started talking about how Christians in politics judge their "opposition" very carefully because our search for God is an individual search and one far more important than any political journey. Politics, he cautioned, should never be a stumbling block for someone else's faith. Coe knew what he was talking about. Like the Jesus he modeled, he counted everyone a friend. If anything, he was most partial to befriending those whom no one else thought a Christian should befriend—dictators, embezzlers, shamed celebrities, and indicted politicians, to name just a few.

He told us about Marion Barry, the embattled mayor of Washington, D.C., who was about to go on trial for buying and selling cocaine in an undercover sting. He had been caught on tape buying cocaine and infamously shouted, "The bitch set me up, the bitch set me up!" He was a political laughingstock. It was so bad that someone else had trademarked "The bitch set me up" and made oodles off T-shirt sales. That night, Doug talked about how Barry was trying to find Jesus amid his brokenness. Coe and Barry would meet by the Jefferson Memorial late in the evenings and walk around, talking about Jesus.

Washington, Coe told us, built up leaders only to tear them down. Power was more fleeting than last week's headlines. Former Cabinet secretaries who were once worshipped were now forgotten. Congressmen with staffs were voted out of office and spent the rest of their lives trying to regain public recognition. White House staffers often spent the rest of their lives trying to get back inside the iron gates so that they could have meaning once more. What lasted, he said, wasn't power, but relationships. We needed less judgment and more love. Those of us who called ourselves followers of Jesus needed to focus more on people and less on politics, as Jesus did.

It was the power of relationships that changed the course of history, Coe proclaimed. Look at Jesus' model, he told us. Look closely. What did he do? He invested himself in a small group of people—twelve to be precise. The twelve disciples were his primary focus. But even within that group of twelve there were three who were even closer to Jesus. Peter, James, and John were the "three within the twelve." Jesus frequently took those men aside, showing them glimpses of his power and giving them special instruction. That model of intimate relationships had been followed by other leaders, but not by the church. He pointed to Hitler, to Stalin, to Mao, to Castro. He talked about the small group of men around each of them who modeled Jesus' example of discipleship and how they begot revolutions. How tragic, he said, that it had been evil men who had modeled Jesus and not Jesus' followers themselves. Do you want to prove your worth? Change the world? Make a real change? Then pursue Jesus, pursue real relationships. Forget about power.

Chuck Colson had made me feel as if I should storm the battlements for Jesus, but Coe inspired me to keep my eyes on Jesus himself. I couldn't fight as if I were in a war—trying, figuratively, to "kill" everyone who opposed me. I had to fight with love, I realized. Loving those who opposed my position, serving anyone whom God put before me, avoiding seduction by the illusion of power—this was my calling. As Martin Luther King Jr. said, "Always be sure that you struggle with Christian methods and Christian weapons. Never succumb to the temptation of becoming bitter. As you press on for justice, be sure to move with dignity and discipline, using only the weapon of love. Let no man pull you so low as to hate him."

I was sure I was ready for Washington.

Three months later, in the summer of 1990, I was in the middle of the national abortion fight. I joined the National Right to Life Committee, the nation's largest, most mainstream and respected pro-life organization. Founded after *Roe* by doctors, scientists, clergy, and laypeople, NRLC gained its reputation as a good neighbor in the abortion battles. It was never too extreme or too nasty.

Working for a pro-life group hadn't been my plan when I arrived in Washington immediately after graduation. Instead, I figured I would get a job on the hill with a pro-life Democratic congressman. I still didn't understand that the Democratic Party had largely closed itself off to people like me. When I went to interview with Democrats, I discovered they just weren't interested in someone who was pro-life, even me with my Kennedy background. But when I tried Republicans, they looked at the "Kennedy" on my résumé and laughed. Capitol Hill was off-limits to me. Somehow National Right to Life found me.

In the fall of 1989, just four months after the *Webster* decision, abortion had been the deciding factor in the only two significant elections in November. Pro-choice candidates defeated pro-life favorites in gubernatorial races in Virginia and New Jersey. Republican leaders like Newt Gingrich publicly grappled with their party's abortion stance while Democratic leaders jumped on the seemingly more popular pro-choice bandwagon. During the next months, million-person pro-choice and pro-life rallies were held on Washington's National Mall. A new political newsletter called *The Abortion Report* became the hot new D.C. publication. Every major newspaper and magazine ran abortion stories every week. Abortion defined politics. Some said it was the greatest political divide in American life since slavery.

And now I was in the middle of it. I had told my employers the truth about my abortion experience during the job interview. I didn't know if it would help or hurt; I had just decided that I needed to tell the truth. I had gotten a young woman pregnant, and she had had an abortion. I regretted it and thought that it was far too easy to get an abortion in America.

It would be the last time for fifteen years that I told the truth about my pro-life conversion. In years to come I would describe my position as one of intellectual, philosophical, and moral conviction. That seemed smarter and more socially acceptable than the truth. It made me sound more like an intellectual than someone who had knocked up his girlfriend, been part of an abortion, regretted it, and was ashamed of it. I wanted people to think I was more like William F. Buckley Jr. than someone on Oprah.

My new job added a twist to the Buckley image. It made me angrier and angrier. I looked for my enemies and found them to be Democrats like Ted Kennedy. One day I found an August 1971 letter from Kennedy to a constituent. In it he had written, "When history looks back to this era it should recognize this generation as one which cared about human beings enough to halt the practice of war, to provide a decent living for every family and to fulfill its responsibility to its children from the very moment of conception." I felt ill. Before *Roe*, he had been pro-life. What a hypocrite! How could he have changed his mind on something so fundamental? I began to see him for what he was—for what conservatives thought of him: he was a liberal, womanizing drunk. And I had interned for him. It was horrible. He was disgusting, and so was anyone who didn't share my now rigid pro-life stand. I felt thoroughly justified in saying these things. It was people like Kennedy, I thought, who helped create the abortion culture that victimized me, my girlfriend, and our unborn child. Ironically, years later it would be a casual conversation with one of his pro-choice nieces whom I had just met, Kathleen Kennedy Townsend, that helped me realize I hadn't fully dealt with my own abortion experience. I am sure I cannot count the number of people I know who have had a similar experience that moved them into pro-life stands. And I marvel at that fact, wondering how much anger on both the pro-life and pro-choice sides comes from personal pain.

Abortion was the dominant force sending Christian conservatives back into the political arena. But it wasn't the only cause. Five years after *Roe*, an attempt by the Internal Revenue Service to consider eliminating the tax-exempt status of private Christian schools also infuriated Christians. *Roe* had convinced many Christians that America was morally lax, and the IRS convinced them there was a Big Brother out to get them.

Those were some of the national issues. What fueled Christian conservatives' mobilization, however, were local skirmishes fought below the national media radar. Most of those issues involved kids: sex education, school curricula, prayer in schools, and textbooks. And most of those Christians' positions were defensive ones.

Future CNN polling expert William Schneider said of them in 1984, "It is significant that virtually every item on the [Christian] Right's social agenda is a protest against a liberal initiative. They weren't anti-ERA until there was an ERA. They were anti-gay only after a pro-gay ordinance passed in Florida. They were for creationism after laws passed mandating the teaching of evolution. Others see them as an aggressive right-wing movement attempting to impose their values, but the right sees it exactly the opposite."

No one capitalized on these defensive emotions more than Jerry Falwell. In the mid-1970s, Falwell, who had once decried any involvement in politics by clergy, gathered pastors and conservative activists together to figure out how to attack the anti-God culture. Someone said there was a "sleeping moral majority" in the country waiting to be loosed—and a moniker was born. Over the next decade the Moral Majority and Falwell would become synonymous with Christian political activism. The night of Ronald Reagan's election, Falwell went on television and made it clear that Reagan owed his victory to the Moral Majority and that they were going to make sure he delivered. At a rally the next morning at his Liberty Baptist University, Falwell was introduced with "Hail to the Chief," the theme reserved for the president of the United States.

Fighting against abortion, the Equal Rights Amendment, and gay rights, while supporting prayer in schools and creationism in the curriculum, the Moral Majority raised $11 million in 1984 alone. But it also veered far from its founding and, in many Christians' eyes, far from Jesus. In 1985, for instance, Falwell went to South Africa to assess apartheid. He met with future Nobel Peace Prize winner Desmond Tutu, called him a "phony," and said he was going to tell "millions of Christians to buy Krugerrands" (thereby supporting the pro-apartheid government). Later that year he traveled to the Philippines, where he met with the corrupt Ferdinand Marcos and praised the authoritarian ruler as a friend of freedom while declaring the Philippines "a paradise." Falwell apologized for the Tutu remarks but defended his trips as an attempt to awaken "conservative Christians in America to the serious threat of Communist expansion in the free world."

By the late 1980s, however, the organization faltered. Televangelist scandals had erupted: Jim Bakker's ministry paid a mistress more than $250,000 for her "services" to the pastor, and charges of embezzlement and fraud caught up with him. Jimmy Swaggart, it emerged, also had a thing for hookers. Televangelists around the country saw their donations dry up. Even Pat Robertson's squeaky-clean *700 Club* saw a 30 percent drop in donations. The year after these scandals, in 1988, Pat Robertson decided to run for president. He raised nearly $30 million yet earned only 9 percent of the Republican primary vote. When his campaign folded, it was widely believed the evangelical political movement was over.

In September 1989, however, during my senior year in college, the Christian conservative movement was reborn in Atlanta. Robertson quietly convened a meeting in Atlanta that included three major evangelical leaders who had also been on the Moral Majority board. Charles Stanley, D. James Kennedy, and Beverly LaHaye shared Robertson's growing conviction that evangelicals needed new approaches, new strategies, and a new commitment to political activism. Robertson held the meeting in Atlanta in part because he was trying to recruit a young doctoral student at the University of Georgia to run a new operation. That student was Ralph Reed, who sat in the meeting wondering why he was there.

Earlier in the year Reed had drafted a plan, at Robertson's request, for a new grassroots political organization but hadn't ever gotten a response. Reed wrote, "There exists in American politics today a tremendous vacuum that must be filled. Estimates of the number of evangelicals range from a low of 10 million to a high of 40 million. Whatever the actual number, there is no constituency in the American electorate with greater explosive potential as a political force." Instead of using a top-heavy organization like the Moral Majority, Robertson wanted to infiltrate the American political system from below. State chapters would foster local chapters. Local chapters would organize by precinct. National activity would be minimal. The whole effort would be done without drawing any attention to itself. The Atlanta meeting was a success. The evangelical leaders signed on and Reed was recruited. A few months later Reed inherited a bunch of debt from Robertson's campaign, an old direct-mail list, and a warehouse in Chesapeake, Virginia. The group called itself the Christian Coalition. No one in the press would report on it seriously for years.

Robertson's decision to name it the "Christian" coalition highlighted the central question of Christian politics in the 1990s. Was it "Christian" or was it simply "conservative" with a religious veneer? Reed advocated against including the Christian adjective precisely because he saw the danger in asserting that "Christian" meant conservative. Regardless, the decision was made, and from that point forward the line between conservative and Christian was indistinguishable. And no one was a more powerful "Christian" advocate than Reed.

At about the same time, James Dobson, head of the $50-million-a-year Focus on the Family ministry, felt he needed to expand upon his somewhat intermittent political involvement. Dobson was a successful child psychologist who began Focus on the Family out of his home when he realized that Christian parents needed advice on how to raise children. To him, discipline wasn't a bad word and spanking wasn't a crime. Fathers needed to be present. Faith mattered. More than a decade later he had amassed a database of millions of Americans who looked to him as their amiable family counselor. The list was uniquely powerful because it was comprised solely of people who had reached out to him. His daily radio broadcast was carried on 1,300 stations. Dobson's religious traditions typically steered clear of politics but as he surveyed the cultural landscape he concluded that one of the greatest threats to children came from liberal government policies. In the late 1980s, Dobson and former Reagan White House official Gary Bauer significantly ramped up a small group Dobson founded in 1983, the Family Research Council, to bring an explicitly pro-family, pro-life, and pro-faith message to Washington lawmakers.

Together, the Christian Coalition and the Family Research Council would take what most thought was a dead evangelical political corpus and bring about an unprecedented revolution. Within five years they would help Republicans take control of Congress for the first time in more than a generation and sweep

Republicans into a majority of the state houses. Within a decade they would be the single most important constituency in electing President George W. Bush.

Though at work I didn't see all of this coming in 1990, I should have seen it coming at church. Much to my mother's quiet chagrin, I was attending a *Southern* Baptist church just outside Washington. Not only had my mother failed to dissuade me from living in the South, but now I was attending the region's unofficial official church, and loving it.

It was a startling experience for someone who came from a Boston church with fifty-four members. Here thousands of people attended multiple services every Sunday. There were more than a hundred people in the young couples Sunday school class I attended with my girlfriend (soon to be fiancée). There were Christians everywhere. They were uniformly white and Southern. They seemed to have known everything about Jesus since they were kids. In college, I sometimes thought about changing into sweats before going to brunch so no one would think I was some religious freak who went to church. These people had done the opposite. If they skipped church they would still dress up for brunch so that people would think they *had* gone to church. I thought our new church was huge, seating a thousand people per service. They thought it was small.

It was a pleasant surprise how much I liked everyone I met. While I had long ago realized my mother's anti-South bias was hugely overblown, I still had an irrational fear in this new place that one day I would be booted out or forced to fly a Confederate flag. Instead, I found deep friendships with people who loved God. All in our early 20s, we played touch football together, studied the Bible together, learned how to manage our finances together, and in many ways grew up together. In all these ways the Sunday school class ended up feeling a lot like college.

We were also united by our struggle to live as Christians in a culture that viewed our faith as anachronistic at best, and bigoted at worst. The cultural estrangement we felt wasn't based on one thing. It wasn't akin to how African-Americans felt before the civil rights movement. No one was denying us a seat on the bus or a vote in an election or a house in the neighborhood. Virtually no one cast epithets our way. Instead, it was the culture itself that bothered us. Every day seemed to bring a new report about some anti-Christian bias. We were H. L. Mencken's "childish theology founded on hate." We read AP stories saying we were prone to "riots, terrorism—and death." We opened the *Washington Post* and found ourselves described in an article—not an opinion piece—as "poor, uneducated, and easy to command." And Hollywood? Its Christians were dowdy, sexually repressed, sometimes psychotic bigots. Even fun movies like *Footloose* found their villain in a little town's Bible-thumping pastor whose principal occupation was outlawing dancing and fun. We understood how easy those characterizations were because we well knew how easy it was to be a Christian and sound stupid. But we also knew those kinds of people were the exception, not the rule.

The biggest surprise for me in my new church was learning that our Christian faith presupposed a common political agenda. There was never any question that everyone in our group was conservative and Republican. Being pro-life was a given. Life began at conception and needed to be preserved as such. Likewise, I learned that a real Christian opposed gay rights. Homosexuality wasn't acceptable to God. We followed Jesus' commands to hate the sin, not the sinner, so we weren't against homosexuals per se—but we were strongly opposed to their sexual behavior and especially to their political agenda. My Christian political education didn't stop there. I learned that Christians were absolutely pro-capitalism and that meant taxes were bad and always needed to be cut. These positions were understood by virtually everyone in our Sunday school class, no matter their profession. Young moms and trial lawyers, a staffer at the Republican National Committee and a management consultant, an FBI agent and an entrepreneur, all held the same views. To hold different views would mean one was liberal. And a liberal was a Democrat. Democrats liked Ted Kennedy, hugged trees, and remembered the words to "We Are the World." Democrats were weak on crime. They were all as insipid as Michael Dukakis. One couple out of our dozens defied these tenets—we loved them but couldn't take them too seriously. Something was obviously not quite right about them.

Somehow, though, I made a seamless transition to embrace all of these positions. It was the same direction I was already moving in. And despite my "sordid" political past, my new friends accepted me. Even though I had been a Kennedy intern and voted for Michael Dukakis, I was on the right path now. After all, I worked at the National Right to Life Committee. To them—and increasingly to me—my Democratic past was an old life. I was once a child of darkness but now I was a child of light. I embraced that notion with gusto, mocking liberal policies and those who advocated them whenever politics came up, which was often.

By and large it all felt very natural—just an extension of my theology. Obedience was a natural part of my Christian faith. A life without lying, avarice, lust, and stealing (among other sins) was just a natural byproduct of my faith. My intimacy with God made those things detestable, or at least less desirable. Similarly, moral wrongs like abortion, homosexuality, and divorce were detestable and needed to be opposed with the same fervor that I pursued God.

Ironically, opposing sin became a sort of substitute for pursuing God. Opposing political policies is very easy when compared to some of Jesus' daunting challenges—loving my neighbor as myself, denying myself and following him, loving those who hated me, serving those who were sick. Jesus required my life. Politics required only my attention. And I really, really loved politics.

My work was increasingly alluring. Though I was just a lowly flunky, I was talking to congressmen, lobbyists, and White House officials. That I was simply the guy who picked up the phone, a conduit to someone else to whom they *really* wanted to talk, didn't matter to me. I was part of the process. I had become what I hoped I could be after hearing Chuck Colson. I was overtly Christian, overtly involved in politics, and overtly trying to change the culture for good. It was impossible to feel anything but blessed. It helped that I arrived during the summer of Souter.

In July 1990, a year after *Webster,* Supreme Court Justice William Brennan retired. Brennan had been appointed by President

Dwight Eisenhower and was one of the first to interpret the Fourteenth Amendment as containing a "right to privacy." This was my first Washington "moment." The capital city was abuzz with everything sexy about politics. Who was President George H. W. Bush going to appoint? Would it be someone who would tip the Court's balance to the right? Would the new appointee be a conservative like Rehnquist and Scalia, and help overturn *Roe*?

It felt to me that there were two centers of power over the appointment. The first, obviously, was the White House. But seven blocks away, in our little warren, the National Right to Life Committee seemed to be the other key broker. Producers at CNN or ABC looking for background information called incessantly. Reporters for the nation's biggest newspapers called. George Will called once while veteran TV newsman David Brinkley was on the other line. I became used to fielding calls from the White House and Capitol Hill. I wasn't in on any meetings. No one cared at all about my opinion, nor should they have. And yet it felt like I was in the middle of the most important political happenings on earth. Every day felt like the rapturous moment after a beautiful woman says yes to a date.

Colleagues from the other side of the office would ask me, "So, what do you hear about Bush's nominee?" I would tell them the truth: "Nothing." They would raise their eyebrows and say, "I understand, I understand you can't say anything about it." It took me a while to catch on. They assumed I knew everything, even though I knew nothing. If I said nothing, they'd keep assuming I knew everything. I asked someone about this odd phenomenon. They said to play it up. "Washington is built on power and the perception of power. Say nothing and more and more people will think you matter." It was an odd game but I would soon master it.

In late July we learned that Bush was considering David Souter, an unknown judge from New Hampshire, to fill Brennan's seat. There were reports that Souter had argued pro-life cases while he was New Hampshire's attorney general and that he had written some pro-life briefs. None of that information was conclusive. Those cases and those briefs were part of his job. Whether he meant them was an open question. He was a "stealth" nominee whose views on abortion were absolutely unknown. For the White House he was a spectacular pick because he avoided political blowback before the midterm congressional elections. A strong pro-life nominee might have hurt the GOP in key states. But for groups like National Right to Life, which had passionately supported Bush precisely because they knew how crucial Supreme Court nominees were to their agenda, Souter was anything but spectacular. He was a nightmare: no one knew how he would vote.

National Right to Life cut a deal. NRLC would support Souter with the private assurance of White House Chief of Staff John Sununu that Souter was opposed to *Roe*. In return, the White House would continue supporting NRLC's pro-life legislative agenda. It was a monumentally risky gambit for the organization. If Souter, like Scalia and Rehnquist, was someone who believed *Roe* was incorrectly decided, it could be just a few years until that case was overturned and one of National Right to Life's greatest goals was achieved. But if Souter wasn't like them, if instead he believed in a fundamental right to privacy broadly covered under the "spirit" of the Fourteenth Amendment, *Roe* might never be overturned. That fall, Souter was overwhelmingly confirmed by the Senate. Though we did not know it, we lost the gamble. He would eventually become one of the most liberal members of the court, part of the block of justices who reaffirmed *Roe* in 1992.

After the Souter moment passed I stayed at National Right to Life another six months. By then I knew I didn't want to make abortion my life's fight. I suppose that as much as I wanted to be an American Wilberforce by ending abortion, I couldn't equate abortion and slavery. Yes, I was still pro-life. But abortion wasn't slavery and it certainly wasn't, as some suggested, like the Holocaust. It simply wasn't murder. For the sake of both mothers and babies, I wanted it to end, but by means of a more caring, compassionate culture rather than by judicial fiat.

I wanted something new. I wanted something bigger. I thought seriously about going to seminary, to study God more closely, but that seemed a bit radical, a bit too extreme. So in 1991, a year after arriving in Washington, I floated. I tried a job at the CIA, but with the Cold War over, and the Agency in transition, it wasn't the place for me. In 1992, I joined a presidential commission examining the role of women in combat. It was just a six-month assignment, but it offered a way to get back from the CIA into politics. And if President Bush was reelected, I would have a shot at a bigger job in the second term. I couldn't imagine him losing, especially to the man I and all my Christian friends knew was a fraud, and who we suspected might actually be evil.

CHAPTER THREE

Buffalo Hunting

"President Bush will not lose to some hick governor from Arkansas!" I swore to my friends. I knew little about Clinton save what I was hearing in my Sunday school gathering and in bits and pieces from the news. He was pro-abortion. Rumors swirled about his infidelity and his wife's possible sexual orientation. These rumors circulated not with questions attached to them but with exclamation points. "Did you hear that Hillary likes other women!" "You know that Bill Clinton has women problems!" Did I ever think that this might constitute gossip? Never. It didn't feel like gossip. It felt like I was helping defend the republic from a pot-smoking communist sympathizer.

The more popular Clinton became, the more incensed we became. When he'd emerged from the Democratic primaries we had laughed. He was clearly a joke, the by-product of all the prominent Democrats who decided not to challenge Bush when the latter's approval ratings topped 80 percent. Clinton had avoided the draft by going to Oxford. He did drugs. His wife didn't even take his last name until his presidential bid got under way. He was liberal on abortion and on gay rights. He stood for everything we loathed. To make matters worse, he called himself a Christian, specifically a Baptist. That felt blasphemous. He was a heretic in our eyes—but America wasn't seeing him that way. All we could conclude was that most Americans were thoroughly deluded.

If my group of friends was even remotely representative of conservative Christians across the country, then lots of Christians were saying these things. We asked ourselves if voting for Clinton could actually be considered a sin against God. One radical Christian group ran full-page ads in newspapers across the country saying, "The Bible warns us not to follow another man in his sin nor help him promote sin—lest God chasten us. How then can we vote for Bill Clinton?"

We didn't know about the ad but we were becoming increasingly certain such a vote would be a sin.

I had lots of fellow worshippers. From late 1989 to mid-1992, the Christian Coalition had grown to more than 350,000 members and a budget in excess of $10 million. In less than three years the group had quietly created a vast network of state and local affiliates. Eschewing media coverage, the Christian Coalition had managed something extraordinary. By the time of the Republican Convention in Houston in August 1992, nearly 40 percent of the 2,210 delegates were members of the Christian Coalition or similar groups like the Family Research Council. Twenty percent of Florida's 97 convention delegates were members of one of the Christian Coalition's twenty state chapters, and nearly a third of Florida's Republican executive committees were under their direct control. It was quite an accomplishment for a movement that had been declared dead just a few years before.

While some evangelicals were Christian and politically liberal, they were a minority and so efforts to recruit them into a politically moderate version of the Christian Coalition failed miserably. Instead of mobilizing millions, the effort mobilized thousands. Existing mainline denominations were parts of groups like the National Council of Churches, but those organizations carried virtually no political weight in conservative circles and just a little bit more than that in liberal circles. The problem with these groups was they couldn't flex any political muscle. We looked at them with pity; they were Democratic Party lapdogs who had been bought off with periodic White House meetings with Democratic presidents. Jesus wanted us to be salt and light and warned that salt that had lost its flavor was worthless. It was obvious to us that they had lost their flavor. We would never be like them.

One August night I settled down to do something completely new—watch a Republican Convention without laughing. The closest I had come to it in the past was in 1984, when I made fun of the totteringly old Ronald Reagan during his speech, and in 1988 when I made fun of George H. W. Bush during *his* acceptance speech. But by 1992, I was a different person. The first night of the Houston convention I sat agog, listening to conservative commentator Pat Buchanan give voice to my feelings.

My friends, this election is about much more than who gets what. It is about who we are. It is about what we believe. It is about what we stand for as Americans. There is a religious war going on in our country for the soul of America. It is a cultural war, as critical to the kind of nation we will one day be as was the Cold War itself. And in that struggle for the soul of America, Clinton and Clinton are on the other side, and George Bush is on our side.

In my little living room I watched the speech with a friend from college. Her politics were the same as they had been in college, which is to say her politics used to be my politics. She was against abortion but figured the best way to fight it was privately, by encouraging teens not to have sex, by loving women with unwanted pregnancies, and by adopting unwanted babies. She wasn't too sure about the gay rights thing. She was, however, confident that Pat Buchanan's nasty tone contradicted Jesus' message.

She sighed and wondered where on earth this guy had come from. I turned to her and snapped, "At least he's not some gay lover from Arkansas." The words shocked me in their vehemence and their crassness. I had never said anything like that in my life and didn't even know I thought anything like that. I was horrified beyond horrified. I sort of apologized and definitely felt ill. But some other part of me began justifying the sentiment. The homosexual agenda was antithetical to the Christian agenda. We had nothing in common. My job was to fight for America and it was a hard, tough fight, a holy fight. I couldn't back down. I was sick of America's destruction, sick of the attacks on people of faith, sick of how far our country had strayed from our godly founding.

Two nights later Pat Robertson spoke. It was a nice speech, but it didn't have the same gusto and passion that Buchanan's had had.

It was odd. I expected religion from Robertson and politics from Buchanan, not the opposite. Robertson talked about governmental bureaucracy, the tax burden on the American family, jobs, term limits, and crime. He mentioned God only four times. One time was in reference to Bush's own personal faith, another saying that the Democratic Party didn't reference God in their platform, another that God is the basis of traditional values, and the last in expressing his hopes that God would continue to bless America. He referred to abortion only in passing.

At the end of the Robertson evening, I watched Bill Bennett speak. I knew him as the former drug czar and Reagan education secretary. A friend from the presidential commission, Kate O'Beirne, told me to pay attention to Bennett. Listen closely, and call me tomorrow to talk about it, she had said.

Bennett hit the same themes as Buchanan, but there was a tonal difference. He reminded me more of the academics I had grown up with than of the politicians I had been hearing.

I called Kate the next morning and told her I thought Bennett was great. "Great. Great. Good. Well, I think you should go work for him."

"What?"

"Yeah, he's looking for someone to help him out. He's fired the last few people who worked for him but I think you'll love each other, love each other. Get me a résumé. We'll set it up."

A few weeks later I sat at a conference room table after having survived two interviews with Bennett's two closest aides. Bennett ambled in, plopped down opposite me, and started talking.

"Kate likes you. Good. National Right to Life and the CIA, huh? Hell of a combination. What are you going to do next, take over a small country?"

I was barely twenty-four years old. I had been out of college two years. I couldn't believe I was talking to the man I had seen on television just weeks before, the man who knew Ronald Reagan and George Bush. I felt dizzy that night I heard Chuck Colson argue for Christians engaging in politics. Now, sitting across from Bennett, I tingled. I couldn't let myself believe he was going to hire me. Such a thing would simply be too great, too miraculous.

"I don't have many questions, I just wanted to look you in the eyes for myself," he said. He looked at me. Then he said he did have one question. "Do you play ball?"

"What?"

"Ball. Football. Do you play football?"

"Yeah, sometimes with friends from church."

"You any good?"

"Yeah." That was a lie—but no guy can admit that they suck at touch football.

"Great, we'll have some fun then."

He shook my hand and left.

Two months later the miracle came to pass. I started working for Bill Bennett—traveling with him, answering mail, getting chicken soup, reading books, or writing letters.

I was in awe. Some mornings I arrived before anyone else and I tiptoed into his office, just to stand in the middle of it and look. Pictures casually decorated his walls. Some were of him atop Colorado mountains he climbed a lot. There were shots of him meeting with Reagan and Bush. His bookshelf contained a few political books and lots of small, worn copies of Shakespeare's plays. Plato's *Republic* was held together with a rubber band. In a corner was a brown leather chair with a straight back. It didn't roll, pivot, or adjust. It looked very uncomfortable. It felt important. I didn't think I was worthy of sitting in it, though I didn't know why. I wouldn't see a chair like that again until I was in the White House standing in the Cabinet Room. They were the secretaries' chairs and their names and titles were etched on a brass plate on the back. After their terms of service cabinet members could purchase them as very rare souvenirs.

In the aftermath of Clinton's win, pundits were atwitter about the upcoming civil war within the Republican Party. At issue, once again, was the religious Right. Postelection griping held that the Houston convention had been so divisive that it alienated moderate voters who, in turn, flocked to Bill Clinton. Though President Bush's poll numbers increased ten points after the convention, it was widely believed that his pro-life, pro-family, and pro-God stands all hurt him. The perception was that every speech was like Pat Buchanan's culture-war speech. Buchanan was perceived to represent the religious Right. Since Bush had lost, the media was quick to label the religious movement dead . . . again.

A major *Los Angeles Times Magazine* story about the disappointment of Christian conservatives gloated, "Robertson and his Christian Right movement—politically conservative fundamentalists, evangelicals, and Catholics—[should] be forgiven for a bit of self-indulgent wallowing. Time had finally run out on their crusade to create a Christian America." Turning to the perceived party split between conservatives and moderates, the article declared, "It could be a decade or more before the looming war between the two camps can be settled." The mainstream media takes a lot of flack, some deserved, for being liberally biased. But that's nothing compared to its antireligious bias. Most reporters continue to think evangelical Christians are from another planet and most couldn't name one as a friend or acquaintance. A few years ago, a *New York Times* reporter commented on President George W. Bush's use of the phrase "people should take the log out of their own eye before taking the speck out of their neighbor's eye." He said it was an odd version of the pot calling the kettle black. It was a reference to Jesus' Sermon on the Mount, arguably the most famous speech in history.

Working for Bennett, I was now in the midst of this battle for religion and the Republican Party. He was one of the main combatants. His position was unwavering. "Pat Robertson isn't going to take over the party," Bennett told a group of reporters shortly after the election. "He's going to get a lot of people working to make inroads, which is fine. . . . Besides, our public policy is not suffering from an oversupply of Christian values at the moment. Nor, certainly, are our TV, news media, books and schools." Bush's problem was that he had failed to carry a coherent conservative message out of the convention. He got scared, backed down, and ended up with no message at all.

Bill Bennett was a Catholic who supported the religious Right as part of a broader cultural message. In this, Bennett and Christian Coalition head Ralph Reed were of the same mind. Reed wrote, "The convention wasn't too conservative. The problem was that

Bush wasn't far enough to the right. And the party has to realize that the evangelical voting block is enormous. One out of every two people who voted for Bush was a white evangelical. No other voting block is bigger, better organized or more disciplined. It's bigger and better than organized labor used to be." Then, sounding a bit too much like Glenn Close in *Fatal Attraction* after she boiled the bunny, he concluded, "We will not be ignored."

The Bennett-Reed position, however, wasn't the typical Republican position. Most Republican leaders were skittish about morals, religion, and culture, especially after the perceived "jihad" at the Houston convention. Republicans liked economics. At some level it seemed that they believed that with enough money, everything would be fine. Ironically, it was an economic determinism that mirrored Marxism. Communism basically believed everything was about money, too. If man was fully cared for and didn't have to worry about his physical needs, then eventually utopia would exist. Republicans believed the same thing—they just wanted man to be richer than the Marxists did. No one was more explicit about this than the shiny, happy, positive former Housing and Urban Development secretary and presumptive 1996 presidential nominee, Jack Kemp.

Kemp, the self-described "bleeding heart conservative," had long championed care for the underprivileged. But for Kemp, economics would be the savior. For Bennett, Reed, and the other cultural conservatives, Kemp had it backwards: values nurtured economics. Around the time Madonna released her notorious erotica book, *Sex*, Bennett joked, "A country where 900,000 people can buy the Madonna book for $50 a copy is not a country in a severe economic crisis—unless you say they're all rich Republicans. A country where that many people are buying the Madonna book for that much money has another kind of problem."

Jack Kemp's economic determinism was part of the Republicanism that made me cringe. The (still-kicking) supply-side notion of trickle-down economics offended me. A "rich get richer" policy wasn't a policy at all; it was justification for greed. It struck me as anti-Jesus. Jesus talked a lot about money. But Jesus' discussions had to do with how one couldn't really pursue money and God at the same time. He couldn't have been much clearer when he said, "No one can serve two masters. Either he will hate the one and love the other, or he will be devoted to the one and despise the other. You cannot serve both God and Money." Yet, again the Republican Party seemed to think that more money would take care of everything. Clearly, I hadn't yet become fully Republican.

The economic Republicans dominated in early 1993, and Jack Kemp was their leader. He himself didn't play the religion card with religious voters, but he basked in his wife's well-known evangelicalism. She was a very strong evangelical Christian, as were all of his eight kids. He was pro-life and pro-family, though he was generally reluctant to talk about those topics.

When Bill Bennett told me he was teaming up with Kemp to start a new organization, I was surprised, dismayed, and, after a few moments, elated. Combining values and economics, virtue and taxes, the new organization would have a potential presidential and vice presidential ticket under one roof. And I got to be part of it. Maybe supply-side economics wasn't *that* bad after all.

The new organization was intended to be one part Reaganism (that is, pro-freedom), one part historic economic conservatism, and one part faith-and-culture conservatism. It would favor tax cuts and a pro-democracy foreign policy, while lifting the poor through economic empowerment. It would uphold traditional American values like marriage and family. Bennett and Kemp's organization would hold Clinton responsible for his activities, actions, and politics while simultaneously challenging the existing Republican establishment.

Not inconveniently, it would also be a grassroots advocacy organization operating in states around the country on important legislative and electoral policy matters. In other words, our group would spend the next four years recruiting conservative grassroots activists in states like California, Texas, Florida, Michigan, Pennsylvania, South Carolina, and Georgia. We would spend a lot of our time in very important Republican primary states that also happened to have a lot of electoral votes.

I got to play a serious role in the organization's creation because there just weren't any other people to do it. There were three of us on Bennett's staff. There were three people from HUD who were going to follow Kemp. But since it was still December 1992, they remained government employees and were strictly limited in what they could do. We were it.

Everything was up in the air with the new organization, including its name. Kemp insisted that "Lincoln" be used somehow. Bennett insisted there had to be something about "American renewal." Endless options were tossed around: the Lincoln Center for Renewal, Lincoln's American Renewal Society, the Lincoln Republican Renewal Society. Nothing quite worked. Then, one afternoon, someone came up with it. We were to be the Lincoln Institute for American Renewal. Bennett was fine with it. Kemp loved it. Other aides deemed it appropriate. The financial backers liked it, too.

I got on the phone with a lawyer to begin the process of incorporating the name. As we talked I began making folder labels for the new group. The lawyer talked and I daydreamed. Since "Lincoln Institute for American Renewal" was too long for a tab, I wrote the acronym. Oops.

We finally settled on Empower America.

As the days wound down in the Bush administration, formerly powerful staffers started calling the office and telling us why they would be important additions to the Bennett/Kemp team. They sent résumés, video clips from their speeches to high school ceremonies across the country, and an occasional fruit basket.

In a way it was humbling. Their jobs were suddenly gone, and so were their lofty positions in the local pecking order. One of those people was a dear friend from church. He had arranged for my job on the presidential commission on women in the military that, in turn, had opened up the door to Bennett. I felt bad for him and for his family, but there wasn't anything I could do to help him. Fortunately, he found a dream job back in his home state of Texas.

But, the transition was mostly thrilling for me. Now I was on the inside and helping determine what the Republican Party could be. I talked to my pastor, who volunteered to lead a Bible study for me with some of the new staff members. He reminded me that building a biblical foundation during these pre-power years would help insulate us from corruption once we were in power. But he also said something else that I didn't like. Our goal as Christians, he said, wasn't to figure out what we wanted to do and invite God into it. Our goal was to find what God was doing and be part of that. I objected. Isn't what we are doing God's work, especially since we are Christians who are doing it? Maybe, he said. Or maybe not. To presume our agenda is God's agenda is a dangerous thing, even for Christians. He could have added "especially for Christians" but he didn't. He made his point. I still didn't like it, but I couldn't put my finger on why.

There was only one drawback to my new job. Right around the corner was the new Clinton/Gore inaugural store. Every time I stepped out for lunch I saw a line of people waiting to get in and buy some new merchandise. Mugs, T-shirts, posters, and underwear were all adorned with the Clinton/Gore logo or the official seal of the presidential inaugural. Fleetwood Mac's "Don't Stop" played incessantly. How did I know this? I kept stopping by and looking around and watching the giddy people. I was rubbernecking at the political wreck that had befallen America.

How could anyone celebrate a Clinton presidency? That smug mug, the corners of his lips turned down, the upper lip covering the bitten lower lip as though he were about to howl or cry or spit: I wanted to slap it. He had Richard Nixon's deliberate cadence, Jimmy Carter's drawl, and he tried to sound like John Kennedy. Could he be a more obvious fraud? I understood that George H. W. Bush hadn't been the most inspirational president. His relationship with the spoken word was strained. He had broken his promise not to raise taxes. He had given us David Souter. But still, compared to Clinton, Bush seemed Lincolnian.

Most mystifying for me was trying to understand God. The Bible made it clear that God chose a nation's leaders. What was God thinking when it came to Bill Clinton? During the dreary days after the Bush loss I pondered these questions with friends. One plausible theory was that Bill Clinton represented God's judgment on our morally loose nation. Sometimes God did that kind of thing. He sent along wicked leaders so that his people would realize just how much they needed him. Eventually the wicked leader would be replaced by a godly one and much rejoicing would follow as the years of drought or famine came to an end. Perhaps that is what would happen here. Perhaps we would learn our lesson, turn the nation around, and be rewarded with a godly leader.

Things only got worse as Clinton's inauguration neared. My Christian friends and I casually wondered aloud about the possible lifestyle choices of Secretary of Health and Human Services Donna Shalala and Attorney General Janet Reno. We were certain that the incoming Commerce secretary, Ron Brown, was corrupt. Then there was Hillary. She made Bill's smugness seem positively humble. We all *knew* what she was really like—her disparaging words about stay-at-home moms still reverberated. We knew *she* thought that staying home and baking cookies was akin to slavery—she had said it, or something close to it. Word emerged that she would play a very active role in domestic policy by heading up a White House task force on health care reform. She was also apparently going to be intimately involved in vetting Clinton judicial nominees. He was intent on reinstating federal funding for abortion, allowing gays to serve openly in the military, permitting the abortion pill to be dispensed, and using U.S. foreign aid money to fund abortions. Darkness and gloom had descended upon the land and God's judgment was sure to follow.

I had grown so passionate about my politics that I had less and less time for God. More and more often, Sunday mornings were spent not at church but in front of the television, watching the "morning shows." It's the political junkie's form of Sabbath worship: watching *Meet the Press, This Week with David Brinkley* (now *This Week with George Stephanopoulos*), and *Face the Nation*. The shows are ground zero for talking heads. They are status symbols—to be an invited guest is a big deal—and they are unscripted, so actual news can be made. After every appearance guests get mugs. Staffers and even big shots throughout Washington want to have one of those mugs.

It wasn't that I was turning away from God, or so I thought. I was simply doing what needed to be done to honor God in my work. Besides, I did get to church, just rarely for the sermons. I showed up for the Sunday school class, after which we would head out to brunch with our friends. We talked about politics. When I had first arrived at church three years before, and heard about people like me who skipped church but showed up for Sunday school, I rolled my eyes. How could you be serious about God if you weren't willing to be part of worship? Now, I was one of them.

The hunger for God and for peace that Jesus had ignited in me was still very real. I still looked to the passage in Matthew where he promised peace for my soul, and I still longed for peace to be true. But instead of searching for it in the Bible or in church or in quiet meditation, I was trying to find it in politics. I spent countless more hours doing politics than doing God. After all, God had called me to serve him there.

Empower America grew bigger and grander with every hour. Not only were Bill Bennett and Jack Kemp involved, so was former United Nations Ambassador Jeane Kirkpatrick. Five governors or ex-governors came on board: John Engler from Michigan, Tommy Thompson from Wisconsin, Bill Weld from Massachusetts, Carroll Campbell from South Carolina, and former New Jersey governor Tom Kean. The media joked that we had almost as many potential presidential candidates under one roof as did the United States Senate.

I was given a new assignment. Bill Bennett came up with an idea to quantify America's moral decline. Economists relied heavily on something called the Index of Leading Economic Indicators. Those indicators included everything from housing starts to sheet metal purchases to lumber. Each predicted something in the future. Taken together, they gave economists a hint about the future growth (or lack thereof) of the economy.

Bennett reasoned that we needed something similar, to get a grasp on what was happening in the culture. Anecdotal information existed about America's moral decline—divorce rates were up, crime was up, educational achievement was down, abortion was up. But that information had never been gathered together in a single place, to build a snapshot of where we were as a people. I headed up the research.

The information I gathered was startling when it was displayed visually. "Divorce is up" is far less disturbing than seeing a chart from 1960 to 1990 that ascends at nearly a 45-degree angle. The same was true of crime, violent crime, abortion, teenage pregnancies, and a host of other social ills. We ran the early data by Jack Kemp to get his reaction. "You've got to compare them to economic data," he said. "They probably were worse when the economy was worse." So we decided to set the statistics against some economic indicator, something of a test of the Bennett versus Kemp approach to life. From 1960 to 1980, the American population grew 40 percent. Gross Domestic Product (GDP) tripled and government spending increased five times, even after adjusting for inflation. But during that same period, there was a 500 percent increase in violent crime; more than a 400 percent increase in illegitimate births; a tripling of the percentage of children living in single-parent homes; a tripling of teenage suicides; a doubling of the divorce rate; and a drop of almost 75 points in average SAT scores. Those were the kinds of numbers that should have settled arguments among conservatives. Laissez-faire, Reagan-style conservatism wasn't enough. Cultural renewal was essential. We showed the numbers to Kemp, who found them interesting but absolutely unconvincing. The economy simply hadn't grown enough, he thought.

As Bennett concluded in the report, "Today the forces of social decomposition are challenging—and in some instances, overtaking—the forces of social composition. And when decomposition takes hold, it exacts an enormous human cost. *Unless these exploding social pathologies are reversed, they will lead to the decline and perhaps even to the fall of the American republic.*"

The report was released in March 1993 and was featured on Rush Limbaugh's talk show, where Limbaugh cited it for "some of the most chilling statistics I have ever read. . . . [The numbers] are like a kick to the solar plexus." He told people to write to us if they wanted copies. Tens of thousands of people did. Many of the notes were on frilly pages, or on sheets of paper with Bible verses printed on the bottom. They were mostly women. And their notes didn't just say, "Please send me a copy of your report." They said, "God bless you for your work." "Thank you for letting people know what is happening to our country." "We need this kind of information." For all the media's focus on the self-appointed Christian conservative leaders, it was grassroots people like these folks who fueled the movement. They followed the Falwells, Robertsons, and Reeds because they trusted the men's Christian faith. Moms and pops trusted them just as they trusted their pastors and Bible study leaders. Their desires were to fix the problems they saw around them: friends' divorces, crime, children living in poverty. Christian leaders were telling them politics was the answer. They believed it.

In the process of putting the report together Bennett had opened up his Rolodex to me. Professors, sociologists, political colleagues, reporters, and theologians became regular phone-conversation partners. A young political scientist at Princeton named John DiIulio, a leading voice for criminal justice reform, directed me to all the necessary information for everything crime-related. His mentor, the famed political scientist James Q. Wilson, helped as well. Reporters like Joe Klein, then of *Newsweek,* and E. J. Dionne of the *Washington Post* helped answer questions on reports, facts, and figures. Theologians like Michael Novak and Richard John Neuhaus, who were already key members of the religious Right, helped me. The diversity of Bennett's contacts reflected his diversity of opinion. Though he was indisputably conservative, he had friends from across the political spectrum who respected him for his willingness to challenge the status quo on virtually any issue. He introduced me to a world wider than I could have aspired to know.

Work on this *Index of Leading Cultural Indicators* also reinforced my belief in the primacy of values. None of this was really about money after all. All of the statistics I had found and analyzed had to do with behavior. Jack Kemp's tax cuts weren't going to decrease divorce. Lowering the tax on capital gains wasn't going to help with drug addiction. Ending the estate tax wasn't going to reduce teenage suicide.

Shrinking the size of government wasn't particularly going to help, either. A smaller Department of Commerce wasn't going to decrease teenage pregnancy. Bennett pointed me to the great Southern novelist Walker Percy to help clarify my thinking. When asked his greatest fear, Percy had said, "Probably the fear of seeing America, with all its great strength and beauty and freedom . . . gradually subside into decay through default and be defeated . . . from within by weariness, boredom, cynicism, greed and in the end helplessness before its great problems."

By and large Democratic leaders avoided these topics. While the emerging Democratic Leadership Council, with the help of Bill Clinton, was working to change popular perception of how the party viewed these cultural issues, they had a tough job. Candidate Clinton presented himself as a "different kind" of Democrat and even took on explicit lyrics in rap music in the form of Sister Souljah. He was, however, the exception. Most Democratic leaders were comfortable talking about children in poverty and the need for greater health care coverage. But when it came to objective facts like increasing divorce rates, increasing teenage suicide rates and the like, Democrats were largely silent and sometimes hostile. When confronted with the challenge of an increase in divorce rates that resulted in too many children living in single-parent homes, the Democratic response would be something akin to Barbara Boxer's, that we need to "make sure abortions are kept legal." It didn't seem to faze most Democratic leaders that 1.5 million unborn children were aborted every year. In fact, they had prevented the pro-life Democratic governor of Pennsylvania from speaking at their 1992 convention. They had drug problems too. The Democrats fought against the enforcement of drug laws as a way to curb drug abuse. When questions were raised about the easy violence and even easier sex in popular entertainment, the Democratic response tended to be, "Censorship!" Nowhere was that made clearer than when Al Gore's wife had to make a trip to Hollywood to repent for her days as head of the Parents Music Resource Center, where she had lobbied for warning labels on music. Tipper Gore, a Democrat, had led a bipartisan fight to clean up cultural pollution. She even got the "Tipper sticker" about explicit lyrics placed on albums. But before her husband could be considered for the vice presidential slot alongside Bill Clinton, she had to apologize for it.

I wondered why the Democratic establishment had gone soft on these important moral issues. The Democratic Party that I was raised in was the party that fought against racial injustice. So too, I figured, they would fight against the ravages of divorce or the horror of drugs. Yet they weren't just absent from those battles, they attacked those who fought them.

It is easy to say that I became a Republican because I went through a religious conversion, felt guilty about an abortion, or just needed a job. Those things are all true. But if the Democratic Party had displayed a similar interest in addressing these cultural problems, I would have run to them. Instead, they embodied a hostility toward these issues and toward Christian involvement in the political world that was increasingly known as the last acceptable form of bigotry.

CHAPTER FOUR

The Last Acceptable Form
of Bigotry

There were notable exceptions.

In August 1993 the fight to end the "last acceptable form of bigotry" against evangelical Christians found its most powerful and unexpected ally. His name was Bill Clinton.

During his Martha's Vineyard vacation, President Clinton strolled around the Bunch of Grapes bookstore in Vineyard Haven looking for some good reads. For some reason he picked out a new and relatively obscure book by a Yale University law professor named Stephen Carter. The book, *The Culture of Disbelief*, argued that American law and politics treated people of devout religious faith as if they were alien-like oddities—or worse, as a clear and present danger to American life. "More and more," Carter wrote, "our culture seems to take the position that believing deeply in the tenets of one's faith represents a kind of mystical irrationality, something that thoughtful, public-spirited American citizens would do better to avoid."

Bill Clinton agreed. He returned from his vacation filled with religious fervor. He told reporters he had read Carter's book, urged all of America to read it, and said, "Sometimes I think the environment in which we operate is entirely too secular. The fact that we have freedom of religion doesn't mean we need to try to have freedom from religion. It doesn't mean that those of us who have faith shouldn't frankly admit that we are animated by that faith, that we try to live by it—and that it does affect what we feel, what we think, and what we do." The president would return to this theme repeatedly during the next six months, not only making *The Culture of Disbelief* a phenomenal bestseller, but elevating the discourse about religious diversity. Ironically, he gave a key Christian conservative political argument a credibility and legitimacy it had never had.

I didn't know what to think. Part of me really wanted to believe Clinton had been converted and that he would soon be singing from the true gospel of faith, crusading against abortions and for the rest of my Christian agenda. But I mostly had to side with my conservative Christian allies who thought Clinton was simply being "Slick Willie" all over again. He was using God for his own political ends. How low could he go? After his hellish first year in office, marked by Whitewater and the Troopergate allegations of marital infidelity, among other things, he was now having a foxhole religious conversion to gain sympathy. Ugh.

As one conservative Christian columnist observed, "Whatever Clinton's motives, his Christian offensive is good politics. He is drawing evangelicals toward him just as the Republican Party, stunned by charges of pandering to the religious right, is pushing them away. Clinton doesn't need to recruit an army of converts. Gaining even 20 percent of the evangelical bloc amounts to millions of votes."

My view of Clinton was hardly in the minority among evangelicals. One evening while in Chattanooga on business I drove out to meet a friend from Birmingham, Alabama (three hours away) at a rib joint halfway between the two cities. We ate, caught up on things, and headed back to our respective cities. However, I accidentally locked my keys in the rental car while filling up the gas tank. It was midnight. I am a six-foot-five half-Chinese man from New York. I didn't blend in. The folks at the service station were very nice. They called the sheriff, waking him up from a deep slumber, and said, "Some Yankee has locked his keys in his damn car. Can you help him out?" As we waited for him to arrive, the gas station owner made small talk.

"So, boy, where you from?" he inquired.

"Uh, Washington, D.C."

"Mmmm hmm. What cha do?"

"Well, sir, I work in politics." I didn't know why I was calling him "sir." I guess it is what a "boy" does in Alabama.

"Politics. Hmm. You work for the Clintons, don't you?"

"Me? No sir. I don't. I work for the Republicans."

He just looked me in the eyes and said, "That Hillary Clinton. She's the Antichrist."

I thought about the appropriate response. I didn't *really* think she was the Antichrist. I thought her husband was. Nevertheless I found myself saying, "Yes sir, I believe she just might be."

The sheriff arrived shortly thereafter. The gas station owner greeted him saying, "This here boy is okay. He hates the Clintons, too." The sheriff smiled, unlocked my car, and sent me on my way with a blessing.

Meanwhile, however, some prominent evangelical pastors met with President Clinton and came away with far different conclusions. One of them, Jack Hayford, a charismatic evangelical pastor of an eight-thousand person church in Los Angeles, left the meeting saying, "It may bewilder some to have it said that this man believes in the Bible and in Jesus Christ as God's Son, the Savior." Another religious leader said, "People asked me, sometimes mockingly, can someone be a Christian and a Democrat? And my own answer is: this president is both."

It saddened me that such good Christians could be so easily duped. Just one visit with the president and they rolled over like a love-hungry puppy. Christians couldn't let presidential power blind them to their role restoring religious values to public life. They had to stay the course. Three of us at Empower America were particularly passionate in our beliefs about this.

One, Peter Wehner, was Bennett's longtime aide. Mid-thirties, balding, a bit paunchy, deeply serious, Wehner was devoutly Christian and devoutly Bennettian. There was a quiet kindness and thoughtfulness to him. He took an active interest in the people who worked with him and for him. He tutored an underprivileged special-needs teenager, with intense devotion. He supplied money, inspiration, counsel, and endless love. Finally, he was unfailingly loyal to Bennett. Any criticism, particularly by a conservative or Christian leader, was greeted with a stern rebuke.

Mike Gerson was the other person in our Clinton-skeptics group. Kemp's new speechwriter, Mike had Beatles-era floppy hair, and an affinity for fountain pens and Ferragamo ties. He was also an evangelical wunderkind. He had read Henry Kissinger's *Years of Upheaval* (all 1,283 pages) when he was twelve. He wasn't into sports or movies or movie starlets, but he was passionately in love with the conservative columnist George Will. When Mike first arrived in Washington in the late 1980s, he occasionally drove to Will's house and parked at the bottom of the hill that was his front lawn, in hopes of catching a glimpse of the writer. Mike had a staggering grasp of history (including church history), literature, theology, and sacred music. He endlessly gnawed on disposable plastic pens, and wrote indecipherable scrawl on yellow legal pads. Mike also had some unique views. He frequently bemoaned democracy, calling it inferior to benevolent dictatorship. We laughed and so did he, but only to a point. He was intellectually serious about it. A noble dictatorship made it much easier to get things done. The impossible problem, he knew, was finding the benevolent leader. He was stuck with democracy.

Mike was a friend but he was also a hero of mine. For several years in the late 1980s, Mike had worked for Chuck Colson. He had actually ghostwritten Colson's *Kingdoms in Conflict,* the book that not only helped define the cultural war in which Christians were engaged but which had also introduced me to my sometime patron saint, William Wilberforce. If I needed any further affirmation of God's hand in my life I had to look no further than Mr. Gerson. God was affirming my calling by putting me in the company of the very people who had opened my eyes to that calling.

The three of us—Peter, Mike, and I—shared a common faith in Jesus. We also genuinely wondered about the line between faith and politics. How far was too far? How far wasn't far enough?

I found a passage in C. S. Lewis's *Screwtape Letters* that scared me. *Screwtape* contains fictional correspondence between a young demon, Wormwood, just learning how to vex Christians, and his more powerful demonic uncle, Screwtape. Toward the end of the book, as the Christian has developed, Screwtape advises his young cousin on how to really derail a Christian.

> Let him begin by treating patriotism . . . as a part of his religion. Then let him, under the influence of partisan spirit, come to regard it as the most important part. Then quietly and gradually nurse him on to the stage at which the religion becomes merely a part of the "cause," in which Christianity is valued chiefly because of the excellent arguments it can produce . . . [O]nce he's made the world an end, and faith a means, you have almost won your man, and it makes very little difference what kind of worldly end he is pursuing.

Even during the titanic struggle of World War II, Lewis was warning Christians to be careful about how they engaged in politics and which part of their heart they allowed politics to influence. I always remembered his words, but couldn't hold on to their message. After all, we were all utterly convinced that Bill Clinton was a terrible blight on America.

At the same time, though, we were genuinely moved by the plight of America's poor, and dismissive of both parties' traditional solutions. Mike steered us to Alex Kotlowitz's book *There Are No Children Here,* a tragic and intimate portrait of life in Chicago's infamous Cabrini-Green housing project. Kotlowitz once asked a boy what he wanted to be when he grew up. The boy corrected him: "You mean *if* I grow up?" Pete told stories about his friend Isaac and the tragedies of his life. My wife added stories about her kindergartners in one of D.C.'s rougher neighborhoods. In the course of one year five of her kids either were shot or saw a family member get shot. Another boy stole everything in sight. She later learned it was because his crack-addicted parents weren't feeding him.

We couldn't help but conclude that the trillions of dollars spent on Lyndon Johnson's War on Poverty had only made things worse, a popular conservative position ever since Charles Murray's book *Losing Ground* had first argued it. We knew that profound political and spiritual changes needed to occur if America was going to change. Some of those changes would require tough love. The only way to get people off welfare was to make them work, even if that meant sending mothers to work. They had to know there was a cost to having children out of wedlock. Welfare needed to stop paying people to have illegitimate children and needed to be a much tougher way of life. We weren't attacking the myth of Cadillac-driving "welfare queens." We were attacking the whole system. It needed shock therapy.

That shock therapy, we hoped, would also revitalize what the eighteenth-century British political writer Edmund Burke called "little platoons." They were the churches and schools, clubs and charities, that served neighbors. They practiced hands-on compassion. Unfortunately, we believed, they had been continually undermined by the expanding welfare state. Government bureaucracies, run from Washington, took over feeding the hungry, caring for the sick, and helping suffering Americans, and so undermined all these little platoons.

We had no idea that we would wrestle for the next decade with how to mobilize little platoons and how to have government interact with them, or that we would all end up working together in the Bush White House. At the time, none of us had heard the name George W. Bush. Actually, Mike might have. He seemed to know almost everything.

Mike's professional purpose in life was to write speeches for Jack Kemp that would appeal to religious conservative voters. Mike's unenviable task was getting Kemp to sound like the social conservative that he wasn't. It wasn't that Jack was against most social conservative positions. He just didn't like to talk about them or believe they mattered. Mike beat his floppy-haired head against the walls of the Empower America offices at 1776 I Street. He chewed on pens, scrawled on his yellow notepad, and generally lost his sanity at this task.

Late one spring evening, Mike lolled down from the Kemp end of our offices to the Bennett wing. He poked his head in the door and wondered whether I would take a look at a speech. It was for Kemp's social conservative "coming out party" at the Southern Baptist Convention's Pastors' Conference. It was a crucial speech.

The Southern Baptist Convention was the single largest and most influential evangelical denomination. Once ardently Democratic, it had become more ardently Republican in the past twenty years, thanks to abortion, gay rights, the attack on traditionally religious people, and the general decline of the culture. Like me, these Baptists had defected from the Democratic Party because the Democrats were, at best, silent on these issues. Mike had arranged for the speech through friends and ensured that Kemp was the only political leader on the agenda.

Mike's draft didn't have the necessary zing to appeal to the ten thousand or so pastors in the audience. Abortion was barely mentioned, values were given short shrift, homosexuality wasn't included. Kemp had vetoed a long section about all these issues, and on the importance of the family. Mike begged and pleaded to have those things included, but he kept running into a brick wall. Compounding the problem was that Mike also couldn't get Jack to talk about his own personal faith. Instead, Jack wanted to talk about economics, empowerment zones, welfare reform, and the Clinton budget.

If Jack Kemp went to Orlando, spoke to a conference of Baptist pastors, and *didn't* talk about his personal faith in Jesus, it would be a disaster. Mike contemplated getting the invitation killed, or temporarily abducting Kemp so he couldn't make it to Orlando. How could we square the circle? How could we make Jack happy and the pastors happy?

Our only hope was to convince the pastors that Kemp's faith was so strong and so clearly central to his life he didn't *need* to talk about it. Just as a pastor could get up and talk without mentioning his own walk with Jesus, we needed to figure out how Jack could do the speech in evangelical shorthand. We inserted snippets of old hymns in economic sections—such as "the solid rock of economic principles." We threw in a few obscure turns of phrase known clearly to any evangelical, yet unlikely to be noticed by anyone else, even Kemp. Phrases like "narrow is the path of wealth." It was code.

Mike's best line of all was the opening joke. Kemp approached the lectern, faced ten thousand Southern Baptist pastors, paused, looked at them, smiled and said, "A politician among pastors. I feel like a lion in a den of Daniels." In those fourteen words, Kemp told the pastors everything they wanted to hear. He told them that he was one of them. It implied that Kemp had remarkable dexterity with the Bible. It fit the mood: perhaps more than any other group these Southern Baptist pastors were tired of being besieged by a culture that viewed them as anachronistic dingdongs. Finally, the joke played to the pastors' egos. Here was Jack Kemp, former football star, larger-than-life Cabinet secretary, and potentially the next president of the United States, recognizing *their* moral authority. He was saying, "Listen, I know I'm running for president, but *you* are the nation's real leaders."

This use of code language wasn't anything new to American politics. Many people in many different ages have used it. What was unique was its resurrection at this particular moment in time. It gave a reluctant political leader a way to connect with the single most powerful evangelical constituency in America. More important, it was also a way of speaking to the evangelical base without the biblically ignorant media picking up on it. Jack Kemp could simultaneously appeal to evangelicals and avoid sounding like he was embracing the religious Right. It was a method of talking about faith that would be used and reused in the years ahead by our future bosses or clients—John Ashcroft, Ralph Reed, Bob Dole, and George W. Bush.

Read the speeches of these men and you'll see phrases: "An America that recognizes the infinite worth of every individual and leaves the ninety-nine to find the one stray lamb," "the American family, the rock upon which this country was founded," "we have this land and are told to be good stewards of it and to be good stewards of each other," "There's power, wonder-working power, in the goodness and idealism and faith of the American people." Each instance may sound like a nice turn of phrase—or just a slightly weird choice of words—but they are much more than that. Many of them draw explicitly upon Jesus' parables. He called himself the good shepherd who left the herd of ninety-nine to find the one who had strayed. He was "the rock" of faith. His parable about being good stewards of God's gifts is one of his toughest. The last one comes from an old hymn: "There's power, wonder-working power in the blood of Jesus." Each of these instances and hundreds of others communicate exactly what Kemp communicated in Orlando. They are each an adept manipulation of Scripture that conveys Christianity without ever mentioning the name of Jesus. Of course, all this has its own irony. The Bible makes it clear that "at the name of Jesus every knee will bow and every tongue confess that he is Lord to the glory of the Father." In the name of what we understood to be God's political agenda, by contrast, we were hiding the Jesus we said we were serving.

This *should* have been driving me nuts. It should have offended me far more than anything President Clinton or the Democrats were doing. We were bastardizing God's words for our own political agenda and feeling good about it. The truth is I didn't think anything of it. I wouldn't for years.

I didn't need to think about it. Things were too good. Everywhere I looked we were making slow but steady progress. Values were a hot topic. Social conservatives were on the ascendancy. Though my part might have been small it felt like I was using my Christian faith appropriately to change politics. One surprising thing was how much I liked the lifestyle. I became more and more involved with Bennett's endeavors and relished the finer things in life—first-class travel, fantastically good food, and his cadre of friends and supporters.

The work was great but I was becoming a lousy husband. I had married soon after arriving in Washington. Jerilyn was quiet and tall, pretty and smart. She had become a Christian when she arrived at college and became my closest friend shortly thereafter. She had known me before I had acquired the political bug. At the time, my life's chief goal was following God, not for any particular thing he could do for me but just because God deserved to be followed. Having a nice quiet family life with time to fish was another major goal. Jerilyn wanted the same thing. Nevertheless, when I had decided I needed to bring my Christianity into the political marketplace she supported me.

After graduation we both moved to Washington. She wondered if she should go to Africa with the Peace Corps. We were both young. But we loved each other and couldn't really imagine life apart. Four months after arriving in Washington we were engaged. Three months later we were married.

But now, nearly four years into Washington life, I was at cultural war and we spent too much time apart. Hours that hadn't been too bad at first grew longer. Once-quiet evenings were filled with phone calls from people at work. Most other hours were spent working on memos or reading the latest important public policy book, article, or journal.

The more I worked, the more I wanted to work, and no one could talk me into doing it less. If I had worked on Wall Street and simply wanted to get rich, someone could have pointed me to any of Jesus' sayings on money and straightened me right out. If I were an entrepreneur starting a new business, someone could have done the same thing. But with politics and most specifically with the *godly* mission I was pursuing, no one could convince me I needed to do less of anything. Less would have felt like I loved God less, loved America less, and was less committed to the reformational calling in my life.

In late 1993, I was given a new assignment. With the *Index*'s success, Clinton's continued nightmare of a first term (Vince Foster's suspicious suicide, ongoing Whitewater investigations, and further "bimbo eruptions"), the upcoming midterm elections, and Empower America's dedication to advocating policy-heavy campaigns, someone came up with the idea that we should start educating potential candidates on how to run for office. I was in charge. The topics we chose were fairly easy. Welfare, immigration, taxes, crime, and cultural issues were the matters of the day. The case we laid out in binders and in conferences was simple: the Clinton Administration was presiding over a national disaster. Crime was through the roof. Welfare was trapping people in poverty. More kids lived in homes without fathers than in homes with fathers. The public schools were a disaster despite all the money that had been dumped into them. That this was the case not long after twelve years of Republican presidential leadership wasn't completely lost on me . . . just mostly. I had to stop to think about that and would even mention it to a friend. But I wouldn't dig any deeper with my questions. Part of me wanted to but most of me didn't want to. Things were going so well, why would I want to jeopardize any of it by pursuing questions that could lead who knows where?

We gave the candidates some essential facts—virtually all derived from the same neutral government statistics in Bennett's *Index*—on almost every issue that they would confront. We gave them quotes—often by Democrats—to back up what we were saying. We quoted Lyndon Johnson in 1965: "The family is the cornerstone of society. More than any other force it shapes the attitudes, the hopes, the ambitions, and the values of the child. And when the family collapses, it is the children that are usually damaged. When it happens on a massive scale the community itself is crippled." We found a quote from President Clinton's own domestic policy adviser, Bill Galston: "The best antipoverty program for children is a stable, intact family."

We offered policy prescriptions: an anticrime package with tougher sentencing, more prisons, and more police. We also proposed discouraging illegitimacy and teen pregnancy by prohibiting welfare to minor mothers and denying increased government assistance for additional children while on welfare. Spending on welfare should be cut, we argued, but not gratuitously. We wanted tough work provisions. To deal with family breakdown we told prospective candidates that there had to be increases in child support enforcement, tax incentives for adoption, strengthened rights for parents in their children's education, a $500 per child tax credit, and a repeal of the marriage tax penalty by which married couples actually ended up paying more in taxes than two single people living together. On the economic front we told candidates to advocate for small business incentives, capital gains cuts, and product liability reform. But the most important thing we emphasized was the culture. We talked about everything from religious discrimination, to abortion, to the idea that Hollywood's values weren't America's values. Prominent Republican pollsters Ed Goeas, Frank Luntz, and John McLaughlin all showed that these issues appealed to religious conservative voters.

Our first conference featured Kemp, Bennett, House Minority Whip Newt Gingrich, and a slew of social scientists and political consultants, all gathered to tell candidates how to run their races. More than two hundred candidates and staff showed up. Actor-turned-candidate Fred Thompson was there. A heart surgeon from Tennessee named Bill Frist wandered in, as did a former football star named Steve Largent. Unknown men and women who were already tired of the Clinton years showed up, too.

Our candidate schools ran throughout 1994. We educated more than six hundred conservative candidates on how to run for office. There was a common spirit and theme among all of them. "We're going to change Washington, D.C." one after another declared, "and we're not going to let Washington, D.C., change us!" There was also a common faith. A definite majority of these candidates talked openly about their religious faith. It animated them and drove their campaigns. We advised them to keep the religious discussions general, not specific, and to use softer, more nuanced language, such as the phrases that Kemp had used. They—and we—dreamed of nothing less than a Republican revolution. Such a revolution seemed more and more possible as 1994 progressed.

One afternoon early that fall, Bennett stuck his head into my office, tossed me hundreds of sheets of paper held together with a rubber band, and said, "Hey, look at this. Ralph Reed wants me to write a foreword for him. See if this is worthwhile." The title page read, "Faith Factor."

It was Reed's first book. His thesis was simple: the religious Right's modern success had been tied directly to Ronald Reagan's ascendancy. With Reagan gone, so was that movement. For it to return it would have to forgo the typical Washington model where organizations are built on direct-mail lists, press conferences at the National Press Club, and a few rallies that might get shown on C-SPAN at 3 A.M. If the religious Right was going to be serious it would have to reinvent itself as a grassroots political machine. Needless to say, it was exactly what Reed himself had accomplished. By mid-1994, less than five years after the founding meeting in Atlanta, the Christian Coalition was a twenty-million-dollar-a-year organization. Its chief weapon was its voter guide. The coalition had distributed forty million of them in 1992, showing where candidates stood on issues like abortion, gay rights, tax relief for families, the balanced budget amendment, and term limits. A network of sixty thousand evangelical and Roman Catholic churches handed them out. Membership in the organization, estimated at about two hundred thousand, was growing in 1994 by about ten thousand per week. The coalition's grassroots network included nearly a thousand chapters in all fifty states, interconnected by phone, fax, and every other communication device available.

Reed used familiar rallying cries. He denounced bigotry against people of faith. He demanded the familiar "seat at the table" for Christians. Once there, he said, the Christian agenda was a mainstream one—nothing that should frighten the average American, nothing religious—a balanced-budget amendment, term limits, and an end to the marriage penalty. Whereas Kemp had used code to appeal to evangelicals, when all he really wanted was libertarian economics, Reed openly represented religious voters but said they only really wanted more pro-family economic policies and term limits. He was arguing for what we at Empower America were arguing for. It was a virtually bulletproof political approach. Who could criticize such a mainstream movement without being labeled a bigot?

I suggested to Bennett that he write the foreword. He had me take a first crack at it. My civil rights and social justice heart poured out: "In reading this book I am reminded of a November, 1956 sermon delivered by Rev. Martin Luther King, Jr., in Montgomery, Alabama. During that speech King said, 'Always be sure that you struggle with Christian methods and Christian weapons. Never succumb to the temptation of becoming bitter. As you press on for justice, be sure to move with dignity and discipline, using only the weapon of love.' In this book Reed does not succumb to the temptation of complaining about the media and the political hostility aimed at religious conservatives. He takes a higher road than his critics. This book is the coming of age of a movement."

I turned in the draft. A few days later, Bennett sent it back with lots of changes and additions. None was more notable than this: "A caution, then, is perhaps in order—one which I believe Ralph Reed shares. When Christians enter the world of politics, they should keep the 'eyes of their heart' on the things that are above. One of the cornerstones of faith is the conviction that we are pilgrims and strangers and sojourners in this world."

Bennett continued, "When the news was brought to him in Carthage that Rome had been sacked, St. Augustine—a Roman citizen and a Roman patriot—knew that the empire that had ruled most of the civilized world for centuries was dying. But he was able to remind his flock of something which we too easily lose sight of. 'All earthly cities are vulnerable,' Augustine said. 'Men build them and men destroy them. At the same time there is the City of God which men did not build and cannot destroy and which is everlasting.' St. Augustine went on to write his master-piece, *De civitate Dei—The City of God.*"

As I typed the words into the computer, I paused. "The City of God." That is what I longed for. It was, I realized, what I longed for when I went to Jesus for the first time. It was home. The peace I wanted wasn't really ever going to be found here. It would be found in another time and in a far different place. That didn't mean I didn't want as much of it as I could get while I was here. Bennett's words, his warning, were right. Giving up anything eter-nal for anything temporal would be the greatest loss. I didn't want that. But, I thought, I wasn't doing that. I needed to stay awake and alert so that I never cross the line, but I definitely wasn't there yet.

Two weeks later my phone rang and a hyperenergetic voice on the other end said, "Hi, Ralph Reed here. Hey, I love the foreword Bill wrote for my book. I just talked to him. He said you helped. He said you were very good and very smart. Do you write speeches?"

"Sure," I said quickly, even though I had never written a full speech for another person—or myself—in my entire life. I had drafted paragraphs here and there, written op-eds, and made sug-gestions for Mike's speeches, but I figured that was good enough.

"Great, great, great. Listen, I've got a big speech at the National

Press Club in a few weeks—just a month before the elections. Can you help me?"

His speech's main theme was the same one Bill Clinton had embraced the previous year: we must end discrimination against people of "serious" religious faith, welcome them into the political debate, and embrace their enrichment of American life. I wrapped it in the language of the civil rights movement: equality, justice, and diversity.

It was the most satisfying work of my young life. As I sat listening to Ralph's speech something felt complete. I was fighting my own little civil rights battle. The Jesus that I had accepted in high school had fully merged with the Christian mission to invade politics I had embarked on in college. On the eve of the 1994 midterm elections I was part of the religious Right and I was proud of it.

Then came the revolution.

In November 1994, Republicans took control of Congress for what seemed like the first time since *Tyrannosaurus rex* walked the earth. At least that is what it felt like. In fact, it was the first time since 1954. More than three hundred of the candidates we had "educated" won races for various offices across the country. Newt Gingrich had taken some of the facts and suggestions of the Empower America candidate school, combined them with other long-held Republican policy ideas and thoughts of his own, and turned them into something called the "Contract with America." Every Republican running for federal office signed it. Against the flailing Clinton administration, Americans knew what Republicans were for and what they were going to do.

The revolution couldn't have happened without the Christian Coalition and other religious conservative groups. The coalition ended up distributing more than 50 million voter guides in that year. Those guides were passed out in churches after services and put on the windshields of cars during services. Though technically nonpartisan, the guides showed religious voters where candidates stood on abortion, gay rights, prayer in schools, and other hot-button social issues. In sheer numbers, it was the single greatest mobilization of religious voters in American history.

Capturing Congress was the fulfillment of one of the Christian conservative movement's greatest dreams. Congress controlled the government's purse strings and set the legislative agenda. Even though the Gingrich Contract was focused more on limiting government than on eliminating abortion, religious conservatives expected that the impossible dream of controlling Congress would be the beginning of reclaiming America for good and for God.

Things were good at Empower America. Newly elected members of Congress called our offices to thank us for what we had done in giving them the ammunition they needed to campaign. Ralph Reed called to see if I wanted to help with more speeches and possibly help him write his next book, for a mainstream publisher. Bill Bennett walked into my office and said that he had recommended me to help write some of Bob Dole's speeches, since Dole was now running for president. Mike Gerson popped in and said he had recommended me to a newly elected senator from Missouri named John Ashcroft. Life was perfect.

CHAPTER FIVE

Struggling to Kneel

I wandered around some unknown part of the U.S. Capitol, an area I didn't even know existed. I was looking for the hideaway where John Ashcroft was waiting to talk to me. I saw the stand used to hold the caskets of esteemed Americans lying in state. The hallways were dark, the ceilings were high, it felt claustrophobic. It felt like the catacombs.

I had never met Ashcroft before. In the evangelical political world he was akin to one of Jesus' disciples. Two-time Missouri attorney general and governor, the son of a Pentecostal preacher, Ashcroft had gone to Yale and the University of Chicago Law School. His devotion to Jesus and the tenets of his own Assemblies of God faith were never hidden. Neither was his political skill. The Show-Me State never gave politicians an easy time, yet Ashcroft managed to be among the most popular figures there.

None of the doors had numbers that I could see. I knocked on one door and poked my head in. Jesse Helms was snoring. He looked like Elmer Fudd. I closed it quietly. I kept wandering. I was late.

These hideaways were private little offices for senior senators. Less senior ones coveted them. They were little retreats where they could go and not be bothered. Ashcroft was borrowing his from a much more senior friend. I knocked on the next door that seemed to fit the description I had been given. I didn't open it. I heard a muffled grumble, sounding like something akin to a rockslide. It was either Barry White or John Ashcroft. I was in luck.

He was seated in such a little hobbit-sized room that I felt I should duck so my head wouldn't hit the ceiling. Ashcroft was seated on a couch. Another man sat on a chair. Ashcroft got up, greeted me with a smile and a handshake, introduced his friend as a former chief of staff, and said, "Uh, it is really an honor and a privilege to meet you." It felt genuine, which in turn felt odd and very un-Washington. No one talked like that, unless they were parodying someone who really talked like that.

Ashcroft told me what he was looking for. Still sounding a lot like Barry White, he explained that he saw politics through two perspectives. One was as a lawyer. The other was as a basketball lover. Politics, he said, was like both. The law part was obvious, basketball less so. "Politics isn't like baseball or football. You don't have scripted plays. The action is continuous. In baseball and football there are just bursts of action that interrupt long periods of inaction. In basketball you keep going and you have to improvise. I want people I can improvise with."

He explained he wanted logical thought and persuasive arguments, and that he liked confidence. He asked about me, my background, my family. I told the story of my father's unlikely and miraculous journey to America. I told him a story I had only recently learned.

My father's best friend in World War II was an American GI named Tom Stevenson. They fought on the same side but didn't know the same language. The last night they were together at war's end before Tom shipped off home and my father went north to fight against the communists, Tom said, "Tell me your dreams for your life." In broken English and basic Chinese my father told Tom that he wanted to study the earth; he wanted to study rocks and how the mountains were made. He had some theories he had developed during the war. Tom smiled and said that was great and they parted. Unbeknownst to my father, Tom's wife was heir to a banking fortune in Los Angeles. She and Tom were part of a small group of anonymous donors who did things to help people. For two years Tom and Sue pleaded with their friends—one of whom presided over the University of Redlands—to admit this unknown Chinese soldier. The friends declined and declined, but eventually they gave in. They sent my father a letter that somehow reached him on the northern front; it was an acceptance letter to college. One miracle wasn't enough, however. He also had to get a visa to the United States. In those days Chinese immigrants weren't welcomed with open arms. He went to the consulate, filled out a visa request form as best he could, stood in line, presented the letter and boat ticket, and asked for a visa. The foreign service officer asked to see paperwork not only for his scholarship, but also for housing and general financial support. "No freeloaders in America." The officer pulled out a stamp, slammed it down, and handed it back to my father. There was a big red REJECTED on his application.

My father tried to get the paperwork. He couldn't. He went back in hopes he might get lucky the second time. Again he was rejected. Finally, a week before the boat sailed he went back one more time to plead his case. The same man who rejected him twice before saw him again. "You have anything new?"

"No," my father says.

The man pulled out the same REJECTED stamp he had used twice before. As he was about to bring it down on the application, however, someone came out from a door behind the desk officer. He whispered something in his ear. The man pulled out a different stamp, and banged it down on the paper. ACCEPTED.

My father never saw the man's name, never saw him again. He believed it was an angel. I told Ashcroft I believed it, too.

"How could you not?" he said.

His eyes started darting and it was clear he was debating whether to reveal something to me.

"The morning I was sworn in to the Senate, my father, who had flown to Washington for the ceremony, gathered some of our friends together. Someone suggested that I be anointed with oil . . . it was something that they did as a blessing for leaders in the Bible. A friend poked around the kitchen to find some oil. There was only Crisco. My father said it would do. I knelt in front of the sofa where my father was sitting. Some stood. Others kneeled. 'The spirit of Washington is arrogance, and the spirit of Christ is humility,' he said. 'Put on the spirit of Christ. Nothing of lasting value has ever been accomplished in arrogance.' With that, I noticed my father, who was so weak, battling congestive heart failure, struggling to get out of the sofa. 'Dad, don't worry, you don't need to stand,' I said. He looked at me sternly and said, 'John, I am not struggling to stand. I am struggling to kneel.' He got down on his knees and prayed for me. He anointed me with oil. He flew home and the next day he died.

"This office, my service in Washington, it is anointed time."

This is not the conversation I expected to have. I expected we'd talk about policy and about how we could beat down the liberals and basically expand Christ's kingdom in the United States Senate. Instead, I was getting challenged by the story of a holy man's submission to God.

I tried to picture the old man with so much faith and resolve that he would use every bit of his strength to get on his knees before God. That picture was such a stark contrast with everything I had seen around me and so much of what was inside me. It was hard to feel humble. "We" had just taken control of Congress. Christians like me were ascending and the liberals who'd ruled for so long were descending. It felt like we were so close to achieving those Christian dreams for a better country.

And yet, hearing the story, I wanted to weep. John Ashcroft's father nailed Washington, politics, and the Christian temptation in politics with three sentences. His father had nailed me and I had no idea what to do with it. I don't think Senator Ashcroft knew what to do with it in his own life, either. That was part of the reason he was telling the story.

Part of me wanted to fall to my own knees. I was reminded for that moment of the God I had known before politics. I remembered getting to know God and how enthralling he was to me. There wasn't any need for God "plus" anything. Pursuing him alone was sufficient. At that moment, if John Ashcroft could have magically given me the choice between working for him or having faith like his father, I'd have chosen the latter.

I don't remember much else about the interview, but I got the job. I didn't forget the story, either. But with time and the pressing needs of politics it became quaint and sweet and lost any cutting force of conviction for me.

Ashcroft wasn't the only overtly Christian member of Congress ushered in by the 1994 "revolution." I had met many others the year before at the candidate schools. Sam Brownback, Todd Tiahrt, Mark Sanford, Joe Scarborough, Mark Souder, Joe Pitts, Saxby Chambliss, John Shadegg, Tom Coburn, and dozens more came to Washington wide-eyed. They weren't going to sell out to lobbyists and special interests. They were sure of that.

Capitol Hill was the place to be. I became part of Team Ashcroft because he wanted a policy director to come up with new ideas, write speeches, and be an intellectual foil, a sparring partner and power forward.

Not only was I starting full-time work for Senator Ashcroft, but I was now writing speeches for Senator Dole as well. Dole needed help with social conservatives. Like Kemp, he was reticent to speak publicly about abortion, the family, and his own faith. Dole had been raised in a different age. Most members of the "greatest generation" kept such things private. But in 1995, running for president, even Bob Dole knew he needed to sound very, very Christian. Christians were the party's power brokers now.

It felt like the social conservative political world had only a dozen people in it and I was working for several of them at the same time. Ralph Reed and I worked on his every speech. In turn he introduced me to Pat Robertson, who, after I wrote one particular speech for him, called and told me it was great. "Brother, brother," he said, "you and I make beautiful music together." I reminded him he was on a cell phone. He hung up.

There were times I was afraid that I had accidentally given one man another man's lines, and that he would be accused of plagiarizing the other guy just because they happened to share a tired speechwriter.

With the "struggling to kneel" story safely behind me, I grew ever more passionate about pursuing policies defending religious freedom, the family, unborn babies, our kids, and the poor, all with the confident assumption that God was on my side. It wasn't that I heard from him daily or needed to. I simply knew that he supported my issues.

Yes, there were Republican things that bugged me. I didn't agree, as many Republicans argued, that cutting government was in and of itself a good thing. While bashing the U.N. was good for conservative applause, I felt the U.N. was a vitally important, if misguided, institution. Praising business was fine with me but sometimes it felt like business was akin to a real Santa Claus in the minds of Republicans—always doing good and helping people. I hardly believed that. The whole death penalty thing also got to me. I understood the Old Testament basis for it but could hardly distinguish why we retained that but didn't retain things like stoning adulterers. Mine wasn't a popular position. One day before I left Empower America, a Kemp aide joked, "Forget the electric chair, let's just get electric bleachers and fry them all."

I didn't talk about these uncertainties. Politics wasn't for purists, it was for pragmatists. I knew I would never find a party that agreed with everything I believed, so those were just differences I would have to accept. Besides, the money was getting to be quite nice. Between my Senate salary and all the speeches, I made almost as much money as college friends now on Wall Street. Granted, this was before the stock market boom, but still, it was nice money. Sometimes I thought about Jesus' words, "What does a man gain if he gets the world and loses his soul?" But they couldn't apply to me, I figured, since I was doing God's work.

I was Ashcroft's compassion advocate, and compassion was quickly becoming a Republican buzzword, thanks largely to Newt Gingrich. In the weeks before Republicans officially took power, Bill Bennett recommended that Gingrich read a little-noticed three-year-old book titled *The Tragedy of American Compassion*, by a Texas professor named Marvin Olasky. Olasky, a former Marxist turned evangelical Christian, and journalism history professor of no particular fame, had spent 1990 researching how pre-twentieth-century America cared for the poor. In days before money could be the answer, human kindness had worked better. Premodern America didn't have the financial resources of modern America. It also had no social safety net through government assistance. Olasky discovered that the precursor to social welfare programs was sacrificial giving by families, churches, and neighborhoods. In some instances that giving was mandated. Early laws in the Northwest Territory, for instance, required relatives to care for destitute family members or face serious fines. Churches fed people. Charities did, too. But they did more than feed bodies; they also nurtured souls. Pointing out that "compassion" literally means "suffering with," Olasky argued that "help" wasn't just about food, but about life transformation through God's power. It was a powerful case for the little platoons.

Gingrich read the book. In his first address to his colleagues as majority leader, he told them they should all read it, too. He went on to exhort them about the need to confront the types of social decay that Bill Bennett had written about in his *Index of Leading Cultural Indicators*. "How can any American read about an eleven-year-old buried with his Teddy bear because he killed a fourteen-year-old before another fourteen-year-old killed him, and not have some sense of, 'My God, where has this country gone?' How can we not decide that this is a moral crisis equal to segregation, equal to slavery, and how can we not insist that every day we take steps to do something?"

No one clapped. Republicans were befuddled about this "poverty" talk. Poverty hadn't been part of Gingrich's Contract with America. The Contract was about crime and taxes and other typical Republican stuff. Democrats were uncertain for much the same reason. Gingrich talking about poverty while cutting government programs? The unrepentant Grinch wanting to be the Easter Bunny?

In fact, Speaker Gingrich was showing Republicans how to co-opt compassion from the Democrats. Government welfare programs had produced poverty, teen crime, illegitimacy, joblessness, and general hopelessness. The way out was through families, churches, and neighborhoods. And while government wasn't the answer, it couldn't run away from the problem, either.

While I found Gingrich's compassionate conservatism thrilling, Christian conservatives were unhappy with Gingrich and the new Congress from day one. They had been the most significant single force behind the Republican ascendancy. And yet the new Congress wanted nothing to do with social issues. By May 1995, Pat Robertson was lamenting that "Congress is ignoring the concerns of Christian and pro-family voters." James Dobson sent a letter to

Haley Barbour, head of the Republican National Committee, reminding him that "43 percent of your votes last November came from evangelical Christians" who "trusted Republicans to deal with their deepest longings and fears." Yet Congress, even a Republican Congress, wasn't fulfilling their desires.

It was a rude awakening for Christian conservatives who were looking forward to big dreams like a Human Life Amendment and smaller ones like crackdowns on pornography and gambling, more prayer in public schools, and teenage abstinence. Now, however, they were learning they would have to lobby Republicans to do good, as hard as they had lobbied Democrats not to do bad. Robertson sent out letters urging his supporters to call their representatives because "even the best members of Congress prefer not to discuss moral issues."

Nothing changed. And Barbour, RNC chairman, said nothing was going to change. Congress, he said, couldn't direct its attention to social issues until it had first dealt with economic concerns.

Even Ralph Reed was growing antsy. Though he had weekly breakfasts with Speaker Gingrich, by mid-1995 Ralph introduced the "Contract with the American Family" to try to move things along. This contract called for crackdowns on child pornography and Internet porn, an increase in the per-child tax credit, and a provision to allow working mothers to establish tax-free IRAs. There was also support for a recently introduced "Religious Equality Amendment" to the Constitution to explicitly end religious hostility against people of faith by reaffirming America's heritage of religious freedom. He included provisions to help the poor, including tax credits for charitable giving. The contract didn't call on Congress to end all abortions. Instead, it urged restrictions on late-term abortions and taxpayer-funded abortions.

It was attacked—by fellow believers. Focus on the Family's James Dobson and the Family Research Council's Gary Bauer jumped on Reed, saying his abortion suggestions weren't aggressive enough. "It would be strange if millions of new voters got involved in the process for an agenda that turned out to be this modest," Bauer said. Pat Buchanan followed: "It sets the hurdles too low. The [Christian] Coalition has given away any boldness in a search for popularity and consensus."

As the year progressed, the divisions between religious conservatives and Congress widened and splits within the movement grew. One side, led by Reed and backed up by Bennett and Ashcroft, advocated pragmatism. They reasoned that slow changes would eventually become great changes. There wasn't any chance a Human Life Amendment would pass Congress. An end to late-term abortions, however, had a real shot. The other side, led by Dobson and Bauer, advocated fighting for everything immediately. What good was power, they asked, if it wasn't used to fight the good fight? Abortion was America's cancer and needed to be nuked. As at the Republican Convention in 1992, it was the ideological and tonal difference between Pat Buchanan's "cultural war" and Robertson's "cultural engagement."

In some ways James Dobson went beyond Buchanan. He had always been pro-life, but slowly and seismically, Dobson grew less and less tolerant that abortions were still performed and change wasn't sure and swift.

In late summer Bennett invited me to Colorado for a hike and to accompany him during two back-to-back radio shows with Dobson. Focus had its headquarters there, a campus including its corporate center, and multiple office buildings. Its $100 million yearly budget easily made it the largest pro-family organization in the country. Dobson effusively praised Bennett. "You are such a godly leader for our country," he said. "You know, we need to talk about you running for president. I sense that God may be calling you."

Bennett shifted. "Mmmm, okay, good, glad you sense that."

"Bill, the country needs you for such a time as this. It really needs you. There isn't anyone like you, and your *Book of Virtues* just proves that. We need you in politics." Bennett's *Book of Virtues,* a compendium of moral stories, poems, and essays, was becoming a cultural phenomenon emblematic of a renewal of interest in "moral" matters. It would go on to sell more than three million copies, one of the bestselling books of the decade.

"I'm not sure that politics is the most important arena, Jim. Maybe we need to focus less on politics . . . and more on . . . the family?"

Dobson looked at him smiling. "Uh-huh. Well, Bill, we need you and I'm one hundred percent behind you."

Just weeks later, as Republicans were debating the possibility that Colin Powell might run for president, Bennett said that he could support him even if he wasn't pro-life. It wouldn't necessarily be his choice but he could support him.

Dobson went ape. He pulled the interviews with Bennett before they were aired. He attacked Bennett on his radio show, calling him a "sellout." He fired off a letter to Ralph Reed imploring Ralph to denounce Bennett. Instead, Reed sent Bennett the letter. Bennett wrote back to Dobson telling him he could not only support a pro-choice candidate, but that it was time to acknowledge that the pro-life plank in the Republican platform probably needed to go. The call for a constitutional amendment banning abortion was a fantasy. The proper concern, Bennett wrote, is reducing the 1.5 million abortions per year. The platform simply allowed Republicans to say that they are pro-life while never being required to actually do anything to reduce abortions. "If a pro-choice candidate of exemplary character used the bully pulpit to talk about, say, teen abstinence, adoption, crisis pregnancy centers, individual responsibility, and the importance of a civilization's common moral code—and did this well—he could have a profoundly positive impact on the nation's cultural condition. And he could do more to lower the number of abortions than a presidential candidate who supports a constitutional ban but does nothing more than pay lip service to the pro-life constituency."

Dobson and others wouldn't hear of it. And when they realized Congress failed them they went in search of a presidential candidate who would address their concerns. They would find their man in George W. Bush.

In Austin, Texas, however, Governor George W. Bush was having compassion problems of his own. The Texas Commission on Alcohol and Drug Abuse threatened to fine, jail, and revoke the state license for Teen Challenge, one of the faith-based drug and alcohol treatment programs highlighted by Olasky. The commission required that any drug and alcohol treatment center had to have licensed chemical-dependence counselors, and that all patients had to be treated through detoxification. Teen Challenge's approach was different. Jesus was their treatment. Pastors and former addicts were the counselors. They worked first on a person's soul, believing that once a person had found God, his addiction would disappear soon thereafter. Who better to treat addicts, they reasoned, than recovered addicts? Teen Challenge was the darling of the compassionate movement.

At first, Bush did nothing. Olasky led a 325-person rally of mostly Hispanics and blacks at the Alamo. Holding signs that read, BECAUSE OF JESUS I AM NO LONGER A DEBT TO THE STATE OF TEXAS, and singing hymns, the group called on Bush and the commission to permit Teen Challenge to keep its state license as an official treatment center. Former addicts gave testimonies. One said, "I was a junkie on the streets of San Antonio for thirteen years. I was a thief. I went to the government programs. They didn't work. Jesus set me free." Another said, "My dad said 'I'm gonna show you how to be a man,' so he tied my arm and showed me how to shoot heroin. Then we were in the pen and he would point me out to other prisoners and say, 'That's my boy, he's just like me.' Now we both know Jesus, and we're clean."

Bush, though, remained silent, and the commission kept insisting that their rules had to be followed. Olasky took to the pages of the *Wall Street Journal* and attacked the commission (but not Bush), touting Teen Challenge's international record of recovery success. Still, nothing from Bush or anyone else.

Months later, the governor came out with a statement that Teen Challenge shouldn't be threatened and deserved to continue operating. His spokeswoman, Karen Hughes, said, "Governor Bush believes that religious faith tends to make people more responsible. He's seen a number of success stories." Months after that, Teen Challenge and the commission came to an agreement that both the organization and Bush touted as a victory for the faith-based movement. Unfortunately, the "victory" meant that Teen Challenge wouldn't be able to classify itself as a licensed treatment program, and as a result the organization wouldn't be eligible for government money. It was a hollow win. For Governor Bush, however, it was the start of something big. He announced that he was assembling a task force to look into the promise of faith-based programs.

It was a passionate and undeniably authentic conversion. The governor invited people like Marvin Olasky to educate him about faith-based groups. Karen Hughes widely circulated copies of John DiIulio's "Build Churches, Not Jails" Senate testimony in which the renowned criminologist argued that the best way to prevent a potential onslaught of youth violence was to use churches to care for "some of these children [who] are now still in diapers."

In short order, Governor Bush would lead Texas to the forefront of government-backed faith-based alliances. He even funded a voluntary program in a prison run by Prison Fellowship. The program, called "InnerChange," requires a commitment to eighteen months of Bible study and six months of voluntary aftercare. In 1997, Bush visited the unit to see it himself. On his way out, a group of the prisoners spontaneously gathered and started to sing "Amazing Grace." He joined in, putting his arm around a man, swaying and singing. The next morning, the *Houston Chronicle* ran a front-page picture of the scene along with the revelation that the man had spent the last thirteen years in jail for murder.

Bush never forgot that man and checked in on him periodically through the program's director. One morning in June 2003, the man, George Mason, walked through the White House gates and into a meeting with President George W. Bush. He had taken a janitorial job at the Mount Zion Missionary Baptist Church in Houston and hadn't so much as gotten a parking ticket since his release.

It was precisely this sort of heartwarming story that was so rarely associated with Republicans. Nothing highlighted that to me more than one day in 1995 when I was watching the Senate's proceedings from my desk in Senator Ashcroft's office. I saw Rick Santorum from Pennsylvania speaking on the floor about welfare. Behind him was a big graph showing that spending was way up. There was a corresponding graph with the increases in illegitimacy. It was a fine show, but it was a sterile one. Santorum wanted tougher job requirements, penalties for illegitimacy, and a cut in spending. His presentation, however, was purely factual. It bored, rather than captivated, viewers. It was typically Republican. Years later, however, Santorum would stand alone as the only Republican senator to support a "pro-poor" agenda.

What we were advocating wasn't sterile, it was moving. We genuinely believed that obliterating the existing welfare system was hurting people and that radically changing it was the very best thing to do to help people. Though there weren't very many of us arguing for ending welfare while still spending amply on different programs—as opposed to just slashing funding for the sake of it—it didn't make us any less excited or passionate about our arguments. And we wanted people to know that our way was the compassionate way. That meant telling stories.

We collected about fifty articles from newspapers across the country detailing various horror stories, such as a child being killed in public housing, or a young mother being abused. Anything bad. We blew them up on big poster boards. Ashcroft went down to the Senate floor to tell the stories. The funny thing about the Senate floor is that 95 percent of the time, when a senator is giving a speech there, the chamber is absolutely empty. All they are really doing is speaking to the C-SPAN cameras and putting into the official record things that they need to put there. We realized that. We weren't going for Senate colleagues. We were going for C-SPAN watchers. Day after day Ashcroft went down to the floor. Not too long after that, other Republican senators started doing the same thing.

Only a few newspapers ever reported on it. By and large it just seemed like some quirky little thing. What happened, however, was far from quirky. Bit by bit we began eroding the Democrats' compassion monopoly. For decades Republicans had been the pro-rich party of big business. Democrats were the party of working people and the needy. Democrats fought for government spending. Republicans fought against it. But as 1995 went on we began claiming compassion as our own, little bit by little bit.

Ralph Reed, Bob Dole, Bill Bennett, Jack Kemp, and numerous other conservatives made the compassion argument. We cited

Robert Kennedy. In 1965 he had given a little-noticed speech in upstate New York. "Opponents of welfare have always said that welfare is degrading, both to the giver and to the recipient. They have said that it destroys self-respect, that it lowers incentive, that it is contrary to the American ideals. . . . Most of us deprecated and disregarded those criticisms . . . but in our urge to help, we also disregarded elementary fact. For the criticisms of welfare do have a center of truth and they are confirmed by the evidence. . . ." I tried to incorporate it or some reference to it in every speech I wrote.

We didn't need everyone to believe that Republicans had a heart. We just needed to sow enough doubt in voters' and reporters' minds that our policies couldn't easily be dismissed as heartless. Compassionate conservatism was taking off.

On one part of Capitol Hill, Mike Gerson, now working for Senator Dan Coats, was creating the "Project for American Renewal," a nineteen-bill package of reforms that included federal grants to states to improve victim restitution, grants to match "communities of faith" with welfare recipients and nonviolent criminals, federal funding of school-based mentoring programs, and a $500 "compassion credit" for taxpayers who donated to poverty-related groups. On another part of the Hill, a young staffer for Congressman Jim Talent of Missouri was starting to dream up the Community Renewal Act, which would provide tax incentives, improved local services, and other assistance to one hundred American communities with high unemployment and pervasive poverty. In addition, residents of those communities would be given special savings programs, increased opportunities for home ownership, and vouchers to take to explicitly religious faith-based organizations for counseling help.

We were busy in Ashcroft's office as well. We heard about a case in New York City where a Catholic foster family was forced to remove a crucifix from their living room wall because it violated church-state lines. What would happen, Ashcroft wondered aloud one day, if we introduced a very simple amendment to the forthcoming welfare bill? When it came to receiving federal government money either directly or through states, faith-based organizations had to be treated exactly like secular ones. They couldn't be discriminated against because of their faith.

Certain safeguards would be required. Absolutely no government money could go for evangelizing or proselytizing. Government money couldn't fund anything that was primarily religious in nature—Bible studies, prayer groups, etc. Pretty much everything else was fair game.

The church-state conflict was intellectual and spiritual. Intellectually we all understood, endorsed, and argued for safeguards against government infringing on faith, and vice versa. At the same time, however, there was the spiritual. Virtually every person helping advance this nascent faith-based argument was an evangelical Christian. That went for Marvin Olasky, senators like Coats and Ashcroft, congressmen like J. C. Watts, Sam Brownback, and Jim Talent, and staffers like Mike Gerson and me.

God tempted us to faith through Jesus and we had happily succumbed. Now we longed for everyone, including those struggling in poverty or addiction, to experience the same personal transformation we'd had. We knew that when they found Jesus— like the reformed Texas murderer with whom George Bush sang "Amazing Grace"—even the most "hopeless" person could be forever changed. Jesus meant a better life. We wanted everyone to know Jesus.

In a way that didn't matter. Everyone comes to politics with a particular set of spiritual or philosophical beliefs motivating them—beliefs about the nature of man and the nature of government, whether derived from Jesus or David Hume, Moses or Rousseau, Kierkegaard, Camus, or Homer Simpson. Everyone seeks something from social policy. That we hoped everyone would one day know Jesus was simply a private goal and didn't mean we wanted public school teachers to have fourth-graders memorize the Gospel of Matthew. This is where so many critics of evangelical political involvement got it wrong. Conservative Christian faith did not mean Christian theocracy was a goal.

But we weren't dealing with education, defense policy, or affordable housing. We were dealing with transforming human lives. More specifically our stated goal was a spiritual transformation of people's lives. No matter how we said it, that meant Jesus. Yet we also recognized our public duty to enforce secular policy. We were committed to the latter while dancing with the former. We knew government couldn't feed Jesus to people, but if we could get money to private religious groups—virtually all of whom were Christian—we could show them to the dining room.

Team Ashcroft named our new proposal "Charitable Choice" because the name was so inocuous. It didn't draw attention to anything religious. Charitable choice was something anyone could support and few people could justify voting against. The name just worked.

The bill was drafted within months. Most religious groups loved it. Scarcely a peep came from liberal advocacy groups. The lack of liberal objection likely also came from the perception that it was just a small, relatively insignificant amendment.

The greatest pushback came from other compassionate conservatives who wanted the bill to allow for *more* religious content. Marvin Olasky, for instance, wanted the bill to be modified so that explicitly conversion-centered programs could be included. If the groups weren't specifically religious, he argued, we would be doing little different from the already "secularized" faith-based Catholic Charities and Lutheran Social Services. Those organizations, who had long received billions of dollars per year, just weren't faith-based enough to be effective, in Olasky's view. They served food but they didn't provide any kind of spiritual nourishment. Marvin had wandered the streets of Washington, passing as a homeless person, where he encountered countless offers of food but no offers of a Bible, prayer, or other spiritual nourishment. He wanted the government to use vouchers so groups could provide spiritual sustenance.

We appreciated Marvin's concerns and shared his desires. But such a bill wasn't practical. As much as we may have liked to do such things—and we did—there was little doubt that they wouldn't pass constitutional muster.

Ironically, the most uncertain voice I ran across was Ashcroft's. His most common saying was "It is against my religion to impose my religion," and he meant it. We tried putting all sorts of religious provisions in Charitable Choice. I wanted to insert language making it easier for explicitly religious groups to use the money for religious material that could also have educational value. We wanted to allow vouchers to let welfare recipients go to places like Teen Challenge where they could receive Jesus. Ashcroft pushed back: "Uhhhh . . . I'm very uncomfortable with some of this."

His resistance came from his theology. One of the basic tenets of our Christian faith is that Jesus alone is the source of eternal salvation. "I am the way, and the truth, and the life; no one comes to the Father but through me," Jesus promised. One day as we drove to the airport, Ashcroft said, "You know, none of us have it quite right. We all think we do. Assemblies of God think that they are just right. Baptists think they've got it right. So do the Mormons. But you know what? No one does have it quite right. We're all off. We're all some shade of gray. I just pray that God is patient." It was a derivation of what Paul wrote in Corinthians: "For now we see in a mirror dimly, but then face to face; now I know in part, but then I will know fully just as I also have been fully known."

Ashcroft's moderate tendencies would be blown away by the movement he helped to lead, however. Religious and political leaders began suggesting that he would be a great presidential candidate. While dismissing the idea at first, he eventually opened up to it. He wasn't sure that he wanted to endure a national campaign or do the politicking necessary to win Republican primaries. As conservative as he was, he knew he would have to sound a lot more conservative to win.

He tested the waters by delivering a series of harshly conservative public messages attacking the "tyrannical judiciary." His staffers blocked the nomination of a liberal Missouri judge. Unfortunately, the judge was black. (The incident would haunt Ashcroft when he approached his confirmation hearings to be attorney general.) He used tough language on abortion and the family. The plan was that he would pick up both the old Buchanan vote and the evangelical vote. The only way to do that, his advisers concluded, was to be more conservative than any other conservative, while also talking up his faith. Charitable Choice, however, was conspicuously absent from his politicking. As one of his closest aides would later say of the decision, "Republican primary voters, most of whom are conservative Christians, don't really care about poverty issues."

As conservative as John was, and as much of a lightning rod as he would become, he was still one of the most low-key people I knew. He wasn't very exciting or dynamic in his personal life. He eschewed parties and typical Washington events in favor of singing kitschy barbershop quartets with a small group called The Singing Senators. A good evening, for him, was sitting in front of the TV set watching basketball. A great evening included the basketball plus a quart of ice cream in his lap. By the world's standards, John Ashcroft was boring.

He was also frugal, verging on cheap, and proud of it. He was known to spy a ninety-nine-cent Big Mac special at McDonald's and order twenty just because it was a good deal. He never paid anyone to shine his shoes. Instead, he could be found bent over his chair at virtually any hour, polishing them himself. And he was the most foul-intensive basketball player I knew, apart from myself. My excuse is "a lack of coordination and ability." That wasn't John's problem. He would put his hand right up to your eyes so you couldn't see. It was called "face guarding." It wasn't legal. It was highly annoying. To call him on it, however, was to be dismissed with a growl. Of course, perhaps it was my lack of basketball prowess that was the real problem.

I was pushing compassion and pushing faith-based programs because at heart I absolutely believed they were the best solutions to the social problems we faced. I kept finding the latest child-related horror story and tying it to the catastrophic welfare system. How much more money do we need to spend, I would ask, before we realized that the problems are fundamentally moral and spiritual? We've spent over $3 trillion in the War on Poverty and there are now more poor people than when we began. This wasn't political fluff to me. It was about my life's calling and my mission.

More and more, though, I found that most of my arguments were with fellow Republicans. They would agree with my premise but then say, "Since it has been such a failure why don't we just abolish welfare altogether?" Pull the money, pull the incentives to stay on welfare, pull it all away, and people will be forced to work. Sure, there might be some "collateral damage," but the overall situation would be so much improved.

No, no, no, I would argue. This isn't about either federal welfare *or* faith-based groups. This is about using both resources at the same time. I had my list of "good" charities. I had a whole spiel about how they changed lives and how with just a bit more money and a bit more this and a bit more that they could be improved.

What occured to me slowly, however, was that the Republicans I was arguing against represented the majority of Republicans. With the exception of our Charitable Choice amendment on welfare, Republican policies and laws still played to the pro-business, pro-rich stereotype.

These policies angered me. But it was a frustration I could handle—at least until Charitable Choice was actually included in the 1995 version of the welfare bill.

For a year I had been busy writing the language and making the arguments about how much better things would be if faith-based charities were given more power, money, and control. One morning, however, it hit me. I didn't actually know any faith-based charities. I had read about some and they sounded good. Those had become my list of good charities. But apart from volunteering at a few soup kitchens in college and a few more through my church, I was largely compassionless myself. I walked around the office one day asking fellow staffers who worked on the issue if they could name five effective private organizations that helped the poor. One person got as high as three. I made some phone calls and asked the same questions. More people knew of more charities, but they all ended up overlapping. We all referred to the same groups. And when I asked them if they'd ever visited them, they had to say no.

Then I asked how they knew that faith-based groups were actually effective. Friends just responded that they were faith based, that that was good enough. I knew virtually everyone in the Washington compassionate conservative movement and yet not one person could present me with a convincing case, based on his or her own experience, that faith-based organizations worked. "They can't be any worse than the curent system" didn't seem to be the most reassuring argument.

None of us had a practical clue as to what we were talking about. We assumed religious charities worked better than secular ones. We wanted people's lives changed through conversion. But we were a million miles away from the action. The reality, as I would learn, was that in 1995 there was virtually no objective data on the efficacy of faith-based social service groups. The sole objective data that we did utilize was from Teen Challenge. We pointed to what they touted—a 1968 Pennsylvania study and a 1975 National Institute for Drug Abuse study that showed phenomenal results. Seventy-five percent of former heroin addicts were drug-free five years later. Yet the study was ridiculously flawed. It didn't sample everyone who had graduated from the program, only those who could be found. And it only surveyed those people who had given their lives to Christ and therefore "graduated" from the program.

What was I peddling? With Charitable Choice, I had helped get a fairly radical provision in the welfare bill. I was writing speeches for Bob Dole and Ralph Reed about the power of faith-based groups. I was advocating these provisions up one side and down another . . . and . . .

. . . it was a February morning in 1996 when I walked into Ashcroft's office and told him I was quitting. I was now father to a beautiful daughter and living in a new house. I wasn't quitting for the sake of my marriage, but in truth my marriage was not great. I was twenty-seven years old. I told Ashcroft that I planned to start an organization to help the poor, or rather to help the charities that really did help the poor. My grand idea was that I would first come up with a way to evaluate how effectively a charity was doing its job. What percentage of addicts from a particular drug treatment program relapsed? Did kids' grades improve after time spent in an after-school program? How many people got jobs through a welfare-to-work program, and then how many kept them? After I did that, I was going to convince charities to let me evaluate them. Then, I was going to raise money so that effective groups got money to do more of what they were doing well and struggling groups would get money so they could improve. I figured I could get the whole thing flying nationally in a year. Of course, I had once argued that Michael Jackson was actually the Archangel Michael.

I wasn't sure it was the most astute career move I had ever made, but it felt like one of the most honest and liberating things I had done in a long time. After playing on the political high wire for a while I was going to actually make a difference in people's lives. I hoped it was a model of Christ's humility and not Washington's arrogance.

CHAPTER SIX

Swirling . . .

Two months later, my charity was struggling and so was my marriage. Almost as jarring was my sudden fall into anonymous anonymity. As a staffer I had lived in the background, and as a speechwriter I had a certain anonymity. But that anonymity was, paradoxically, well known. It put me on the inside and made me a player. Now I couldn't believe how quickly I was simply anonymous and relegated to the "outside." It's ridiculous that people in Washington think of D.C. as "inside" and the rest of the country as "outside," but they do, and I did. I was in crisis because I missed the insider life.

Far worse than the withdrawal was the slow-to-arrive realization that not all my friends really liked me. The longer I had been in the capital the more friends I thought I'd amassed. New friends invited me to lunch or dinner. I was given tickets to events. Nice party invitations were exceedingly common. I assumed people liked me for my personality, not for my so-called power (or proximity to power). But now entire days went by without a phone call from these "friends." Invitations disappeared. At first I chalked it up to my own busyness or others'. Then came the dreaded revelation that "friends" weren't friends.

For counseling on all these things, I headed to the mysterious home of the Fellowship.

The Cedars has inspired all sorts of stories. One version had Howard Hughes owning it, then selling it to a Mafia family, at which point the IRS indicted the family, and someone from the Fellowship befriended the family, who gave them the estate. Another story had the enormous white-columned mansion being built by

George Mason, Virginia delegate to the U.S. Constitutional Convention and "Father of the Bill of Rights." It stayed in his family for more than two hundred years before being donated to the Fellowship by one of his great, great, great, great-grandsons (give or take a generation or two). The true story, as accurately as I could figure out, was a combination of all of the above. George Mason built it, Howard Hughes owned it, and it ended up in Fellowship hands. The Mafia part I wasn't so sure about.

Its guestbook was among the most diverse in the world. During his brutal confirmation hearings Clarence Thomas sought solace there with his wife. Apparently Yasser Arafat had stayed there; Mother Teresa, too. Corrupt African dictators were commonplace. Anwar Sadat, Menachem Begin, Mikhail Gorbachev, and Nelson Mandela were all said to have slept there. Word was that the CIA once used it as a safe house.

Most of those things are true. So is the fact that I arranged for Michael Jackson to stay there after 9/11, when he was in town for a concert event. He loved the house, but he awoke in the middle of the night, afraid. At three A.M. he knocked on the door of the couple that serve as house hosts. "Is this house haunted?" he said. "There's something different about it. There's some spirit." The host told him it wasn't haunted but there was a spirit that lived there. The spirit's name was Jesus. They spent the next three hours talking about him. For me it was a Forrest Gump moment. I had crossed paths with the Michael Jackson I had long ago lauded to my Christian youth group, and now I had unwittingly arranged for him to learn more about Jesus.

My problem, that spring morning, was just finding the place. I had made all the appropriate twists and turns and ended up on a very ordinary suburban street. I looked around for some secret Batcave-like entrance that would magically lead me into a hardened bunker guarded by supersecret police.

Instead, at the end of the street I found two brick posts on either side of a steep driveway. To the right was a Cape Cod–style clapboard house I would later learn was the Carriage House. The Fellowship's head, Doug Coe, and his wife lived in its small basement apartment. Then there was the mansion. It bore a striking resemblance in size and architecture to the White House. It turns out they were both built around the same time.

I was looking for Foth. Dick Foth had been many things: pastor, college president, seminary adviser, and author. He had given that all up, however, to come to Washington to work with the Fellowship and be a "friend" to the powerful and powerless. Coincidentally, his childhood buddy John Ashcroft was elected to the Senate a year after Foth arrived. Foth was with Senator Ashcroft the night he was anointed and a few days later was the one who told him his father had died.

Foth had become a friend and occasional counselor to me as well. We talked about God and politics and how the two came together for good and for bad. Foth lacked a political agenda and his religious one was muted as well. He loved Jesus but he wasn't about to force him down anyone's throat.

I needed Foth's advice on how to handle my transition to being an outsider. While I remained in regular contact with Reed, Ashcroft, and Bennett, and was developing new relationships with people like Rick Santorum, J. C. Watts, and Steve Largent, I wasn't part of the rush, the buzz, the biz. For a while I could fake it. I pretended I knew what was going on. One day I realized, however, that the only person I was pretending to was me.

There were many positives to my new situation. I didn't have a boss to report to all the time. There wasn't some ladder to climb, nor did I covet some new, more powerful post. I clung to my dream that I would be able to identify and help countless charities by activating all the wealthy Republican donors I had gotten to know.

I had also tiptoed into exploring my own beliefs and voice. Up to that point my professional advancement was based on my ability to become like those around me. For Ralph Reed I sounded and wrote like Ralph. For Bob Dole it had been the same, and so too for John Ashcroft. Now, though, I had to learn what I myself sounded like and what I believed. There wasn't any sudden revelation that anything I had done was particularly great or evil, only the vague sense that I probably couldn't go back even if I wanted to.

• • •

Foth ushered me into a sitting room known as the Lincoln Room because of the original front page from an April 15, 1865, newspaper displayed there, carrying the words, "Lincoln Dead." I laid out my problems bit by bit. Foth, whose gentleness overwhelms any other physical description of him, listened and nodded. Then he started telling stories. That's what Foth does.

He started with one about former Secretary of State James Baker. As Baker rode to the White House early one morning, his chauffeured car passed a man walking alone on Pennsylvania Avenue. Baker knew the man. He was once one of the most powerful men in Washington. He had ruled the White House with an iron fist. Now he walked alone outside the White House gates looking wistfully in. Baker vowed to remember power's fleeting nature.

I remembered the story. It was the story Baker told at the prayer breakfast I had attended my last semester in college. It seemed more sweet than stirring at the time. I was twenty and ready to attack Washington, and I was thrilled to learn that the secretary of state was a Christian like me. Now, nearly a decade later, I heard it with wiser ears; I understood it a bit. It was a version of Bill Bennett's warning to me that everyone, absolutely everyone in Washington is expendable. I didn't like that idea at all. The belief that I was at least sort of indispensable was much more palatable.

Foth added, "So you're on this journey with Jesus. You've hit a moment. What are you going to do with it? How are you going to change? What needs to change? And what will you carry with you—maybe even as a scar—as you go forward?"

Thankfully he didn't want an answer, even though I really wanted to lay out a five-point plan for self-improvement. He was too wise to have believed it and I was too confused to give it.

Over the next months Foth told me dozens of other stories and introduced me to my new friend Doug Coe, the Fellowship's head. In Coe's basement apartment or Foth's backyard I struggled with what it was that God intended for my life, what I had done with it thus far, and how I was going to get things going on the right path again. I wanted answers—and to be honest, I also wanted access to some of the donors connected to the Fellowship.

I just needed a bit more money to give my charity, now named The American Compass, a fighting chance. But Coe knew that, loved me anyway, and challenged me to read Jesus' Gospels again and examine what he really said.

Without my realizing it the Fellowship began subverting my ideas of power and, more specifically, of Christian power. I had arrived in Washington figuring the best way to serve Jesus was by gaining power, passing the proper laws, eliminating the social evils I saw, and reforming all of American society. Despite some questioning moments, like when I had heard Coe for the first time, it was politics and then Jesus for me. Coe and Foth practiced a very different model.

Coe's early relationship with Chuck Colson gives the best insight into their approach. At the height of Colson's own political power in 1972, one of his biggest enemies was a Democratic senator named Harold Hughes. Hughes, a recovering alcoholic and born-again Christian, was a vocal antiwar, anti-Nixon critic with a special disdain for Colson. The next year, in the throes of Watergate, Colson became a Christian, too. Doug Coe became a spiritual shepherd and told Colson he needed good Christian friends, men like Harold Hughes. Colson thought Coe was nuts. Meanwhile, Coe was also working with Senator Hughes. Upon hearing that Colson had become a Christian, Hughes remarked that he wished no one had bothered to tell Colson about Jesus; he didn't deserve the benefits.

Doug eventually succeeded in putting together a meeting. Jesus or no Jesus, neither man really wanted to be friends with the other. Finally, Hughes challenged Colson to convince him his new faith was real and not contrived. Colson succeeded. "That's all I need to know," Hughes told Colson. "You have accepted Jesus and He has forgiven you. I do the same. I love you now as my brother in Christ. I will stand with you, defend you anywhere, and trust you with anything I have." The men went on to become dear friends and ministry partners.

There didn't seem to be a lot of that happening in the Washington I had seen.

• • •

One day that summer of 1996, Doug called and asked if I wanted to go on a fly-fishing trip out west. A friend of his owned a ranch and Coe wanted me to come along.

Fishing. There was a lot of politics in my life. There was some God, too. But I had completely forgotten about fishing. I wanted to say no. One of the important Washington lessons I had learned was to always appear busy. If you were busy you mattered. I really wasn't that busy. Fund-raising for my charity hadn't been successful enough for me to start my big dreams. I was still writing speeches to pay the bills and I was helping someone write a book. But I wasn't busy. I remembered my fishing-filled youth, decided to violate one of the Washington rules, and said yes.

Two weeks later, after an airplane trip and a two-hour horse ride, I was deposited at the only private ranch in Yellowstone National Park. The ranch consisted of seven brown clapboard and stone buildings. One was a barn chock-full of vintage racing cars and buggies. They had been towed in on wagons decades earlier, and were kept in running condition although there weren't exactly any roads available. Another was a stable. The main lodge was straight out of a very expensive Ralph Lauren catalog. Enormous animal heads adorned the walls and floors. A massive stone fireplace big enough to park a Humvee in dominated the room. It also had electricity, hot water, and a member of the United States Supreme Court. Sandra Day O'Connor was seated at a square wood table passionately involved in a card game with her husband. "Ah! John, you old poop!"

Justice O'Connor came over to say hi as Doug and I entered, apparently frustrated enough to take the excuse of hospitality to leave the game. Doug introduced us. "Justice O'Connor, nice to meet you," I peeped. "Call me that again and I'll slap you. Let's go fishing. Got a pole?"

She took me out the door, pointed me to one of her fly poles, and said, "Let me see you cast." Before I had a chance to explain to her I knew nothing about fly-fishing she said, "Okay, go."

I flailed the rod back and forth, managing to get fly line tangled around a hitching post.

"Oh no! You call that casting?"

She came up behind me, pressed her front side into my back one and grabbed my arm.

"Relax!"

Sure. Sandra Day O'Connor is draped around me, gripping my right forearm like it was a stick, flailing it back and forth. It was very relaxing. She persevered and soon had me guiding the rod back and forth between an eleven o'clock and a one o'clock position. She stepped away to examine my form from the front. "NO! NO! NO! Damn it, David. Don't flail the rod like it is some pussywillow branch. Punch it! Punch it! Punch the rod to a stop. Punch it!"

That was how I learned to fly-fish.

During the next week the six of us went out in groups or in pairs or alone to fish an untouched and private stretch of river. Many mornings I rose before anyone else, grabbed my rod and some food, and headed out. The place felt holy.

I got the hang of the fishing. I also remembered some simple things. My first interest in politics came from a desire to make people's lives better. I hadn't had a particular ideology, just a specific inclination, and my religious faith was related to that. Like a lot of people I had found a job and had done what it took to make myself successful in that job. I had been successful up to that point, but now I knew things needed to change. The small steps I had taken toward discovering my own voice and my own beliefs needed to continue even if they took me away from the lucrative and comfortable conservative political world I had inhabited. Or, even if they *kept* me there.

All of this meant leaving politics for a season or, perhaps, forever. As C. S. Lewis warned in *Screwtape,* my faith had become a means to a political end, and not an end unto itself. When that happened, Lewis warned, the enemy almost has his man. I needed that to end before I lost my soul.

Among other things, I realized I had some apologizing to do. I had said and written many nasty and hateful things about the Clintons. They ranged from mocking their marriage and their personal religious faith to calling them personally corrupt and downright evil. Even if all of my assertions were absolutely true—which, of course, they weren't—Jesus commanded his followers to "speak the truth in love." Instead, I had spoken mistruths in hate. It had been so easy to do. To a conservative audience, all I had to do was throw in something about Bill with a little Hillary, a smack of sarcasm and just a pinch of a punch line, and I had them rolling in the aisles. That had to stop. If I ever could, I knew I ought to apologize for doing it.

I also absolutely had to throw myself into my charity. It didn't matter whether it became big or not, whether it was monstrously successful or ridiculously tiny. I needed to raise money for other charities.

Finally, I had to do whatever it took to make my marriage work. If it was too late it was too late. But I had to do whatever I could to try to win Jerilyn back.

I left Montana knowing all these things.

Four weeks later I was sitting across from Dan Quayle, who had heard about my efforts through the Fellowship. He was interested. With no Secret Service, no bodyguards, and no staffers, Quayle held court in a simple office at one of Washington's countless law firms. I explained to him Olasky's work and his thesis, and Ashcroft's Charitable Choice, and my own plan to analyze and then help small charities. He stared at me and nodded. "Could I visit them?"

"Absolutely," I exclaimed. "That would be great. I don't know how much time you have, but they would love to have your attention."

"Would they mind the press?"

"No, I think they'd love attention on their work."

"Great. But do you think they'd mind if I notified the press about my visit? Here's what I was thinking. I'm going to send out a letter to my friends, ask them each for $25,000 to fund the operation. Then you'll find good charities in every city for me to visit. They can host a fund-raiser where they can use my name to raise money. Then I'll get to meet their donors. We'll have the press come in and cover my visit. Then we can put together a list of the charities that I've helped. Maybe we can put them into a book. That will be good."

"Yes, absolutely, great," I said. Yet my heart was sinking. The little internal voice that had convinced me of my need to apologize to the Clintons was screaming for me to tell Dan Quayle no. His heart may have been perfectly pure. His entire goal may have been just to raise money for these groups. God may well have given him that vision. But that wasn't my vision. Still, I wasn't having a ton of luck raising the millions required to fund my dream. I said yes because I knew he could raise a lot more money than I could on my own, and he could give me more financial security in my own life. So I supposed that I was now part of Dan Quayle's presidential aspirations for 2000.

He gave me a list of three dozen of the biggest Republican donors, and he sent off a letter to each of them asking for $25,000 to help the charities and to help his fund-raising efforts. Some of the donors, such as Richard Farmer, head of Cintas Corporation, and Pat Rooney, who ran Golden Rule Insurance, gave north of $500,000 to the Republican Party in every election cycle. So did Wayne Huizenga, the trash and Blockbuster Video titan, and Foster Friess, mutual-fund magnate.

Those donors, however, proved much more enthusiastic about politics than grassroots assistance for the poor. Of Quayle's list, no more than three gave. And the only one to give the full $25,000 amount was Foster Friess.

Friess, operating out of Wilmington, Delaware, was investing huge sums of money in small, faith-based organizations. He ran some of them himself. One helped people find permanent jobs, another paid the homeless cash for helping clean up the city—providing both a public service and a job. Another one helped single moms. But Foster was unique not only as a human being but also as a wealthy Republican donor.

Part of that difference came out of his faith. For him, loving Jesus meant loving the poor with his own hands. He couldn't figure out another way to serve God. In the process of serving, he learned what I had been learning since leaving politics—people are more important than great political debates.

I'd used people's stories and their lives to bolster my political arguments for changing welfare. Now, however, I was running into the people themselves, and I realized that using anyone's tragedy for political gain was cowardly.

At first I assumed I was the reason Quayle's donors were holding back. I was young. I had never run an organization before. And though I had impeccable conservative credentials, my business plan wasn't exactly FedEx's. After a while I assumed that the problem was Quayle. These donors didn't like him any more and wanted to give their money elsewhere.

But after scores of conversations with Quayle's donors and with potential donors I had contacted on my own, another conclusion presented itself—big Republican donors were not interested in funding anti-poverty programs. Had I called with a proposal for a new political organization that took on the Clintons, funding would have been lavish. That wasn't speculation; it is what donors told me.

I decided it was time to take a bigger step toward finding my own voice. In early 1997 I went to the Op-Ed page of the *Washington Post*. I spewed it all out. I had enthusiastically been part of the conservative policy world and had my wish list of welfare reforms. But when I left government, statistics became stories that belonged to people I was getting to know through my charity work. My experience made me realize that while conservatives like me had done a great job critiquing government welfare, we had not taken the time to examine the private sector. We knew government was bad, but was the private sector good?

It was an important question because I now knew a few of the lives that depended on the answer. I started hanging around a particular after-school program in one of D.C.'s rougher areas. Gazing out the window one day I saw kids on a playground of broken cinder blocks. One Halloween evening I hosted a party of kids in a program our group sponsored. One of my favorite kids didn't show up, and so I went to his home to try to find him. He was packed in with his stoned family in a dark, dirty apartment located in an even darker and dirtier housing complex. Stories like this broke my heart and scared my conscience.

Getting more involved in communities, I wrote, had made me a little more sympathetic toward those liberals who helped deliver services, if only because they actually backed up their words with service. Liberals tended to populate the paid and volunteer staff of virtually every social service group I had seen. That involvement had also made me a little bit less sympathetic toward conservatives. At the end of the day, I argued, if things don't markedly improve, conservatives like me would have to share a large part—perhaps most—of the blame. Unless we became more involved in putting our ideas into action, into rolling up our sleeves and getting involved, we would have failed the country and failed those in need. It was our welfare system now.

I turned in the piece to the *Washington Post* on a Tuesday. Just as I did, Dick Foth called. "There's going to be a small dinner tomorrow night before the National Prayer Breakfast. Franklin Graham, Bill Bright of Campus Crusade for Christ, Jack Hayford, and Senate Chaplain Lloyd Ogilvie will be there; so will Frank Wolf and Tony Hall." The evening had a specific purpose: to discuss how we could start working together to love Christ and love each other. Hall, a liberal Democrat, and Wolf, a conservative Republican, were both members of Congress. Their friendship endured despite policy disagreements—sometimes serious ones—and political fights. Underlying it was Jesus. Foth wondered whether all these religious leaders could do the same. "The world," Foth said, "does not see our religious leaders caring for each other. They see a lot of fighting and opposition. They don't see love." Part of the problem Foth was addressing, without saying it outright, was the increasing shrillness of Christians in politics.

The next night I walked into a small room with four round tables in time to hear Ogilvie and Hayford speak. The two men were in their sixties and both loved Jesus, but they couldn't have been more different. Ogilvie was a formal, stiff, dark-haired man who spoke with a rich, deep voice that one could imagine was the voice of God. He was a Presbyterian. He looked like someone who bathed in a suit and tie. Hayford, on the other hand, looked like a Californian. He was tan and wispy-haired. He wore a tie but was no more comfortable in it than Ogilvie would have been in flip-flops. He was also charismatic. He believed people could still speak in tongues. He raised his hands during prayer and worship to honor God and became visibly emotional and demonstrative when preaching and when singing. This is not to say he played with snakes, however.

The two men had been successful pastors in Los Angeles. Ogilvie headed Hollywood Presbyterian, Hayford, the Church on the Way. During the 1970s neither man much liked the other. Ogilvie thought Hayford was a nut. Hayford thought Ogilvie was a prig. Over the years, however, a friendship developed. They found that they really liked each other. As each man grew older, he grew more certain that his way wasn't the only way. They started referring people to each other's churches. If someone came up to Hayford and said they were looking for a more "traditional" service, he sent them to Ogilvie. If someone approached Ogilvie and said they wanted a church with more "spirit," he would send them off to Hayford. They took turns telling the story. At the end someone in the room asked how they reconciled their theological differences. The response was similar to Ashcroft's: "Well, we kind of figure that God is a lot bigger than whatever our theological differences might be."

Before the conversation could continue, a side door opened. One stern-looking man in a suit entered. A blond-haired woman in a suit followed, with another grouch behind her. The grouches were Secret Service. The woman was . . . *oh crap it is the Antichrist. It is Hillary Clinton.* I looked around to make sure I hadn't actually voiced those words. *You wanted a chance to apologize to the Clintons for what you said. Oh double shit!* As the Secret Service agents took their posts on either side of the room, Mrs. Clinton took a seat. Before long she got up and started speaking. She said something about God or Jesus or being a Methodist. I didn't hear. All I could think about was my prayer to have a chance to apologize to the Clintons for what I had written in other people's speeches. It had sounded good at the time. I had even meant it. Be calm, I reasoned, she's up at that table and you are back at this table and I'm sure you'll never get a chance to apologize. She stopped speaking. We all got up and clapped. Then she shook hands with her friends at the table where she had briefly sat, and got ready to leave.

Suddenly, inexplicably, horribly, she changed course. She started shaking hands with people at another table. She started working the room. I held out hope she wouldn't reach my table, which was unlikely given that there were only four of them. Before I knew it she was in front of me.

She looked up at me, smiled, extended her hand and said, "Nice to see you, thank you for coming." I looked at her with a smirky grin. She looked up at me with a quizzical look. I was still holding her hand. She wanted it back.

"Ummmm . . ."

"Yes?" she said, removing her hand from mine.

"Ummm, Mrs. Clinton. I need to . . . I'm . . . I need to apologize."

Knowledgeable in how to work a room, she had already reached to clasp another person's hand. She stopped, took a step back, and looked curiously at me. "Why?"

"For the last four years I've written a lot of speeches for a lot of politicians that have attacked you. I'm not talking about policy attacks. Those are different. I mean personal attacks, jokes, mean things. I'm very sorry."

She squinted at me and just stood there. It was probably only for two or three seconds. But she was still looking at me. "Okay," she said and her eyes darted around trying to find a word. "Okay. Okay, thank you."

Off she went. More hands were shaken. I sat back down feeling better about life, and enjoyed my flan. All done.

The next morning I arrived at the hotel after the breakfast (and the lunch, too) to find Foth. "You just missed Mrs. Clinton talking about you."

"WHAT?!?!"

"Yes, she just gave a very moving speech about forgiveness and told the story about you last night."

My life flashed before my eyes. My career was ruined. Hillary Clinton had just talked about me apologizing to her . . . in public? I was ruined. I knew that I had said I didn't want to do politics anymore, but . . . Oh no.

"Don't worry, she didn't mention your name."

I sighed. "Foth, does anyone else *know*?" The Bible says that when the time for judgment comes everything that we have ever thought and done will be on display for everyone else to see. That will be an awful moment. If all goes well, however, all those things will be forgiven and we'll be welcomed into the everlasting Kingdom of Heaven. God's love, in forgiving our wrongs, will overwhelm our despair at all we did or did not do. This was not like that.

He assured me that no one else knew and everything was fine. Apparently, however, my apology had triggered quite an avalanche in the White House. Mrs. Clinton got in the limo that evening for the short ride back to the residence and started yelling. She yelled about me . . . but mostly about what I represented. All the personal attacks, all the political ones too. She went back home and talked with her husband about it.

At some point in the night, however, she had a different thought. She had been guilty of the same things her enemies had done. On the way to the hotel that morning the president threw out his prepared remarks for his breakfast appearance, and she did the same for her lunch. President Clinton said that Washington is "ripped with people who are self-righteous, sanctimonious, and hypocritical . . . I plead guilty from time to time." His speech was highly personal, and so was hers. She recounted the story of our meeting and said, "What I should have said was, 'I don't know you and I don't know anything about you, but I want you to forgive me also, because I am sure that in my moments of frustration and anger I have said terrible things about people like you—and I have thought even worse.' " She talked about the personal hurts she had experienced, including the claim that you can't be a Christian and a Democrat. "I have to confess that it's crossed my mind that you could not be a Republican and a Christian from time to time. . . . Yes, faith and following the example of Christ can lead to transformation. But even after transformation we have to be humble, and we have to work hard to make sure that we don't elevate ourselves now that we have been transformed."

I read the specific quotes the next morning at breakfast with a conservative friend. He plopped down opposite me in a booth, grabbed the *Post,* and tossed it to me. "Can you even believe it?" he sputtered. "The flipping *Washington Post* puts the Clintons on the cover talking about prayer and forgiveness. And if you read the story you'll see some jackass apologized to Hillary. Whatever. Are the waffles good?"

Splashed there on the front page was the article, "Applying the Salve of Prayer: Clintons Use Gathering to Speak Out Against Anger, Cynicism." It was the little apology that wouldn't go away. Of course a year later, on the *Today* show, Hillary Clinton blamed most of her and her husband's problems on a "vast right-wing conspiracy." Forgiveness is an ongoing process.

Two days after, the *Washington Post* published my article. I had two conflicting emotions. Absolute pride was one of them. I said what I thought and what I felt and what I knew. That was good. The other emotion was sheer terror. I would probably never get another job in Washington again. Everyone in the conservative world would realize I was actually a closet liberal and that would be that. Then they would learn I was the idiot who'd talked to Hillary, too. I was done.

Sure enough, there were phone calls the next morning from people wondering whether I had gone off the deep end. "Why are you pissing away your career over something like poverty policy? Geez," one friend said. Ralph Reed called and told me to be careful about doing this sort of thing.

But then he said something else. What if the Christian Coalition launched a pro-poor, pro-minority agenda?

It wasn't what Gary Bauer wanted. Though Bauer argued that "[when President Clinton trounced Senator Dole] we came across as a party of accountants instead of a party that cares," his cure for appearing to be an unfeeling party was to push a relentless cultural agenda in Congress that included a Human Life Amendment, school prayer, tuition vouchers, limits on AIDS and arts funding, and legislation providing parents more control over schools. Anyone who opposed him, he warned, would be targeted by his new political action committee. "We're not going to turn down the volume," he said. "To lower it would be to make it imperceptible."

Not to be outdone, Paul Weyrich, a veteran activist of the religious Right, threatened to start a third party. "What I hear from the grass roots is that the powder-puff Republican Party that social conservatives elected won't stand for anything, won't fight for anything, won't rock the boat and only wants to be pleasant and make friends with Democrats," Weyrich said. "The party is traumatized, and Gingrich has evaporated from sight." Even Ralph was ticked, accusing the GOP of "timidity, of retreat and of muddle-headed moderation."

But Ralph's response was different. Whether it was his unparalleled strategic vision to see that focusing on race and poverty would allow the Coalition to expand, or that Ralph had been genuinely moved to address these issues is a question only Ralph can answer. I believe it was both. Regardless, I didn't care. The Christian Coalition was at the height of its power and what it launched mattered. I wanted to help give it substance and words. The policy result might include millions of dollars in tax credits to spur charitable giving, new money for drug treatment programs, and full scholarships for children in America's one hundred poorest schools to attend any school of their choice.

"The thing that is going to combat the social pathologies and the evils and the national sins . . . isn't going to be any political party," Ralph said in a major speech before African-American church leaders, soon thereafter. "It's going to be the church of Jesus Christ on its knees praying, with a sword and a spear in one hand and a breastplate of righteousness and a helmet of salvation and a revival that sweeps across the nation . . . What we need in our inner cities . . . is not another government program or a 'War on Poverty.' We need God's spirit to come crashing down." He called the initiative the Samaritan Project.

Yet it sputtered. Ralph resigned from the Christian Coalition in May 1997. His goal to raise $10 million from his two million members fell short by more than $9.5 million. Politically involved Christians just didn't want to give their money to minority-oriented poverty projects. Still, it could attract votes, even if it couldn't feed the hungry. African-American church leaders were eager to embrace any conservative Christian Republicans who talked about the poor. Somewhere in Austin, Texas, George W. Bush's political advisers must have taken note.

CHAPTER SEVEN

"Just When I Thought I Was Out . . ."

By early 1998, a year after I found my voice on the op-ed page of the *Washington Post* and in a hotel ballroom apologizing to Hillary Clinton, my political sabbatical continued and my spiritual one had just begun. Somehow I thought that righting things with Mrs. Clinton and giving voice to the inner me in print was going to be a great leap forward. Instead I ended up firing Dan Quayle, getting divorced, and ditching God.

First there was the former vice president. I thanked him for his interest in what we were doing and told him how much I appreciated the money he tried to raise. But his vision wasn't mine. I wanted to find, fund, and evaluate great charities and be a resource for them. He wanted to do something different and he had. He had raised money for several charities by hosting fund-raisers and speaking at dinners. That was great and I'm sure he went on to do many more. I would have returned all the money his donors gave to him but that would have been challenging since there was so little to start with.

My marriage ended. There is rarely anything good that can be said about divorce, and our case was no different. I should have been a better husband. I should have cared for her more and for work far less. I should have fought harder for it. We were committed to being friends and to putting our two young daughters ahead of everything. It was a most civil divorce. We never, ever yelled at each other. We never cried in front of each other, either. Maybe that was because we did so much of it when we were apart. It was the bitterest irony; I came to Washington to fight for "the family" and destroyed mine in the process.

Instead of running toward God in the midst of all of this, I ran away. The spiritual intimacy with God that flourished during my time with Foth and Coe and that had led me to my apologizing and writing evaporated. There was only shame, except when there was anger. My faith felt like a mockery. I had said I believed all these things about God. But now, divorce? I didn't feel I could talk to God, be near to God, or relate to God. And some of God's people didn't exactly help my spiritual journey. By and large my Christian friends went underground. That was better than a phone call I got from a pastor I had never met at a church I no longer attended. He left me a voice mail saying, "I am the voice of God in your life" and then went on to accuse me of utter moral bankruptcy. I had screwed up, but I didn't think I was that bad. Regardless, for the first time in my life I was living without God . . . at least in my own mind. Since I partially saw myself as a prodigal son running away from home, I determined I was going to live like one. I was going to drink and meet all sorts of women and have wild parties and live it up. The truth is that I sucked as a prodigal son. Mostly I ended up staying home in the evenings. Sometimes I went to a movie.

I also relocated to Atlanta for six months, when two major donors there said they wanted to fully fund my charity and turn it into a Christian version of the United Way—not exactly the same plan as mine but, at that point, close enough for me. My almost ex-wife and I agreed it would be a good thing. I would fly home most weekends to be with my daughters. I had come to Washington with wide eyes and a passion for saving the world. I left Washington feeling embarrassed, defeated, tired, confused, and alone.

Flying became my occupation. I flew around the country raising money. I flew home to Washington on weekends to be with my girls. Sometimes I flew for fun; I would hop on a plane from my Atlanta home and see friends in Los Angeles or Boston, or see family in New York. A few times I flew just so I could get a few more miles to qualify for a free trip so I could fly somewhere else. After

Jenny left him, Forrest Gump went running. After my life fell apart, I went flying.

One day I found myself in Denver International Airport's Concourse B, listening to my voice mail. The first message was from a good friend in Washington, wondering when I was going to be in town next so we could get together. The second was from a woman who said her name was Geneva Van den Hovelstein, or something like that. She was with Governor George W. Bush in Austin, Texas, and wanted to know if I could fly down to meet with him. They had some speeches I had written for someone else and wanted me to talk with the governor and someone named Karen Hughes about writing for him.

To this day I have no memory of who actually left me the "hey, let's get together for dinner" message. My brain had to dump that information to try to grasp what I was hearing in the second message. George W. Bush was calling *me*? I stopped walking, sat down on the shiny black-and-white speckled rock floor with my back up against a wall and listened to the message over and over and over again. Surrounded by clicking heels, roaming bags, and the fat-frying smell of a food court, I felt happy. Every time I replayed the message I felt happier and more content. I was so excited I completely forgot that I was taking a break from politics.

Though the presidential primaries wouldn't begin for another two years, George W. Bush was emerging as the de facto choice for a Republican Party wanting to unite behind anyone who could end the Clinton-Gore years. Even though he was largely an unknown, he best embodied what virtually all conservatives were looking for—a winning candidate. Oklahoma's Governor Frank Keating summarized it well: "Republicans are so hungry to win and Republican governors are so tired of timidity and fear that we want someone who can raise the money, advance the agenda and kick them [Democrats] into the river. George Bush is our man." The Bush name meant guaranteed fund-raising via his father's old political network. All of Texas, including women and Hispanics, loved him. About the only people who were even mildly suspicious were Texas social conservatives who had been disappointed by how little of their agenda he had accomplished.

The questions for me in Denver and in the days that followed were basic. Do I go and reenter this political world? Do I stick with my charity and try to make it work? Do I do both? Ralph Reed insisted that working for Bush was the opportunity of a lifetime. Most everyone I knew said it would be stupid not to talk to the governor. "God can't steer a parked car," some said. Maybe they thought that writing speeches for a nascent presidential campaign would jolt me out of my funk. Maybe they had heard from God that I was supposed to do it. I didn't know.

A week after the call I crammed myself into one of Delta Air Lines' smallest and most cramped seats at five A.M. and two hours later found myself sitting in Austin in the governor's office waiting for my meetings. So much for turning my back on politics; it appeared I could take a longer break from God than I could from politics.

I knew how this sort of meeting worked. The whole "the governor wants to meet with you" thing is the political equivalent of the come-hither look. It is genuine. It just doesn't necessarily mean what we might hope it means. I wasn't really going to be sitting down with a busy Texas governor and having a long get-to-know-you session where we shared family stories and made s'mores together around the campfire. I would meet with his aides—probably this Karen Hughes who was apparently his communications director—and then, if they found me appealing I would get to see the man for ten or fifteen minutes. If they deemed me unappealing I would get five minutes, after which Bush would suddenly get called into an "urgent meeting."

The receptionist let me know it was time for my meeting. I walked through a dark, wood-paneled doorway, turned left past a couple of desks, passed by a tall glass partition, and entered a large office. On the wall to my left were scores and scores of autographed baseballs, each in its own glass case. It was like a crossword puzzle of baseballs. Before turning to see what else was in the room I spied a "Willie Mays" autograph out of the corner of my eye. Next to it were "Sammy Sosa" and "Nolan Ryan." Then, just as I moved closer to the glass to see a ball that might have had "Jackie Robinson" on it, I heard someone clearing his throat.

"Like 'em, huh?"

Smiling, casual, appearing completely unstressed and even more unwrinkled, and wearing a standard-issue dark blue suit, George W. Bush stood in front of me, shook my hand, walked toward his dark wood fortress of a desk, and told me to sit down.

"Karen Hughes, my communications director, is going to be here in a minute. We just wanted to talk to you a little bit and see if we might work together on some speeches.

"I have a chief of staff, Joe Albaugh," he continued. "He's over there." Bush pointed across the room to an office with a closed door. "The thing is, though, that I don't believe in a strong chief of staff. They get ideas that they are the one in charge."

I was still stuck on the fact that I was talking to him already. I knew he needed a speechwriter and I knew they'd read some of the stuff I had written and liked it, but this was unusual. I was supposed to be meeting with staff. Why did I feel like I was the one being charmed?

Obviously, he said, things were in motion then that might lead him to seek the presidency. At the same time, he emphasized, he had no idea if he was going to run. That, he said, was something he would have to hear from God.

I had been around a lot of prominent politicians before. There was a certain sameness to them. The ones in elected office had a certain frenetic energy about them. They were a lot like I was at that moment of my life—they were running and flying and moving and talking, and most of them lacked depth. Deep down they were very superficial.

Bush seemed different. He spoke slowly, reflectively, quietly. He seemed to grapple with what was before him. "I don't know if I really want to do it . . . I know, you know, I know . . . I know what it means if you run. Then I know what happens if you win. I've seen it all up close. Do I want to spend the rest of my life in a bubble? I like walking to work. I like my life. It is a good life. I just don't know if I can spend the rest of my life in a security bubble. I'll never walk down a street alone. Never again. Politics, you know, is nasty. Don't wanna get beat up but if running for president is what I'm supposed to do I'll do it . . . I'll punch back, too.

111

"I learned a lot of other things from the old man, though. He had a lot of political capital after Iraq. He didn't use it. You've got to use it up and use it up for something that matters."

He asked about me, about my family, my story. We were doing everything that I thought we couldn't, except for making s'mores.

I told him about my father—fighting both the Japanese and the communists in China, escaping on the last boat to leave Shanghai before it fell to Mao. I filled him in on my mother—the Jefferson Davis descendent who fought for civil rights in the 1950s. We talked about my obsession with the New York Mets and my undeniable love of politics. I confessed that I had been all over the ideological map and that I had actually voted for Michael Dukakis in 1988 over Bush's father—though I had redeemed myself in 1992. He said he had had many worse confessions. I told him about my charity and that it would be hard for me to give it up but that I could potentially do more with government.

"Yeah, safe to say that you could raise more money from the Department of Treasury than a bunch of political donors."

At that Karen Hughes arrived. "Karen," he said with a twinkle, "is the enforcer. If you get through Karen then you are in."

Karen was tall and chinny, with twinkling eyes and serious makeup. Her downturned mouth looked exactly like the governor's. She exuded the intensity and intimidation of a union boss from times past. I decided it was good to be afraid of Karen Hughes. She was also Bush's alter ego. He said she knew him better than anyone. Like him she wasn't pretentious, but unlike him she wore her wariness up front. She held up a speech I had written for John Ashcroft a year before and asked, "Did you write this speech?"

I laughed. She just looked at me. "Of course I wrote it," I said. "Call John and ask him."

"We have," she chuckled. "I just want to know if this is the work you are capable of doing."

"I hope so."

"We need more than 'I hope so.' Is this or isn't it?"

"It is." I wanted to say "ma'am."

Karen accepted the answer happily, looked at Bush, and then

floated in and out during the next couple of hours, monitoring, watching, listening.

"I'm sorry Karl isn't in town," the governor said. "He's my political guy. But you'll meet him and you'll like him. And he'll like you," he said with a chuckle. "He'll like that you make Karen nervous."

I smiled and took it all in. He kept rolling on. "I can't do this unless I know that God is calling me to do this," he said. "The sacrifices are too intense, the strain on Laura, my girls would just be too great."

Bush defied easy description. He seemed not just charming, but weighty, seductive yet pure, likeable but mysterious. I couldn't tell whether his disclosures were private revelations to someone he liked or just part of a pitch to someone he might need. I didn't much care. I loved him.

My sole issue was that after all the sitting and talking for who knows how long—I couldn't glance down at my watch and there wasn't a clock I could see from my seat—I was getting uncomfortable. I had to use the restroom. They had given me a big bottle of water when I had arrived and I had drained it. Enough said.

Two conversations began to overlap. In one he was talking out loud about his vision for politics. In the other I was trying to figure out how to excuse myself.

Him: "Yeah, the old man had a problem with the vision thing . . ."

Me: "How the heck can I ask him if I can be excused to go to the bathroom? I've *got* to go to the bathroom . . ."

" . . . vision is important . . ."

"My bladder is starting to hurt."

" . . . my old man's problem . . ."

"Maybe if I uncross my legs it will help."

" . . . never used his political capital on domestic matters after the Iraq War . . ."

"Maybe I could discreetly unbuckle my belt to relieve pressure?"

" . . . I would never make that mistake. I believe in the vision thing."

"Please shut up! I'm going to stain your chair."

" . . . political capital has to be spent on something big; otherwise it is . . ."

I gave up. "Excuse me sir, I'm sorry for interrupting, but may I excuse myself for a minute to go to the bathroom? I think I saw one in the hall outside the reception area."

"No, no, I've got one right over there, use it."

I have never been more grateful for a bathroom in my life.

I repositioned myself in the chair as he finished up a call. He had been talking to Bishop T. D. Jakes, a prominent African-American evangelical pastor in Dallas. "Just made T.D.'s day!" he said with a grin. "Giving away a bunch of the money I made from selling the Texas Rangers. T.D. is a good man. Gonna buy this ranch outside of Waco, Texas. It is in a little town called Crawford. One day gonna be where I live the rest of my life.

"Yesterday," he said, "I was down at a juvenile detention facility talking to some kids. Places like that aren't where governors typically hang out. Anyway, as I was getting ready to leave, this little black kid raised his hand. I pointed towards him and asked if he had a last question. He said he did. 'What do you think of me, Governor Bush? What do you think of me?' "

Behind the desk he shifted and his eyes looked around and it looked like he was chewing on the inside of his cheeks. "You know what? I didn't have an answer. I still don't. I said something but I don't remember exactly what it was. But I have to have an answer to that. There has to be something done about the gap between the rich and the poor. There has to be something done about racial justice, economic justice, social justice . . . something has to be done. I just don't know what it is. Maybe you could help."

I was hooked. It didn't matter that he didn't have an answer for the ultimately unanswerable question of racial harmony, poverty elimination, and global oneness. It just mattered that he cared. That care meant answers would come because he would demand them. I had longed to hear words like that coming from a political leader. I longed for them so deeply that I had tried to put them in speech after speech for other men. I thought that if I wrote them enough for other people then those other people might actually believe them and then they would act.

Bush was the real deal. He loved Jesus. He wanted to help the poor. He was the embodiment of the Christian political statesman I had dreamed of finding and dreamed of being.

"I'm giving a speech tonight, fly down with me. Let's talk some more. Stay at the mansion tonight."

Aides bustled in and out of his office, trying to get me on the plane. As it turned out, because I wasn't a government employee, I couldn't fly on the plane. So the governor said, "Drive down and meet me there tonight and at least get a sense for what I'm saying."

I got up, floated back to my car, and headed to Texas A&M University, a few hours away. I was in love. I called my good friend Joe Klein and babbled like a 1960s girl who had just seen the Beatles on the Ed Sullivan show. I relayed the whole conversation. I told Joe that I had found him, I had found the next Bobby Kennedy, I had found a son of privilege with a heart for the poor, with an understanding of racial, social, and economic justice. Things couldn't be any better.

"Joe, he actually used the words 'racial, social, and economic justice' . . . voluntarily!"

Joe, a couple of decades my senior, listened with the patience of a father. He listened and listened and pronounced it great. "But," added the author of *Primary Colors,* the novel about the 1992 Clinton campaign, "do not let him break your heart." Joe's novel was penned, in part, from his own disappointment with Bill Clinton. "Promise me. He may be what you say he is but just promise me that you won't let him break your heart."

My friend worried too much.

I listened to Bush that night and heard the next president. It was hard to remember exactly what he had said. He talked about opportunity and tried to talk about the story from the juvenile detention facility, but he didn't have any answers and that made him sound uncomfortable in a public setting. He clearly preferred answers to questions. But here was a man humble enough to ask the questions anyway.

I drove back to Austin the next day and flew home. Just a few days later I was working for Bush.

My first assignment was writing about economics for a speech before the Republican National Committee in San Francisco. Ugh.

I always found in my writing that if I didn't passionately care about what I wrote I didn't write it very well. Perhaps it was laziness or evidence of merely adequate verbal ability. It made some speeches wonderful: If I was writing about social justice or faith's power or racial reconciliation, I liked to think the speeches could sing. But when it came to economics or most foreign policy, I just went flat. I think my writing sounded like something off a cereal box.

That didn't change with Bush.

The first speech wasn't a home run. The second one was better. The third he gave verbatim. I went back to Austin to fly around Texas with him, listening to him talk and give speeches. It was me, him, a security guy, and his young personal aide.

The governor and I sat in two opposite seats of a turboprop airplane bouncing this way and that over the all-brown state. He opined about the state of the world and I listened, wrote, ate bologna sandwiches, and recorded it all so I could better capture his voice. "If I could pass a law making people love one another, I would. But I can't. That's why we've got to mobilize people to help each other and care for each other."

I liked him no less the second time around than I did the first. He was more in business mode that late spring day but he was also more fully in campaign mode. He hopped up in front of one group in a firehouse and said exactly what he said on the plane. He wanted people to love each other, he was proud to have worked with both Democrats and Republicans in the Texas legislature, and he believed that people needed to come together to solve problems.

It was remarkable. It was either that he was always on or never off. For most politicians there is a performance aspect to their speeches. They get fired up, they change tone and cadence. Bush didn't. His voice was louder only because of electronic amplification. Other than that he was the same giving a speech as he was when huddling privately. But what did that mean? Was it that he was forever performing for the public and those around him? Or was it that he simply was who he was?

I'm inclined to think that the George W. Bush I met in those days was just a confident man who knew himself. Part of that confidence was the comfort with who he had been. Watching him, I couldn't miss the evidence of the former drunk, the lost soul who had fallen to his knees sobbing before God; the sinner who had become God's own. He didn't wear a badge or a scarlet letter or hand out written copies of his testimony. It just permeated normal conversation. "Now I see," "I used to be blind," "I know what it means to hit bottom," "I know the power of faith to change lives," "I now know who I am."

He displayed this most clearly when he came across an addict of some sort. Whether that addict was clean or not, the governor would slow down. His cadence would change. He would put both of his hands on the man's shoulders and look into his eyes. Any swagger disappeared. Something softer and perhaps more genuine took its place. He listened to each story and nodded. He seemed more like a counselor than a politician. When this happened—just a few times when I was around—he didn't hurry and didn't rush. It was one of the more Christ-like things I had ever seen a powerful man do.

I went back to Austin another time or two in 1998 to talk about speeches. We talked about the possibility of my moving down to Austin, but that was a nonstarter for me. Austin was way too far from my girls. They needed someone completely devoted to them and I couldn't be that if I moved. I was also still involved with my charity and didn't want to do politics full time.

Full-time politics in 1998 was pretty disgusting. A sitting president had had an affair with a young intern, lied about it to the American people, lied under oath, and attempted to obstruct justice. He was impeached by the House and acquitted in early 1999 by the Senate. In the midst of this, there seemed to be a sort of barely contained glee by many of his critics; he had finally been caught and now he was going to pay.

Politically conservative Christians like me had it in for Bill

Clinton from day one. That made the Monica Lewinsky revelation something of a relief. We had been right all along. As angry as Democrats felt—or perhaps still feel—about President Bush's disputed 2000 election victory, we Christian conservatives were angrier about Bill Clinton. He was a moral affront to us as a human being. His policies only made things worse. One prominent evangelical leader actively hawked a video called the *Clinton Chronicles,* distributed by a Christian film production company, which insinuated, among other things, that some of the Clintons' political opponents had been killed. Former Clinton associates were paid by Christian-backed organizations like Citizens for Honest Government to tell stories about Clinton's indiscretions in Arkansas. In terms of apoplexy, this beats Alec Baldwin's (still unfulfilled) promise to leave the country if George Bush were elected president—although some recent remarks by the Dixie Chicks, Barbra Streisand, and George Clooney indicate Hollywood is very quickly catching up.

In an odd way, though, President Clinton helped save the religious conservative movement. Their anger at the Republican Congress, at Bob Dole's 1996 defeat, at Bill Clinton's increasing popularity, and at the general lack of progress on their social agenda was threatening to fracture them, pre-Lewinsky. But in 1998 he gave them common voice with his litany of indiscretions, lies, and blatantly stupid actions.

Just before the scandals broke, James Dobson had accused Speaker Gingrich and his leadership team of "moral and philosophical collapse" for their failure to restrict abortion, abolish the National Endowment for the Arts for funding offensive art like "Piss Christ," a photograph of a crucifix suspended in a jar of urine, and repeal the military's tolerance of closeted gays. But by the time the impeachment hearings were over a year later, Dobson was praising House Republicans. "Considering the effectiveness of the [Clinton] spin machine these past thirteen months, it is remarkable that Republicans in the House had the courage to stand on their principles . . . I believe millions of Americans join me in expressing admiration and appreciation to [them] . . . they are heroes to many of us."

While evangelical leaders warmed up to congressional Republicans, those leaders could only scratch their heads over the American people. Despite the president's lies and the obvious affairs, the American public wasn't going along with the campaign to impeach him; polling showed about 75 percent of Americans opposing impeachment. More than half of religious conservatives opposed impeachment. All of this infuriated religious conservative leaders almost as much as Clinton himself. By the time the controversy ebbed, Dr. Dobson was left to conclude, "Our people no longer recognize the nature of evil."

When some prominent evangelical leaders stood up and denounced what President Clinton had done but then called for absolute forgiveness, a new discussion began. My old friend Pete Wehner wrote, "What we have is an attempt to use God's forgiveness which is something we all are in need of as a pretext to excuse moral wrong. That is a dangerous heresy. Essentially, it rejects the moral law as a relevant part of Christian experience. The thought that God's grace would justify licentiousness has been considered contemptible by saints and scholars throughout the ages. And rightly so."

His position was well justified. As theologians pointed out, when Jesus forgave the thief hanging on the cross and promised him that paradise awaited, he did not supernaturally remove the thief from the cross. Jesus let the civic punishment stand even as absolution was granted. In the same way, Pope John Paul II visited prison and prayed with the man who shot him. He did not, however, lobby for his release.

Perhaps my own past sins gave me more compassion or perhaps they blinded me to sin—I couldn't build up enough rage to want to see the president go down. I understood and was disturbed by his deceit and dishonor. But on the other hand, Bill Clinton hadn't been trying to corrupt the government, undermine democracy, or stage a coup. He had been exposed as an adulterer after trying to do everything he could to hide that fact. I could relate. I certainly didn't want anyone to know I had been part of an abortion a decade before and I didn't want to talk about the divorce I was going through that year. But Bill Clinton and I shared a common faith in Jesus and in the belief that, though we erred time and again, he was making us more like him at every moment. It wasn't an easy faith or a feel-good faith. The things that we did wrong had serious consequences: an abortion meant a child who would never smile; a divorce, a family that disintegrated; adultery, the betrayal of a spouse; lying, the loss of trust, and so on. But we also knew that if we truly regretted what we had done and threw ourselves upon God's mercy with the earnest desire to never do it again, we would find forgiveness.

Bill Clinton did that publicly at a White House gathering of clergy in September 1998, saying, "I don't think there is a fancy way to say that I have sinned. It is important to me that everybody who has been hurt know that the sorrow I feel is genuine: first and most important, my family; also my friends, my staff, my Cabinet, Monica Lewinsky and her family, and the American people. I have asked all for their forgiveness. But I believe that to be forgiven, more than sorrow is required—at least two more things. First, genuine repentance—a determination to change and to repair breaches of my own making. I have repented. Second, what my Bible calls a 'broken spirit'; an understanding that I must have God's help to be the person that I want to be; a willingness to give the very forgiveness I seek; a renunciation of the pride and the anger which cloud judgment, lead people to excuse and compare and to blame and complain." Of course even that apology was debated: was it genuine? It seemed genuine to me.

Clinton's repeated use of religious symbols and rhetoric brought a stern rebuke from an unlikely mix of more than 150 theologians and ethicists. The group, which included numerous liberal academics and others who had voted for Bill Clinton, declared, "We believe that serious misunderstandings of repentance and forgiveness are being exploited for political advantage. The resulting moral confusion is a threat to the integrity of American religion and to the foundations of a civil society. . . . We fear the religious community is in danger of being called upon to provide authentication for a politically motivated and incomplete repentance that seeks to avert serious consequences for wrongful acts." Their final warning was about Christians in politics. Gabriel Fackre, a theologian in the liberal United Church of Christ, wrote, "God help us if we give evidence for the Marxist charge that religion exists to provide cover for the powers that be."

The whole affair was alien to what I had once hoped for from Christians in politics. Everyone, it seemed, emerged smelling bad and looking worse—especially Jesus. Part of the blame lay with Bill Clinton, who leaned heavily on religion to prove his repentance. Another part lay with Democrats who seemed fearful of stating the obvious—that Clinton had lied—and instead decided to fight Republicans because it might be more politically advantageous to do so. And part lay with politically conservative Christian leaders who mobilized against Clinton with remarkable viciousness, failing to display the love Jesus modeled in his parable of the prodigal son in which the father welcomed the wayward son with open arms and no questions. And part of it lay with Republicans in the House who seemed to relish Bill Clinton's humiliation.

The Old Testament prophet Micah said we should do justice, love mercy, and walk humbly with our God. I'd always hoped that Christians would carry into the fights Jesus' commands to radically love even those we called enemies. Of course, I hadn't done so. When it came to the Clinton-Lewinsky scandal, there was far too much hatred.

Ultimately, of course, President Clinton got to stay in office as a tarnished, lame-duck president. The religious Right was apoplectic. In March 1999, Paul Weyrich, a founder of the Moral Majority, wrote a bitter postimpeachment letter addressed "Dear Friend" and placed it on the foundation's Web site. "Politics itself has failed. And politics has failed because of the collapse of the culture. The culture we are living in becomes an ever-wider sewer. . . . Suffice it to say that the United States is very close to becoming a state totally dominated by an alien ideology, an ideology bitterly hostile to Western culture."

As this happened, the mainstream media was again quick to write one of their favorite stories: the religious Right is dead. One major paper's editorial began, "Until recently, Tinky Winky— one of the stars of the wildly popular *Teletubbies* kids' TV show— symbolized nothing more than the triumph of silliness. Now, the amorphous purple space-munchkin has come to signify something else: trying times for the Religious Right. [Falwell had criticized the *Teletubbies'* character Tinky Winky, calling him a homosexual.] Christian conservatives suffered a shattering defeat in the impeachment trial of President Clinton. The mercurial Reverend Pat Robertson has been forced to reclaim the presidency of the Christian Coalition after a lengthy hiatus. And Reverend Jerry Falwell's decision to attack Tinky as a sexually ambiguous advocate of the gay lifestyle drew coast-to-coast snickers." Christian groups' absolutism "scares the hell out of voters in the middle" of the political spectrum, independent pollster John Zogby declared.

By 1999, nonetheless, George Bush was still the Republican front-runner, whether or not his evangelical beliefs scared anyone. I was no longer working for him, however. My admiration and respect for him hadn't changed. In fact, it had increased. As the presidential primaries drew closer and more and more people lauded him, he still talked about compassion and serving others. For me, though, the speechwriting hadn't worked out. I couldn't adequately nail his voice even if I thought I understood his heart. Fortunately though, he found someone who could. Mike Gerson signed on, moved down to Austin, and made sure compassion wasn't going to be forgotten. To boot, I was about to become silly rich. I had joined a dot-com. Value America had all the extravagant promise of its era. Not only would it have billions of dollars in revenue, or so the founder promised, but it would give away 1 percent of gross revenue to charity. That could mean billions per year. I was to be in charge of the charitable giving and corporate communications—a natural combination. I moved back to Virginia, where the company was based, and became a corporate guy.

Ultimately, however, our story was the story of most dot-coms—a wild ride and a spectacular flameout. I spent the last night of the twentieth century eating Chinese food, reflecting on the people I had been forced to fire that day.

CHAPTER EIGHT

Looking in All
the Wrong Places

George W. Bush's religious orientation was the most carefully controlled aspect of his public image. For him to win the Republican nomination, religious conservatives would have to be convinced that his religious faith was genuine and evangelical. But to win the general election, Bush needed to be seen as mainstream, and not "too" religious. The Sunday morning he announced his presidential exploratory committee, for instance, he was at the ten-thousand member Second Baptist Church in Houston. The evening before he had gone to church with another six thousand or so members of the same church. What took him to both services was the preacher—himself. "Faith gives us purpose—to right wrongs, preserve our families, and teach our children values," he proclaimed in both services. "Faith gives us a conscience—to keep us honest even when no one is watching. Faith changes lives. I know, because it has changed mine. I grew up in the church, but I didn't always walk the walk."

Seventy-eight members of Congress, five U.S. senators, half the Republican governors, and countless others had already endorsed him for president. Hundreds of reporters awaited his political announcement in Austin. And not one of them from the national media would write about his sermons. The media was still convinced the religious Right was largely dead, humiliated by Clinton's Senate acquittal and 70 percent approval ratings. No one in Austin was upset by the oversight.

A rapidly developing field of potential Republican presidential candidates that included Dan Quayle, Lamar Alexander, and Steve Forbes was talking openly about God and the need to reclaim moral values. Forbes said he wanted to post the Ten Commandments in classrooms and that America's schools had to let "faith and values back in." Alexander, a former Tennessee governor and onetime U.S. education secretary, complained, "Our standards of right and wrong have all but disappeared." Governor Bush, however, was saying little publicly. His overwhelming reelection the previous November, with two-thirds of voting Texans supporting him—including a large percentage of women and Hispanics—was based primarily on education and not on any controversial social issues. This alarmed some religious conservatives, most notably Dr. Dobson, who chided Bush to come out and say where he stood on abortion, gay rights, prayer in schools, and other issues important to Dobson.

While Bush said the right things when asked about the issues, he didn't dwell on them. On abortion, for instance, he embraced the conservative Christian position, saying he was against it except for special circumstances, and he was in favor of a constitutional amendment banning abortions. Yet he quickly followed that statement by saying that Americans wouldn't go for it, and it was pointless to talk about it. To Dobson he was being wishy-washy. But to most other Christian political leaders he was being smart. They all knew better; they knew his heart.

That was because out of the public eye Governor Bush was doing a lot of spiritual sharing. Whether he was meeting with religious leaders in Austin, or speaking to church groups, he emphasized a single thing: his personal faith in Jesus Christ. He told fellow believers his story: In his late thirties he reached a point in his life where he knew he wasn't living right. He drank too much. His marriage was good but his career unremarkable. Billy Graham asked him if he was right with God, right with Jesus. Bush said he didn't think so. A year later, he woke from his fortieth birthday party hungover; that was it. He chose Jesus over booze. For the pastors with whom he spoke, it was all they needed to hear. George W. Bush was a brother in Christ, a sinner who had been redeemed, and they knew he supported the right positions simply because he had to—he was a Christian, what else could he do?

He modeled this same approach throughout his presidency—quietly reassuring Christian leaders and audiences of his passionate personal faith while trying to preserve a moderate public image. In so doing, he was playing the religious card more than any other American president. It was just that he didn't do it very publicly. What George Bush and his campaign knew was that evangelical Christians were horrified at Bill Clinton's policies, appointments, and moral failures. They wanted changes to abortion policy and conservative judges and the family to be protected. But more than anything, they wanted a good Christian leader in the White House. The story he told Christians wasn't a story. He was giving them his testimony.

When Christians like me share the stories of how we came to believe in Jesus and what his presence means in our lives, it is called a testimony. It is deeply personal, deeply intimate, and shared with fellow Christians as well as with those we hope are open to accepting Jesus. Bush tweaked its purpose—he was using it to encourage Christians to accept him.

Some of the Christian leaders who accepted Bush became informal evangelists for him. Major leaders like Ed Young, pastor of Houston's largest Baptist church and past president of the fifteen-million-member Southern Baptist Convention, televangelists James Robison and John Hagee, and informal Bush adviser Ralph Reed recruited other pastors to be part of the Bush team. This missionary effort didn't just allow Governor Bush to win over potentially powerful political allies, it also gave him the freedom to avoid dwelling on the hot-button social issues such as abortion, gay rights, and prayer in schools that appeal to the social conservatives who dominate the Republican primaries but can alienate more moderate voters. It was a quiet campaign, conducted out of the media's glare. And it worked. In March 1999, the same month he was preaching in churches, *Business Week* called Bush "semi-spiritual," unlike social conservatives like Dan Quayle or Steve Forbes. This approach irked Dobson but thrilled Pat Robertson.

"He's committed to the [social conservative] agenda," Robertson reminded Christian conservatives, "but at the same time, he's running for president. He's aware that he needs to be portrayed as a centrist candidate."

Part of Bush's centrism was his compassionate conservatism. When he talked about the need to rally "armies of compassion" and lauded faith-based social service groups in the sermons he gave in Houston, that message wasn't directed primarily at politically motivated Christians. They, the campaign hoped, would already know about Bush's deep personal faith. The primary target was suburban women and "nontraditional" Republican voters: minorities. It was so important that it was the subject of the very first policy speech of his campaign.

In July 1999, while I was dot-comming in Virginia, Governor Bush went to Indianapolis, home of Mayor Stephen Goldsmith's "Front Porch Alliance." The Alliance created partnerships between the city, faith institutions, community groups, neighborhoods, and community members to address local problems. With that as the backdrop, Bush launched the boldest, most radical agenda for the poor of any major presidential candidate since Robert Kennedy. While he nodded toward economic conservatism, noting that he believed in tax cuts, he said, "I know that economic growth is not the solution to every problem. A rising tide lifts many boats, but not all. . . . The invisible hand works many miracles. But it cannot touch the human heart." The remarks were blatant slaps not only at Jack Kemp–style economic conservatism but at the Republican Party's economic focus in general.

The governor talked about all the people who felt the American Dream wasn't for them, people who lived in places where "despair is the easy path, and hope the narrow gate." But they still have hopes, he said, and "in their hopes, we find our duties. In their hardship, we must find our calling, to serve others, relying on the goodness of America and the boundless grace of God." He made the case that the only way we were going to tackle deep human need was locally and personally and rooted in faith. "We found that government can spend money, but it can't put hope in our hearts or a sense of purpose in our lives. This is done by churches and synagogues and mosques and charities that warm the cold of life. A quiet river of goodness and kindness cuts through stone." It would be these faith-based and community groups that would lead his administration's "determined attack on need . . . rally[ing] the armies of compassion." They were remarks as distant from the Clinton-Lewinsky saga as the East is from the West.

Then he did possibly the most radical thing of all, at least for a Republican: he wanted to extravagantly fund efforts that reduced suffering. "It is not enough for conservatives like me to praise these efforts. It is not enough to call for volunteerism. Without more support and resources, both public and private, we are asking them to make bricks without straw." He then promised about $8 billion per year in spending. Tax credits to encourage giving would total $6.3 billion, and $1.7 billion per year would be for specific programs to help the poor. In addition, Bush proposed $200 million a year for a "Compassion Capital Fund" to help small charities (faith-based or secular) expand their work with the poor.*

At the heart of it all were two proposals aimed at increasing giving to poverty-related groups. One was a charity tax credit that would allow all Americans to give part of their state tax bill directly to poverty-fighting groups. The other was a way for the 70 percent of all Americans who don't claim itemized deductions to receive the same treatment as wealthier Americans who do itemize their deductions and get a tax benefit. The way most Americans file their taxes is by adding up how much they've made, taking the personal exemptions and standard deductions, applying any child tax credits, and determining their tax bill. Doing it this way, they don't get to itemize their charitable giving and get a deduction for it. The Bush proposal would change that, giving credit for current donations even if one doesn't itemize, thereby encouraging further donations. Estimates suggested it could mean billions more per year in charitable giving.

In addition, Bush promised initiatives to help children of prisoners, expand after-school programs, expand drug treatment pro-

* Ronald Brownstein, "Charity Begins at Church, Gov. Bush Says," *Los Angeles Times,* July 23, 1999, p. A13.

grams and maternity group homes, and set up new prison programs like Prison Fellowship's InnerChange initiative. To top it off he promised to get rid of rules that discriminated against faith-based groups.

He concluded, "There must be a kindness in our justice. There must be mercy in our judgment. There must be love behind our zeal." It was Christian statesmanship and leadership unseen in American society since Martin Luther King Jr.

His rivals thought he had gone loco. Senator John McCain called the endeavor "a bit nonsensical" (but then again he thought sending a man to Mars should be a NASA priority). Steve Forbes called it a Democratic-style "big government" solution. Senator Elizabeth Dole's press secretary, Ari Fleischer, dismissed the proposals with the quip, "The governor will make a great future president—of the American Red Cross."

From my dot-com perch, I read the speech with total wonder and satisfaction. The pro-poor policies we had been dreaming of for nearly a decade were the centerpieces of Governor Bush's campaign. My original impressions of him, his heart, and his desire to help the poor were absolutely on target.

By the time 2000 began, Bush's evangelical support had been largely solidified. Dan Quayle left the race after finishing eighth in the August 1999 Iowa straw poll. Gary Bauer was a nonfactor, garnering only a few thousand votes in Iowa and 700 in New Hampshire. It was good Bush had picked up their support because he would need it in South Carolina.

McCain trounced Bush by 19 points in the New Hampshire primary and headed into South Carolina with momentum on his side. Suddenly, that sole primary campaign, for a single Southern state, took on immense significance. If upstart McCain could best front-runner Bush a second time, they wouldn't be calling Bush the front-runner anymore.

Bush's first stop was at ultrafundamentalist Bob Jones University, a place that had sued for its right to deny entry to blacks in the 1970s and still forbade interracial dating and called the Catholic Church satanic. When asked about the seeming incongruity of a compassionate conservative leader going to Bob Jones, a Bush spokesperson said the candidate opposed their policy banning interracial dating, "But this is a school that has a lot of conservative voters, and it's a common stop on the campaign trail." In his speech there Bush didn't address race or anti-Catholic bigotry. One prominent conservative commentator remarked, "It's one thing to lurch to the right. It's another thing to lurch back sixty years. You could make the case that 'compassionate conservatism' died February 2 when Bush appeared at Bob Jones U."

In the days that followed, the campaign in South Carolina only got uglier. Rumors swirled that the Vietcong had brainwashed McCain and that he was an unstable man. Other rumors about his past included that he was the father of an interracial child. No one admitted they knew where the rumors were coming from, even though everyone knew where the rumors were coming from. Beyond any doubt, it was people affiliated or associated with Bush's campaign. Exactly who they were and how they were paid was never established.

It got so bad that Gary Bauer ended up endorsing John McCain because of his disgust with the smear tactics he believed were coming from the Bush camp and because he felt he needed to restore a certain sense of honor to Christian conservatives. The conservatives, in turn, turned on Bauer, one of the most important men in the 1990s resurgence of politically active Christians in the first place. One religious conservative leader said in an interview after South Carolina, "Gary is an enigma, as opposed to being a good or evil person. For years, he was clearly on the basic team as everyone else in the social conservative movement, and suddenly it's like, 'Do we really know you, Gary? We don't know how to figure you out.' "

If all of this had occurred simply among Republican conservatives whose sole goal was a more conservative America, it would have been bad enough. That it occurred among proud and professing Christians was unspeakably damaging to the Jesus they served. People on the ground and media around the world reported on Pat Robertson, a Christian, saying McCain would destroy the Republican Party, on a Christian professor who launched a string of e-mail attacks on McCain's character, on Christian activists jeering McCain, on Governor Bush telling McCain, "John, it's only politics" before one of the South Carolina debates.

Bush won South Carolina but the notion of him as a compassionate conservative suffered badly. Every bit of religious and conservative nuance was dropped from the Bush campaign. It haunted him for months.

In heavily Catholic Michigan, McCain's campaign highlighted Bush's Bob Jones visit with recorded phone calls saying, "This is a Catholic voter alert. Bob Jones has made strong anti-Catholic statements, including calling the Pope the 'Antichrist' and the Catholic Church a 'satanic cult.' John McCain, a pro-life Senator, has strongly criticized this anti-Catholic bigotry, while Governor Bush has stayed silent, while gaining the support of Bob Jones." Meanwhile, Governor Bush leaned on Pat Robertson, who recorded calls urging people to vote for Bush.

McCain attacked religious "agents of intolerance," saying that "neither party should be defined by pandering to the outer reaches of American politics . . . whether they be Louis Farrakhan or Al Sharpton on the left, or Pat Robertson or Jerry Falwell on the right."

Bush responded by lashing out at McCain, accusing him of "playing the religious card."

Bush lost Michigan badly. He wrote a letter of apology to Cardinal John O'Connor of New York, saying, "On reflection, I should have been more clear in disassociating myself from anti-Catholic sentiments and racial prejudice. It was a missed opportunity causing needless offense, which I deeply regret."

It was striking to me that for all the Christian discussion of whether or not President Clinton's public apologies for the Lewinsky affair were valid, I heard almost no Christian discussion about Governor Bush and Bob Jones, nor of the transparent political act he'd engaged in by writing and then releasing his "private" letter to O'Connor.

Yet his "apology" seemed to be exactly the sort of thing my friend Pete Wehner had critiqued about Clinton. Bush was using forgiveness and penance to win votes. As I had learned in my own life, one of the hardest parts of serving God in politics is ensuring that God reigned over politics rather than having politics reign over God.

Bush's penance was Catholic mistrust of him. The first four years of his presidency were spent trying to regain those disenchanted Catholic voters.

One June day in 2000, after Bush had wrapped up the nomination and Republicans were back to being a happy family intent on destroying Al Gore, I was in the middle of thinking about writing a book on my wild Internet experience. I was back in Atlanta. Mike Gerson called. By that point, he had been with Bush for nearly a year, and the two of them had melded minds. Somehow the swaggering Texas governor and the guy who had read Kissinger at twelve and probably didn't know the difference between a curveball and a knuckleball were political and spiritual soulmates.

Gerson asked if I wanted to start writing speeches again.

I told him it depended on the audience. He said it was the NAACP. I said yes. The new millennium was bringing some sort of karmic completion: I was living in Atlanta, the city of my mother's civil rights horror, and was to write the speech a Christian political leader who cared about race and poverty would deliver to the NAACP.

I drove around Atlanta and tried to see the city as my mother had once seen it. That, I figured, was the only way I could write about what any Republican talking to the NAACP needed to say—that we are sorry for all we didn't do. The Republican Party had been Lincoln's party. It just hadn't behaved like Lincoln for a very long time. It all came down to a highway in Atlanta. On one side there were small rundown houses and apartment buildings, almost all populated by blacks. Men and boys hung out on street corners. There were long lines at what looked like a church soup kitchen. On the other side there were new buildings with glittering glass and Starbucks and places that served $12 hamburgers for white men and women. It made writing the speech very easy.

> My goal this morning is to talk about the future—to share with you my heart and my head about matters of economic justice, racial equality, and unlimited access to the American Dream. But before we can get to the future, we must confront our past. In the darkest days of America's civil war, the Great Emancipator pleaded to a nation to remember that "we cannot escape history—we will be remembered in spite of ourselves." One hundred and forty years later, that's still true.
>
> For our nation, there is no denying the truth that slavery is a blight on our history and that racism, despite all the progress, still exists today. For my party, there is no escaping the reality that the party of Lincoln has not always carried the mantle of Lincoln on matters of racial and economic justice. Today we live in cities where highways divide third world squalor from information age wonder. Highways of cars separate communities of prosperity from communities of poverty . . .

I turned it in. Mike loved it. Bush loved it and he gave most of it. Phrases like "economic justice" and "racial justice" didn't survive the cut, nor did the discussions of poverty and wealth. But Governor Bush became only the second Republican presidential candidate to address the NAACP in twenty-five years. That made up for any policy disappointment, or the fact that the NAACP speech was a part of his ongoing political penance for the Bob Jones visit.

Then again, I may just have been in a good mood. Her name was Kim McCreery. She was a beyond-beautiful brown-haired, brown-eyed Kansas girl who had gone off to Stanford and then overseas to study in London, ending up in Washington on a lark as an intern for Bob Dole. For me she is the only answer to that common question, "If you had to live on an island with one person and just one person for the rest of your life, who would it be?" We were back in Atlanta because she was working at a high-tech start-up. I had persuaded her to join me at Value America in Virginia. After that, I figured if she still wanted to be married to me, I had to follow her to Atlanta.

Kim reminded me of two past loves. On the morning of my birthday I awoke to oddly shaped packages spread out in our room. Before I opened them she wanted me to know that I had forgotten something in my life and she wanted to fix that. She found fishing for me. Months before we had been away for the weekend at a bed-and-breakfast. As we toured the grounds she had seen my eyes light up at a man fly-fishing on a trout pond. Now she was giving it to me—the rod, reel, waders, flies, everything.

The other thing she helped me find is God. Though I like to say I was tormented about remarrying because my first marriage failed, it isn't true. I wanted to be married to Kim so much I even found myself talking to God on occasion, asking him to help me out by having her say yes to the proposal. After she accepted I told her about my brief conversations with God. She offhandedly mentioned that in some cultures talking to God is also known as prayer.

I wasn't the only one praying. The most interesting part of the campaign wasn't what happened in Florida but what happened with God. He was everywhere and it wasn't only Governor Bush and his followers who were talking about him. Vice President Gore talked about his life as a born-again Christian on *60 Minutes*. To the *Washington Post* he said he often asked himself what Jesus would do on certain matters. Senator Joe Lieberman, his running mate, was an Orthodox Jew who brought up God and the Hebrew Scriptures at virtually every event. About the only nonreligious voice in the race belonged to Bush's running mate, Dick Cheney.

On Election Day, though, the most observantly religious voters went overwhelmingly for Bush. Sixty percent of his votes came from evangelical Christians, devout Catholics, and observant mainline Protestants. Eighty-four percent of regular church-going evangelicals voted for Bush.

One day in January, after Bush's inauguration, I stopped at a gas pump to fill up my car. My phone rang and it was Joe Klein. "Guess what," he said. "John DiIulio is going to head up the president's faith-based office. Bush looks like he is certainly the real deal."

CHAPTER NINE

Breaking Down Gates
of Bronze

"Hey Kuo, I've got a great idea."

It was April 2001 and Joe Klein was on the phone again. We had just spent two weeks in Florida going to golf school and watching New York Mets spring training. Naturally I figured his latest idea centered around a new trip. "Where are we headed?"

"Not we. You. You need to go talk to Brother John."

"Brother John" was DiIulio. He looked like Newman from *Seinfeld*. It was not a passing resemblance. When you looked at John you looked at Newman. He was a big South Philadelphia guy. When he was a kid he and his buddies used to try and catch big water rats. It was an urban version of catching a greased pig. He had gone to college just because someone told him he was smart. Graduate school at Harvard followed because he couldn't figure out whether he wanted to open a hot dog stand or work construction. Then he got a Ph.D. and landed a job at Princeton. He was twenty-five. Within a year he noticed a lot of his colleagues were being denied tenure after seven years, and were left searching for someplace else to go. He went to the dean and said he wanted to be considered early for tenure. If not, he told the bemused scholar, "I'm still young enough to get a real job in construction or something." A year later he was tenured. Construction would have to wait.

He denied having a photographic memory. A photographic memory, he said, meant you could recall virtually anything at any moment. In order for him to pull from memory an entire chapter of a book, he had to be given the first line.

Those things were part of who he was, but they weren't the essential parts. The essential parts were revealed in the hours he took to teach poor kids in high school, volunteer his time in inner-city schools, and fight to get funding for charities that served the poor. Someone said he talked like a longshoreman, reasoned like Einstein, and cared like Mother Teresa. It was a good description.

During the 2000 elections, he helped write both Vice President Gore's and Governor Bush's speeches about faith-based charities. Not surprisingly, both men came out for virtually the same things: more money to help small faith-based groups, an expansion of Charitable Choice, and some tax credits to spur charitable giving.

After Bush's win, John helped advise the transition team on creating the new Office of Faith-Based Action that Bush had promised during the presidential campaign. The process did not go smoothly.

The controversial election, settled only in December by the Supreme Court, shortened the traditional transition process. Three weeks after the voting, Dick Cheney announced the creation of a privately funded and technically "unofficial" transition office. Things had to move quickly, he said, or "we will pay a heavy price for the delays in planning and assembling the next administration." A week later, Bush declared to reporters that he'd "pretty well made up his mind" on whom to name to his White House staff. Things were moving quickly. To help with the truncated transition, President Clinton signed an executive order creating a special transition council to provide further assistance.

The work of putting together an entirely new government is, as DiIulio described it, "a buzzing confusion." Every federal department needs a new secretary and more than three thousand political appointees. In addition, the entire White House needs to be put together. That means appointing all new leadership to the National Security Council and Office of Management and Budget and essentially recreating the Domestic Policy Council, Economic Policy Council, and all of the individual offices like political affairs and public liaison that round out the entity known as the Executive Office of the President. To get all of that done, transition teams had been created for each of these different areas. That is, every area had a team except for one—the president's poverty-fighting, compassionate-conservative, faith-based agenda.

George Bush, however, continued to talk about it as one of his top priorities. In his first address to the nation as the president-elect, on December 13, 2000, he said, "Together we will address some of society's deepest problems one person at a time, by encouraging and empowering the good hearts and good works of the American people. This is the essence of compassionate conservatism and it will be a foundation of my administration."

A week later, he hosted a small gathering of ministers in Austin. Before it began Bush said, "This is not a political meeting. This is a meeting to begin a dialogue about how best to help faith-based programs change people's lives."

The closed-door discussion began with Bush talking movingly about his desire to heal the country and serve the poor. "I understand people don't trust me—that black Americans don't trust me. I understand that. There has been a . . . we have a credibility problem. But I hope that a year from now no one is going to be able to say that this was all just smoke and mirrors." He talked about the same things that he had discussed with me that day in Austin. "What is justice?" he asked. "How do I speak to the nation's soul?"

While the meeting ended without any specific commitments or plans to follow up, even skeptics left the room impressed. Jim Wallis, evangelical advocate for the poor and a regular critic of Republicans, wrote a private letter to Bush a few days later, lauding him for the meeting. "Our meeting showed me you are a person who listens. It wasn't the photo-op that one sometimes experiences with presidents and politicians. It was instead a serious conversation." Highlighting the policy and political opportunity before the president-elect, Wallis attacked Democrats: "Frankly, the Democrats talk a lot about poverty, but have done little about it." Even the American Jewish Congress, another traditional critic of many things Republican, reached out to senior transition officials, saying that they were interested in working with the president and the

White House on the faith-based initiative despite some initial concerns.

Even with the speeches and meetings, officials in charge of the Bush transition were ignoring the faith-based effort. In late December, Josh Bolten, later to become deputy chief of staff for policy, head of the Office of Management and Budget, and then White House chief of staff, responded to a pastor's inquiry about the initiative by saying, "As far as I know, no one is in charge of the undertaking yet." His disregard was surprising not only because he had been the campaign's top policy guru but because he had the same role during the transition. As it turned out, it wasn't just that nobody had been named to shepherd the initiative through the crucial transition period, it was that nobody at the senior levels of the transition team was even paying attention to the problem.

Finally, down in Austin, Don Willett, a thirty-something Texas lawyer and longtime Bush aide, stepped up to address the problem. Son of a widowed mother, Willett grew up poor in a small Texas town. Funny, kind, and smart, he was a onetime professional drummer and rodeo cowboy with an almost encyclopedic knowledge of old-school hip-hop music. He also liked giving rap-type nicknames. A White House fellow and Marine Corps major named Roberta Shea became "B Sheady" after Eminem's Slim Shady. I was Yo-Yo Kuo or LL Cool Kuo.

Willett wanted to spend his time finding, vetting, and helping confirm federal judges. But he saw the neglect of the faith-based initiative and felt compelled to approach Bolten to help design and launch the office. He knew the faith-based world. He had long advised Bush on a dizzying array of legal and policy issues, including faith-based ones.

In the last days of 2000, Willett got started. He drew up plan after plan for the promised White House office. Some of them would model the office after that of the drug czar—it would be a coordinating agency with a powerful head responsible for pulling together all of the administration's compassion efforts. Other plans put the faith-based office alongside the domestic and economic policy offices. On a good day one plan after another was rejected. On most days they were simply ignored.

In early 2001, the president-elect continued his meetings with clergy and charity leaders. Bush wanted their thoughts on how to help Americans who had been left behind. He lauded his forthcoming faith-based office.

Willett's initial proposal for a staff of 25 was whittled down to 23, and then 18, and then 12. In early January, Bolten told Willett he needed to cut yet more staff. Things had to be "lean and mean." Willett wrote back, "I see the definite virtue in having a lean and mean WH set-up—<u>absolutely</u>—but I also see virtue in re-ordering priorities and giving some muscle to what will be the fulcrum for one of the President-elect's signature and highest-profile initiatives." Bolten never responded.

One of Willett's senior Washington friends, Wade Horn (later to become a high-ranking official at the Department of Health and Human Services), reminded him, "The first question that needs to be addressed is placement. Where in the chain of command is it [the faith-based office] likely to be placed? The higher up the food chain . . . the easier it will be for the office to actually make a difference—offices lower down on the food chain have difficulty being taken seriously." By mid-January the question was whether it would be on the food chain at all.

The neglect would not only delay the office's launch, it would also limit its size and importance. The total number of senior White House staff is fixed. In 1978, Congress established it at 127. The first internal fight, therefore, is for those positions. The way things were going, Willett and his team of volunteer friends who were trying to put the office together didn't technically have to do much planning. Their office would simply consist of whatever staffing slots remained.

Stephen Goldsmith, former Indianapolis mayor and a leading figure in the compassionate conservative movement, had also been a top domestic policy adviser to the Bush campaign. Eight days before the inauguration, Goldsmith wrote to Karl Rove, Bush's campaign manager (and the "Karl" Bush had spoken of back in our Austin introduction). Goldsmith explained to Rove his plan for a small White House office of ten people, "Karl, you absolutely must sell this design as the <u>minimum</u> required to do the job and fill the top positions with the best and brightest talent we can find. Given how dicey this mix of issues is and how every word and action will be dissected, this Office must boast a sharp and diverse staff."

In Indianapolis Goldsmith had gained national prominence for his antipoverty battles, drawing on a diverse community in his "Front Porch Alliance." He was a veteran battler, but he quickly realized he wouldn't win this one. Retrenching, he fought to get the office at least some financial clout, by securing its funding. That too was quickly shot down.

On January 20, 2001, George W. Bush became President George W. Bush, the forty-third president of the United States. The longest section of his inaugural address dealt with compassion:

> America, at its best, is compassionate. In the quiet of American conscience, we know that deep, persistent poverty is unworthy of our nation's promise.
>
> And whatever our views of its cause, we can agree that children at risk are not at fault. Abandonment and abuse are not acts of God, they are failures of love.
>
> And the proliferation of prisons, however necessary, is no substitute for hope and order in our souls. . . .
>
> Government has great responsibilities for public safety and public health, for civil rights and common schools. . . . .
>
> And some needs and hurts are so deep they will only respond to a mentor's touch or a pastor's prayer. Church and charity, synagogue and mosque lend our communities their humanity, and they will have an honored place in our plans and in our laws. . . .
>
> I can pledge our nation to a goal: When we see that wounded traveler on the road to Jericho, we will not pass to the other side.

Every other White House office was up and running. The faith-based initiative still operated out of the nearly vacant transition offices.

Three days later, a Tuesday, Karl Rove summoned Willett to his office to announce that the entire faith-based initiative would be rolled out the following Monday. Willett asked just how—without a director, staff, office, or plan—the president could do that. Rove looked at him, took a deep breath, and said, "I don't know. Just get me a f*%#ing faith-based thing. Got it?" Willett was shown the door.

That night Rove got an e-mail from Peb Jackson, an influential evangelical fundraiser and networker as well as a genuine supporter of the initiative. Peb had heard about the problems, knew politics, and thought he knew how to help. "Great weekend!" he wrote, of the inaugural. "Inspirational, historic, emotional, encouraging. One of the spontaneous events we attended was a brunch late Sunday morning . . . [with] Bob Rowlings, Michael Stevens, the Foster Friess [*sic*], the Ed Atsingers, the Elsa Prince's [*sic*] . . . etc." (They represented several billion dollars of evangelical Christian net worth.) Jackson went on to talk about the group's enthusiasm for the faith-based initiative. For these Christians, several with long histories of serving the poor, the initiative was the boldest possible proof of Bush's private Christian testimony.

"You may already know this," Jackson continued, "but this office is going to be overrun by response and I hope it is going to be staffed sufficiently to handle the opportunities which will come." Understanding better than anyone else how to get things done, Jackson concluded, "A by-product, politically, will be an ongoing interest . . . and even more support by this group which will be necessary for Republican victories in the Congressional elections in 2002 and the next general election in 2004." Translated into plain English, Jackson was saying, "Staff the office, give it power, and it will bring in donations and reap big political dividends down the road." He was trying to speak the political language the White House understood.

Twenty-four hours later, John DiIulio got another call from senior administration officials. DiIulio was a close friend of Goldsmith's. On top of his other areas of expertise—crime, social welfare policy, faith-based initiatives—DiIulio was a leading scholar of government administration. He understood the potentially vexing public, political, and policy problems a new Office of Faith-Based Action would encounter. During the campaign he advocated against such an office, fearing that it would ultimately hurt, not help, attempts to implement faith-friendly efforts like Charitable Choice to help the poor.

Now, however, DiIulio was being asked whether he wanted to head the office now renamed as the Office of Faith-Based and Community Initiatives. After negotiations, he agreed, subject to three understandings.

First, given personal health issues and his desire to continue his "street-level" research and fund-raising on behalf of what he called urban "sacred places that serve civic purposes," DiIulio would serve for only six months, or as long as it took to complete a White House report on whether qualified faith-based nonprofit organizations were treated fairly in the federal grant-making process. To get the snap-to-it cooperation from the federal agencies he would be auditing, and to ensure the initiative would be taken seriously, he required an appointment at the rank of Assistant to the President, the highest-ranking staff position in the White House, technically on par with senior adviser Karl Rove and counselor Karen Hughes.

Second, Goldsmith, whom the president was to name as Chairman of the Board of the Corporation for National Service, the Clinton-created agency that ran the "paid volunteers" Ameri-Corps program so loathed by many Republicans, would lead the administration's overall compassion agenda.

Last but certainly not least, the initiative and the office would remain strictly bipartisan. It wasn't to be used as a political tool and no new legislation on faith-based issues would be sought until after the report detailing the relevant facts about federal grant-making was released.

Chief of Staff Andrew Card agreed. "Big John," as the president lovingly called DiIulio because of his ample physique, was the new director. On January 29, 2001, the president was on his way to make the DiIulio-Goldsmith announcement. Minutes before he arrived, then White House counsel and now U.S. Attorney General Alberto Gonzales noticed that Big John's paperwork wasn't complete and no one had asked him the usual questions about his past life or whether he had done anything that might embarrass the president (e.g., been especially sexually active). DiIulio looked at him, smirked, and said he was "a fat, boring guy." Gonzales was pleased.

There was only one more question. What about anything criminally related?

DiIulio couldn't resist. "Indictments or convictions? After all, I am a fat, boring South Philly guy."

Gonzales blanched. DiIulio relented with a sly smile and a reassurance there probably wasn't anything bad.

The president concluded his remarks this way: "This is an effort that will be an effort from now, the second week of my administration to the last week of my administration, because I am confident that this initiative when fully implemented, will help us realize the dream that America, its hopes, its promise, its greatness, will extend its reach throughout every single neighborhood, all across the land."

The executive order creating the office didn't allow it to open until mid-February. That wasn't an accident. The office couldn't be up and running before then. Nothing was in place for it to start.

Coming during the president's second full week in office, the announcement got enormous media attention. Over the next few weeks, the bipartisanship Bush had touted and DiIulio had required was reinforced by numerous White House statements and symbols—all arranged by DiIulio. During the president's first address to both houses of Congress (known as the State of the Union in every year except a newly elected president's first year), Philadelphia's Democratic, African-American mayor, John Street, was seated next to first lady Laura Bush in the gallery. The president used the quip Big John had written for him about how Mayor Street had helped Gore defeat Bush in Philly by over 400,000 votes. But Street, like Bush, believed in empowering faith-based groups to work with government to serve their own needy neighbors. That was to be the initiative's central message. Unfortunately, when it came to Bush's discussion of the Compassion Capital Fund, things had changed. DiIulio, watching the speech and following along with the text, waited for the president to talk about the $1.5-billion program. DiIulio had spent much of the last month in pitched battles for its existence and was satisfied with the funding levels. He convinced Street to attend and give bipartisan support to Bush based on the president's stated commitment to keeping his compassion promises. The president, however, announced a $70-million-a-year program. When DiIulio inquired about how and when it had changed, someone replied, "It just changed."

Even with nonpolitical bipartisanship on display, the delay in opening the office was rough. Every major paper and magazine ran huge articles about the initiative. News shows everywhere were abuzz about it. Was it a massive violation of the church-state wall? Had the president been trying to buy off religious voters in the 2000 campaign? What kind of radical proposals were going to come from the new effort? What was the initiative *really* about? Instead of being shielded from the media and political glare inside the transition, the faith-based announcement became everyone's focus. It was an easy controversy, combining religion, politics, and a new president. More than seven hundred articles appeared in just the first week of the initiative. By and large the coverage was negative. The *Atlanta Journal-Constitution*'s editorial summed up many people's sentiments: "We do not need government officials sitting in judgment of religious groups, deciding which to support and which to reject. We do not need religious leaders addicted to federal money, always lobbying Congress for more. We do not need politicians using taxpayers' money to buy the support of religious leaders. And most importantly, we do not need a government that requires taxpayers to fund religious groups whose doctrines they find objectionable."

The more the initiative was covered, the more small charities heard the news and let their hopes grow. This could be a new way for them to meet some pressing needs. The White House switchboard was deluged with phone calls from small churches and ministries across the country wanting to know how they could apply for grants. "We would like to get $5,000 to fix the leak in our ceiling," wrote one center-city after-school program. "We would like to apply for a grant for $3,321.20 to repair the air conditioning in our drug rehabilitation facility. We're located in Phoenix and it is hot," wrote another group. The letters piled up as a skeleton crew of three volunteers tried to manage the entire office.

No White House press staffers had been assigned to this beat, so they were caught flat-footed. Religious conservatives universally praised the president for acknowledging the importance of faith-based groups and sending the unmistakable message that religious groups were welcome in his administration. But many Christian conservatives were also worried that "with government shekels come government shackles." In other words, they feared that Christian groups might lose their essential religious character-istics if they took government money and become religious in name only. The other concern had to do with religious diversity among grant recipients. As Pat Robertson wrote, "The same government grants given to Catholics, Protestants, and Jews must also be given to the Hare Krishnas, the Church of Scientology, or Sun Myung Moon's Unification Church—no matter that some may use brainwashing techniques, or that the founder of one claims to be the messiah and another that he was Buddha reincarnated."

In the face of the explosion, Karen Hughes, who was the media chief in addition to counsel, pronounced that the White House would "go dark" on all things faith based. For the next two months there were absolutely no public events. But as the communication crew discovered much to their chagrin, not saying anything about an issue doesn't mean the press won't write about it. The onslaught continued.

In late April I was sitting in a restaurant near the White House waiting for John. My name had come up at a friendly intervention that some of John's friends held for him. These friends, who included Vice President Cheney's communications chief, Mary Matalin, told John he needed staff help. My name came up and I happened to be in town with my wife for some meetings.

Over dinner DiIulio filled me in on the plan he had gotten the West Wing to approve: no legislation right out of the gate, a faith-based report, and bipartisanship. Meanwhile, he wanted the president to begin following through on his funding promises from the campaign. The president's budget would prove to a skeptical charitable community that he was, in fact, serious about compassion.

Then John told me how things hadn't gone quite as planned. The White House wanted legislation first, because legislation was political proof the president was following through on his promises. Then, once a bill passed, it would inoculate them against any criticism that they weren't working hard enough on the initiative. Eager conservative staffers in the House also wanted legislation because they figured an evangelical president could make the existing faith-based laws even more faith friendly. What that really meant was they wanted to allow evangelism-heavy programs to get federal money. John worried that some of their specific proposals were blatantly unconstitutional. He thought the White House would back him, once the disagreement reached the Oval Office, because he was sure nobody would want George W. Bush to be the first president to have the Supreme Court overturn one of his policies while he was still in office. Though the initiative was still technically bipartisan and nonpolitical, it seemed to be getting less so daily.

"So, sounds like fun, huh? When do you want to start?"

My first thought was of the timing, perhaps the Divine timing. We sat there talking about my coming back to politics on the night of my mother's sixty-ninth birthday. Here was the best chance I had ever had—and might ever have—to help the kind of poor, hurting people she had fought for decades earlier. My second thought was that my book was going to be released in the fall and I needed to travel to support that, so I couldn't do it. My third thought was that it couldn't have been a more natural job for me. It was everything I had ever worked on rolled up into one neat package, with me sitting behind a White House desk. There was the social justice passion of my Kennedy days, the faith-based work of my Ashcroft days, and the charity work of my most recent days. John would be my boss. And I would be working for President Bush, a man whose passions for those things equaled, if not exceeded, mine. I wanted to scream, "Yes!"

But there was the personal side. I feared that returning to Washington, especially to the White House, would once again tempt me in all the wrong ways. I had done pretty well for a staffer in Washington during my first stint there. But I had seen too much too fast and had done too much too fast—at least for me. I got God and politics confused. My priorities were twisted. The Icarus in me took me higher and further away from home and from God and I had crashed awfully hard. I didn't want any of that to happen ever again.

Conveniently, I didn't have to accept or reject anything formally. John still had work to do to see if my hiring was a legitimate possibility. The White House was a bureaucracy and positions were at a premium. There were plenty of reasons it might not work.

I went back to Atlanta, kept talking to Kim, who thought it could be exactly what I was supposed to do, and talked to God, who had already accepted back his tremendously boring prodigal child.

It happened accidentally. Earlier that year I had stumbled across a small book and read the opening lines, "Some years into our spiritual journey, after the waves of anticipation that mark the beginning of any pilgrimage have begun to ebb into life's middle years of service and busyness, a voice speaks to us in the midst of all we are doing. *There is something missing in all of this*,' it suggests. *There is something more*.' " It summed up my spiritual life in less than sixty words. The words were from *The Sacred Romance*, by Brent Curtis and John Eldredge.

I knew there was something more because I had glimpsed it. One morning during my time out in Montana, I had gotten up long before anyone else and slipped out to fish. Something rustled the brush next to my trail. A baby moose poked its nose through, gave me a baby snort, and kept on walking. Mama moose followed closely behind. Foxes ran all about. Someone wrote of Norman Maclean's *A River Runs Through It*, "It was the world with dew still on it, more touched by wonder and possibility than any I have since known." It was like that. God was there. Except that out there, God wasn't small and practical. He wasn't a ticket to heaven or an ear to hear my prayers. He was huge and wild and big enough that I could get lost in him. That little glimpse of God inspired me to say and write things I never thought I would. It took a wild God to get me to apologize to Hillary Clinton.

But that glimpse of God quickly faded away, and with it I faded away from God. Now, after divorce, and with daughters living in a different city, and the dot-com collapse, I needed Jesus to come and pull me from what felt like an awfully dense thicket. There was only one problem with the whole thing. I had no idea what that meant. I knew I had to let Jesus come after me. That meant telling him I needed to set out of the thicket. It also meant allowing myself to receive the love he promised me he wanted to give.

I discovered another paragraph in *The Sacred Romance*. "It is possible to recover the lost life of our heart and with it the intimacy, beauty, and adventure of life with God. To do so we must leave what is familiar and comfortable—perhaps even parts of the religion in which we have come to trust—and take a journey . . . on a search for the lost life of our heart."

Leaving what is comfortable and familiar, going on a journey with God, that was it. That was what I wanted. I imagined going back to the wilderness to be reminded of God's raw greatness. I imagined running from bears or dancing with wolves.

Those were the images in my mind when John called again. "Karen Hughes is on board, Karl Rove is on board, Chief of Staff Andy Card is on board, Mike Gerson is on board. Everyone is on board. And you just stay until your book tour begins. We'll both leave at the same time. When can you start?"

It was a late afternoon day in May. I was on a golf course. And I was alone. I told John I would have to get back to him and hung up.

Now that it was in front of me, I realized I really *didn't* want to go back to Washington. I was terrified. Then a thought—what if leaving what was familiar and comfortable and taking a journey meant going *back* into politics? Did my journey deeper into God go through Washington once again?

I walked back to my car in the dusk. My phone rang. It was a dear friend from California. I told her the dilemma.

Martha Williamson was my accidental friend. We met at a

conference the year before and Kim and I hit it off with her and her husband Jon Andersen. It was a little disturbing. I thought I knew about her from my pre-apology days as the New Age guru who, it was said, helped Hillary Clinton channel the spirit of Eleanor Roosevelt. Kim and I tried to keep an open mind even while we kept telling ourselves to beware of becoming New Agers ourselves.

Over time, however, we realized she wasn't *Marianne Williamson*, the New Age guru. (And in fact, even Marianne never actually helped Hillary Clinton channel anyone. Nothing like that ever happened, though the story circulated for quite a while in evangelical circles.) Martha produced a television show for CBS called *Touched by an Angel*. At the time we were oblivious to its existence, even though it had been a top show for years. Now she was my spiritual guru.

"Just one question for you, sweetie: was David a better king before or after Bathsheba?"

Huh? I remembered the story. King David was in Jerusalem when his army was at war. He spied the beautiful Bathsheba. She got pregnant. He had her husband killed. God told David how angry he was. God pronounced death upon David and his heirs. David repented. He was *really* sorry. God relented in part. But condemnation came. David remained repentant and in the end God lifted him up.

"Huh?"

"Sweetie, was David a better king before or after Bathsheba?"

I didn't remember. I guessed the answer she was after.

"Right. He was humbled. He was repentant. He became a different person. You are a different person."

I wanted to tell her that she really didn't know me that well. But I hoped she was right.

In the end my hopes trumped my fears. My faith that God was leading beat back the voices that screamed I was going to screw up worse than I had the first time around. I accepted the job.

The next day Kim got a job offer from out of the blue in Washington, to work with a friend for a major trade association. Ten days later, on the eve of my first day at the White House, I couldn't sleep. Fear and hope were battling again and fear was ahead by a nose. I was excited, and very nervous.

I grabbed a Bible and prayed that God would speak to me through the first words I set my eyes upon. The Bible opened to the Book of Isaiah, the forty-fifth chapter, and my eyes settled on the second verse:

> I will go before you and will level the mountains; I will break down the gates of bronze and cut through the bars of iron. I will give you the treasures of darkness, riches stored in secret places, so that you may know that I am the LORD, the God of Israel, who summons you by name.

I didn't know the exact biblical context, and I found the "treasures of darkness" thing quite disturbing, and I also knew that opening the Bible randomly to a certain place doesn't equate with encountering a burning bush. As I sat there that evening and focused on the verses, though, I was certain they weren't an accident. God had led me to where I was going. There weren't a lot of other explanations.

There wasn't anything I could do that night on my knees that could ensure my faithfulness. The only way to guarantee that was to make sure I got back on my knees and returned to God again and again and again. It would be a daily—an hourly?—practice. And this time I would keep practicing, I promised myself.

CHAPTER TEN

Tripping on Marble

I imagine the West Wing visitors' lobby to be something like the waiting room to heaven—in the unlikely event heaven has a waiting room. No matter how "important" or "unimportant," that first visit to the lobby lets visitors know they are neither.

The unimportant are elevated. History, mystique, and the palpable sense of power are inspiring, surreal, and wonder filled. What a place to be!

Those same things humble the important. The place feels huge and they can't. History, mystique, and the palpable sense of power are sobering and fearsome. What a place this is.

Both types of visitors sit far closer than they probably realize to the president of the United States. Through just one door, down a short hallway and to the right, is the Oval Office. Within fifty feet of where they sit are the national security advisor, chief of staff, press secretary, vice president, and several other people of note. Visitors don't know it but they sense it. They can't miss it.

On June 5, 2001, I was wonder filled. Everything felt different. The carpet felt plusher and the couches softer. I watched serious staffers stride purposefully through the doors and tried to imagine what important things they were doing.

Too quickly, a woman introduced herself and said I was to meet John at a briefing. I thought my first day would begin with bagels, not a briefing.

We headed west out of the lobby, down a couple of half-flights of stairs, past a Secret Service station in the West Wing basement, across West Executive Avenue, and up the fifty stairs into the Old Executive Office Building, where the vast majority of the president's staff is actually housed. From there we headed to something called "450."

The White House—defined as the East Wing, West Wing, Residence, and Old Executive Office Building—is filled with mysterious rooms behind heavy doors. In one place or another in the complex there is a florist, a woodshop, a bowling alley, a photo shop, a bank, travel agents, two gift shops, a post office, a doctor's office (actually three), and unimaginable caches of firearms and weapons. Room 450 was one of those surprising places. Situated on the building's top floor at the end of a hallway and through old oak doors, 450 was an auditorium. It had cushy theater-style chairs that still managed to squeak with even the slightest movement. The ample stage could be transformed into virtually anything. On the back wall a bank of heavily draped blue curtains shielded the two-inch-thick windows able to withstand bullets, cannons, missiles, or rockets. Behind the stage were two holding rooms: one for general use and one for the president.

I took a seat on the stage with five colleagues. John was seated farthest away from me and shot me a grin that screamed, "Surprise!" I had no idea what to say to this group. I had learned they were a combination of wealthy Christian donors and entrepreneurial Christian ministry leaders there to learn about the president's passion for his faith-based compassion initiative. But what little I knew of what was really happening wasn't fit for public consumption.

At my appointed time, I got up, took a few steps toward the lectern, and thought about lapsing into Bush-speak. "Government can't love people. Only people can love people. People should love people. People loving people makes people good people. People who love government aren't conservatives. I know that. Heh, heh, heh. Faith is good. Government shouldn't fear faith. We need faith. I need faith. I've got faith. We've got faith. In God we trust. Heh, heh, heh."

Instead, I tried to remember all the things I said back in 1995, when we created Charitable Choice. Religious groups shouldn't be discriminated against just because they are religious. The best, most compassionate way to help suffering Americans was through neighborhood groups, charities, and churches. They are the best of America and President Bush recognized that, which was why he had taken the political risk to create the Office of Faith-Based and Community Initiatives. It was fun to be talking about this again.

Then men appeared in the doorways on both sides of the room. They were big and looked sturdy, and appeared to be a bit lumpy around the middle. The lumps suggested Matrix-like weapons, stored under their jackets. They stared at me, looked down at a little piece of paper in their hands, and looked up again. One of them whispered something into his sleeve. I started talking faster and soon I sat very still and very quiet. The room fell silent.

Someone came out from behind me, walked up to the lectern where I had been standing, and attached something I couldn't see to the front of it. He deposited some papers on it and adjusted the microphone. A cup of water was placed on a shelf and plastic wrap was peeled off it. He disappeared.

The thing on the front of the lectern was the presidential seal. People's eyes widened. Breathing patterns changed, becoming more rapid and more shallow. A weird vibe filled the air—electricity, anticipation, awe, uncertainty, hope. No squeaking from chairs was heard.

A disembodied, booming voice then announced, "Ladies and Gentlemen, the *President* of the United States." We shot to our feet. It was like we were pulled up by our heads. A door immediately behind me and to my right opened, and there, striding through, looking out at the crowd with a sly smile, and giving a determined wave, was President George W. Bush.

The sturdy guys descended down the aisles and took up spots stage right and stage left. The president turned from the audience to glance at his staff. He looked me in the eyes and started to smile and tip his head toward me. He was ready to move on to the next guy but stopped with a look of startled uncertainty in his eyes. He knew he knew me but the context was off. "Kuo!" he finally said, stopping dead in his tracks. "How the heck are ya? Good to see ya. Long time! Didn't know you'd be here." For a split second he paused, waiting for me to say something. I mumbled. He slapped me on the shoulder and moved quickly down the line. I didn't know if he was surprised I was at that particular briefing or if he was surprised I was at the White House in the first place.

The orderly march of the president to the lectern had been interrupted for just one moment. As I would later learn, my surprise presence was a breach of the rules of conduct regarding the president of the United States. The president is never, ever to be surprised. He is always to be in control. He is given briefing memos—preferably less than two pages—about the topics being discussed, the people present in an audience, the staffers he'll see onstage, the timing, any potential controversy, everything. He is given talking points or speeches for absolutely everything: authors dropping by the Oval Office, NBA teams getting their photo taken with him, meetings with his children.

Then there was security. The United States Secret Service has a dualistic worldview. There is the president, and then there are the people who could hurt, kill, maim, injure, or otherwise bother the president. They are known as "everyone else." It is an official term. It includes staff, audiences, family members, and sometimes pets. For me to be on the stage, that close to the president, without the Secret Service knowing—this didn't make them happy.

The staffer to my left, whom I had met only moments earlier, looked me up and down as the president waved to thunderous applause. "How does he know *you*?" He leered at me. Another one looked at me suspiciously. It seemed personal.

I watched President Bush from behind as he spoke. His highly polished right black loafer (no tassels) was on its toe as he leaned in to the lectern—left forearm on the top like a cowboy who had just sidled up to a bar. The loafer sometimes tapped, sometimes twitched, and sometimes went back to its rightful place directly underneath its owner—only to pop right back onto its toe.

I watched the audience—big eyes, mouths semi-agape. There was no whispering. There was no note taking. He had their rapt attention as he talked in generalities.

"The government shouldn't ask 'What do you believe?' It should ask 'How well do you do it?'" He went on, saying very little, and sounding somewhat awkward.

I expected more. He wasn't faltering or incoherent, and he

knew what he was talking about. He just seemed like another officeholder giving a talk to donors.

The more I listened, the more I heard and saw the same guy I had met in Austin three years before—the son of a president, the politician, the Texan, the baseball lover. He just didn't seem to be the *President* yet. The *President* was the Wizard from Oz—grand, mighty, powerful, awesome. The *President* struck fear and aroused wonder and awe. I didn't sense that.

After fifteen minutes or so, he wound up his remarks, jumped off the little stage, shook some hands, hopped back onto the stage, shook the staffers' hands, and whacked me on my right shoulder. "Really good to see ya. Come see me." Then he was gone. The audience that had initially been hypnotized by the president's introduction didn't seem overwhelmed anymore. They chatted casually as I walked through the crowd looking for a friend. The snippets I heard from people were, "Good," "I liked it," "Glad to have heard from him," not "Wow," "Amazing," "Spectacular."

I found John DiIulio backstage and asked as casually as I could, "So, how long does it take for a man to actually *become* the President—to live up to the office?" John thought for a moment, probably reviewing several history books in his mind, and said, "Historically? About six months to a year—some sooner. Some never."

"Some never?"

Thus began my White House crash course.

Moments later it continued in another meeting. John marched us through another of the Old Executive Office Building's oversized, unmarked oak doors, and into a large conference room. Karl Rove was sitting at the middle of a twenty-foot table. Every other senior official or their most senior representative was there. I slid into a seat on the side of the room and nearly sat on an old friend.

"What are you doing here?!"

It was Juleanna Glover-Weiss. She was Mary Matalin's top deputy, well known for being ferociously effective at getting what she wanted, and utterly silky smooth at the same time.

"I just started working here."

"And you were going to tell me *when?*"

I tried to explain quietly how quickly it had all happened, but before I could she whispered, "Well, you are sitting in the most important meeting the White House holds."

"What is it?" I asked quietly.

"It is the 'message meeting.' Every decision is based on the message. Watch, you'll see."

It was a taxing day at the White House. A couple of weeks earlier, Republican Senator James Jeffords of Vermont had announced his intention to leave the Republican Party and become an independent. Jeffords's defection tipped the balance of power in the Senate over to the Democrats. That day the change of control became official.

Senator Charles Grassley, Republican from Iowa, who had waited to become chairman of the Senate Finance Committee for more than a decade, reportedly choked up as he handed the gavel to his friend Senator Max Baucus, Democrat from Montana. Now the message meeting debated whether the president should say anything about the change in power. Karl Rove volunteered that there wasn't any reason to say anything. People around the table agreed. The president didn't need to say anything. Margaret Tutwiler, former press secretary for James Baker at the State Department under George H. W. Bush, cleared her throat and said, "You can't be serious?"

Tutwiler was there as Karen Hughes's temporary tutor on how to handle the Washington press corps. "You just lost the damn United States Senate. The president of the United States needs to say something about it. Why don't you have him call [Senate Minority Leader] Trent Lott? Show leadership. Take responsibility." Tutwiler had an ambassadorship waiting for her and she wasn't afraid to tell anyone what she thought.

One set of heads in the room spun toward her. The other set bowed slightly and looked at her out of the corner of their eyes. Karl just smiled.

"What about [new Senate Majority Leader Tom] Daschle? The president doesn't have to call *him*, does he?" someone I didn't recognize had piped up.

"Yes, he has to call him, too. It is called leadership, and he's willing to work with the Senate. It ain't gonna be pretty but it has to be done."

Everyone agreed. He would make the call.

"Message," as it was called in White House parlance, was all about the White House's public face. The White House was intent on driving the news. It wanted to dictate what everyone was talking about and in what terms. If the White House wanted to focus on education, for instance, the day's first events might be at a suburban school to highlight how students' test scores have improved because of a focus on basics like writing or arithmetic. The president might sit down with the students and help them with their classwork. By doing this, the White House tried to ensure that news coverage would be not only about education in general but about teaching fundamentals in particular. The White House communications shop would e-mail a synopsis of the event to media outlets, along with a small fact sheet. They would also send talking points to friendly pundits, policy makers, lobbyists, and congressmen and their staffers, so that they would be saying the right things in the right way if they were interviewed.

The message meeting was aimed at coordinating all of this, and the main tool was a five-week strategic calendar. Each page showed a week running Sunday through Saturday, with each day's public events laid out. There could be as many as seven or eight events per day though typically there were three to five. Each day, one event was usually highlighted and coordinated with the "message of the day," which was shown in a special box. One week, for instance, might include two days devoted to the economy, one day on homeland security, another on energy, and one on education.

This proactive media strategy was ingenious—unless it was derailed by something unexpected such as Senator Jeffords's defection. When those things occurred, the debate was between those who believed that the message of the day would still trump something happening on the outside and those who believed the message needed to be scrapped and outside issues addressed. One senior West Wing friend said to me early on that it was "policy for the media, not media on the policy." In many areas—particularly in domestic policy—this White House didn't exist to advance a certain philosophical agenda. It existed to advance a positive public perception of the president and itself. It wasn't putting the proverbial cart before the horse, it was making sure the cart and horse were under television lights, gleaming, happy, and smiling.

Then it was evening and that was my first day.

Every morning during the summer of 2001 I went to work in a suite of offices sandwiched between the Political Affairs suite and Public Liaison office on the first floor of the OEOB. Those other two offices were the epicenter of White House political life. Political Affairs' sole purpose was expanding President Bush's direct political power—real and perceived. To that end it deployed presidential assets for political gain. They ranged from fund-raisers by the president, vice president, or senior aides like Karl Rove and Karen Hughes to presidential trips to important states or key districts. They were also experts at stroking the egos of important people in every American state, county, and precinct by means of trinkets, photo opportunities, and meetings. Most of the people seen on television greeting the president were preselected VIPs or wannabe VIPs placed there by Political Affairs. They were kept happy so that they would give the White House whatever it wanted when the time came.

Public Liaison's job was to keep all of America happy. Every special interest, including businesses, sports teams, the entertainment industry, minority groups, majority groups, religious groups, and every other conceivable group had someone in Public Liaison assigned to make them feel important and in the know. They are one part therapist, one part evangelist, and one part spinmeister. Like a therapist, each Public Liaison staffer must be trusted by the constituencies they service. The Jewish community, for instance, will be most comfortable with a fellow Jew. The high-tech world needs someone who has been successful in that world, and so on. This trust assures the communities that the staffer is really one of them. As such, they grow comfortable in venting their frustrations to a friend in the White House as opposed to someone they perceive to be a political flunky. The more they vent in private, the less likely they are to vent in public. Each staffer also has to have the enthusiasm of an evangelist. Their "god" may not be omnipotent but they've got to convince others that he is pretty close. Finally, they've got to be able to spin. When something happens that a particular interest group doesn't or isn't going to like, they have to help their friends see things the right way.

The idea of the Public Liaison office has evolved slowly over the past forty years. The general consensus is that this Bush White House perfected it. One reason is that for the first time it fell under the control of the same person who was heading political affairs, in this case Karl Rove. In addition, Karl ran "strategic initiatives" and "intergovernmental affairs." The former was something like an internal White House think tank. The latter was responsible for all White House communication with mayors and governors. Rove's official title, Senior Advisor to the President, belied his power. No other aide since the 1940s had been given such a vast White House portfolio. No one made any decision on anything without at least considering what Karl would think about it. Andy Card was the technical White House chief of staff but Karl was the chief of all White House staff.

Though I expected to be given a desk somewhere in a corner of the crowded offices, John housed me in his own office. He had arranged for two identical wood desks and chairs. Our computers were even placed on the same spots of our respective desks. His desk overflowed with paper and books. It took a few days for mine to have the same appearance.

It was flattering and frightening. There couldn't have been any clearer message to everyone who came by the office that I was DiIulio's guy. Given how much I admired and respected him, that felt really good. But it was also frightening because I wasn't him. If he was finding the White House hard, given his abilities, what could I possibly do to help?

From John's perspective, my job was to use the practical political experience I had gained during my first Washington tour to help him do his job there. He had found that his academic expertise in government administration carried him to a point. But beyond that point were things he just didn't understand. One of those things was how to work in a world of conservative Republicans.

Conservative Republicans were in the midst of derailing his carefully laid plans. One thing they wanted was more Charitable Choice—that is, a broader range of religious charities eligible for government grants. Though versions of Charitable Choice had been attached to three Clinton-era bills, that administration had blocked its implementation. In other words, it was a law that had never been enforced. Now, with a conservative evangelical president in the Oval Office, with Republicans controlling the House and nearly the Senate, some conservatives thought it was time to allow "real" faith-based groups to receive federal funding. In short, they wanted to allow groups that aimed to convert people to a particular faith to be able to receive direct federal grants— which was far beyond what Charitable Choice was actually intended to do. They also wanted numerous large federal grant programs converted to vouchers so that grant recipients could have access to plainly religious groups. Finally, they wanted to give all religious groups receiving public funds an unfettered right to hire and fire people based not only on their professed religion but on whether they lived according to the "rules" of their religion (i.e., no gay Catholics, pork-eating Orthodox Jews, bug-killing Jainists, leather-wearing Buddhists, or drinking Christian fundamentalists). They wove these objectives together into a single, highly partisan bill. It wasn't exactly the legislation-free bipartisanship that Brother John had hoped for.

To make things more challenging, we not only had to figure out a way to modify and pass—or perhaps just pass—the House bill, we also had to pass billions of dollars in charity tax credits. They weren't part of the president's first $1.7 trillion cut. They should have been.

In my third day on the job, President Bush signed the huge tax cut that had been one of his top priorities. He invested in it whatever postelection political capital he had. A recession had begun in 2000, and the president believed tax cuts would jump-start the economy. There were cuts in capital gains taxes (profits from the sale of stocks and land). The inheritance tax was cut, with the exemption slowly increasing to $3.5 million ($7 million for couples), and there was an across-the-board reduction in income tax rates. But something was missing: the president's promised $6 billion per year in tax credits for groups helping the poor. Those tax credits had been the centerpiece of compassionate-conservative efforts for years and the centerpiece of the president's own compassion agenda during the campaign. The best estimates projected that the proposal would create more than 11.7 million new givers throughout the country, stimulate an additional $14.6 billion in charitable giving in the first year and more than $160 billion over ten years, and increase current giving levels by 11 percent.

Unfortunately, those charity tax credits weren't listed by the White House as must-haves, so the House skipped over them. They did make it into the Senate's version of the tax bill, but only because then Senate Finance Chairman Grassley insisted on it. He assumed that the White House had omitted the charity provisions by oversight.

When the White House and congressional negotiators sat down to hammer out the details of the final bill, however, Assistant to the President for Legislative Affairs Nick Calio told Grassley to get rid of the charity tax credits. Republican and Democratic jaws hit the floor. Russ Sullivan, chief Democratic staffer to the Finance Committee, and Mark Prader, his Republican counterpart, both asked Calio if he was serious. Each man had worked hard to ensure that those provisions were in there. Yes, Calio said, he was absolutely in earnest. The White House didn't want them anymore.

The public line: Those charity tax credits were so loved by everyone they would pass later with no problem. No need to make the big tax bill any bigger. After all, over ten years the $60 billion price tag for generating all that charitable giving would amount to almost 3.5 percent of the total tax cut. That 3.5 percent was needed for something else—the over one-hundred-billion-dollar cut in the estate tax.

In 2001, about 2 percent of all estates paid any tax after someone's death. The reason the number was so low was that there was a $675,000 exemption. The vast majority of estates just aren't that large. Nevertheless, the tax cut included both a reduction in tax levels for estates that are taxed and an increase in the exemption to $3.5 million ($7 million for couples). The estate tax changes were costly to charities, because they crowded out the charitable tax deduction and so were also costly because they reduced charitable giving. The inheritance tax had been a huge financial incentive for the wealthy to give more money to charity. According to some estimates, estate tax cuts cost more than $5 billion per year in charitable giving (and were therefore opposed by such wealthy philanthropists as Warren Buffett and Bill Gates).

The net effect of the tax cuts, by omission and commission, was brutal on the charities that Bush had said were among his highest priorities. First, the promised incentives for Americans to give more to charities was nixed. Second, giving would actually decline because of the change in the inheritance tax.*

Heirs to the Mars candy, Gallo wine, and Campbell soup empires had started lobbying for estate tax repeals back in 1992 with the help of elite Washington lobbying shops, but in 2001 our lobbying coalition on behalf of the president's faith-based agenda was a bit different. Powerful Christian conservative efforts focused on judges, abortion, stem cell research, and gay rights, not on lobbying for tax credits to help the poor or for new programs. Those conservatives had, however, supported the president's tax cut package. After its passage, Dr. Dobson wrote to his supporters that the president was to be commended for the cuts despite the opposition of "liberals in Congress." Most liberal advocacy groups were actually worse in also leaving us stranded. Though they lauded Vice President Gore's campaign endorsement of Charitable Choice, they were virulently opposed to President Bush's initiative.

We were left with a motley crew of poor ministers, tiny charities, and small advocacy groups to help us convince Congress to spend billions more to increase charitable giving and pass new

---

* In early 2006, the Republican-controlled House of Representatives passed a White House–backed $290 billion bill for full repeal of the estate tax, despite the fact that the existing $3.5 million level ($7 million for couples) exempted 99.7 percent of all estates.

laws enabling small charities to access government funds. But these allies had no political clout. The poor don't have a lot of money to spend on big-time lobbyists. But they weren't *supposed* to need political clout with this initiative. They were supposed to be able to count on George W. Bush's White House to fight for them, and get for them what they could never get on their own. It was a core promise of compassionate conservatism. I was sure that this was the kind of fight President Bush's White House would launch on their behalf. After all, we were "restoring honor and dignity" to the White House.

In early June the biggest problems not related to charitable giving centered on the hiring and firing issues. Existing federal law permitted churches and other faith-based organizations to hire only people who shared their faith. Houses of worship are the most protected. By the Constitution and by law, they have an absolute right to hire and fire whomever they wish to based on religion. Religious organizations have a particular "exemption" from the nondiscrimination provisions of the 1964 Civil Rights Act. They cannot discriminate on the basis of race, but they are free to discriminate on the basis of creed. An Orthodox synagogue cannot be forced to hire a Southern Baptist, nor a Methodist church to hire a Buddhist. The Supreme Court unanimously upheld this law in the early 1970s. Senator Ashcroft's Charitable Choice bill reiterated this "right to hire." Now, however, staffers for Republican representatives Tom DeLay and Dennis Hastert told us their bosses wanted to let organizations hire and fire based on "beliefs *and practices.*" They wanted the law to allow organizations to require that its employees adhere not just to the religious beliefs, but also to the practices of the organization.

These changes would effectively allow an organization to fire someone if they weren't "Buddhist enough" or "Baptist enough" or even "conservative enough." It could allow for a very broad, or very narrow, definition of acceptable practices.

Critics insisted that this provision targeted gays and lesbians. The staffers said, no, quite the contrary, it was just about protecting religious organizations' rights and beliefs in general. Behind closed doors, however, everyone knew what it was about, and why they were pursuing it. For evangelical House members, their staffers, and for the conservative Christian advocacy community, preventing expansion of gay rights was an almost peerless priority. As they saw it, the single greatest threat to the American family came not from divorce, pornography, gambling, workaholism, materialism, or faithlessness, but rather from the mainstream acceptance of gays and lesbians. The most powerful Christian interest organizations (as opposed to charities), such as the Family Research Council, the Traditional Values Coalition, and everyone else, from the home-schoolers to the private Christian school associations, agreed.

Their beliefs were hardly concocted for political opportunism. As the analyst William Schneider had said years before, they viewed this as a defensive stand. During the 1990s they famously fought the New York City schools chancellor to remove two optional elementary school books featuring same-sex parents. They believed the homosexual lifestyle was simply akin to such sins as adultery, alcoholism, and lying, and needed to be parried. It didn't hurt that gay rights issues helped conservative groups raise a lot of money from their constituents because it was a fight against an identifiable "enemy." By contrast, as Ralph Reed's experiment with the aborted Christian Coalition Samaritan Project showed, grassroots conservatives with a political bent couldn't be counted on to help lobby for the poor.

Opposing the right-to-hire plan were civil rights groups such as the ACLU, NAACP, and Human Rights Campaign, the nation's largest lesbian and gay rights advocacy group. Their battle was largely political as well. While there were two or three isolated lawsuits across the country alleging discrimination against gays and lesbians by Christian social service organizations, this was hardly a major issue for them. They knew what conservatives and the social service organizations knew: no charity trying to feed the hungry, clothe the naked, or heal the sick was going to turn away anyone offering help. These organizations on the frontlines of the poverty war were so underfunded, understaffed, and neglected that any volunteer was put to work.

Both sides also knew that such a hiring fight mobilized their funders. The gay, lesbian, bisexual, and transgender (GLBT) inter-est groups needed the Christian Right, and the Christian Right's donors were afraid of the gay community. Neither could really stay funded without the other.

That covered just the hiring issue. The other items on the House conservatives' agenda were no less controversial. Direct funding of expressly evangelical groups with government money was in the realm of the unfeasible. Clarence Thomas would vote against it in ten seconds. So, too, the idea of converting massive federal pro-grams to vouchers.

However, for House conservative leaders like Tom DeLay, who wanted the most powerful wedge issues he could find against the Democrats, it was a fight with no downside. If the bill passed, it would be the most "faith-friendly" legislation ever. If it didn't pass because the Democrats succeeded in blocking it, a great political purpose would have been served. As one conservative said in a meeting, "If the Democrats object they'll just be the anti-God party."

White House Legislative Affairs knew all of this and laughed about it. "Oh, those crazy guys," the woman assigned to cover compassion issues for us in the House chuckled when I suggested she use her influence to encourage them to back off from some of their more controversial positions. "Tried before but can't really do it now," she said. "We're going to have to twist their arms later on other important stuff." It felt as if someone had just piled the stupefying onto the surreal.

I couldn't believe what I was seeing and hearing. I had actually been present at the creation of Charitable Choice and knew very well what we intended and why we worded everything the way we had. Regardless of our spiritual motivations for allowing faith-based groups to receive government assistance, our public purpose was very clear: we wanted to help people trapped in poverty, hooked on drugs, unable to put down the bottle, and caught up in despair. We took great pains to put walls in place between govern-ment funds and any overtly religious activity. We took even greater pains to ensure that the legislation was consensus legislation, not fracturing legislation. And we succeeded. When Al Gore announced his support for Charitable Choice in early 1999, he said it was wonderful that it wasn't "a political thing but a consensus thing." Yet for our House Republican friends, the initiative was primarily useful for politics, and for some of my White House colleagues, the initiative wasn't even on their radar screen.

As I reported all of this back to John DiIulio I began to realize I was simply describing his own frustrations. He had been facing these same dilemmas and questions since January. I also reported the problem during one of the biweekly domestic policy meetings chaired by Margaret Spellings, assistant to the president for domestic policy. Spellings, another longtime Bush aide from Texas, was laid-back, gregarious, funny, and an education expert. She helped Governor Bush pass sweeping reforms in Texas and was one of his favorite people. Everyone loved Margaret. It was hard not to. Her "aw-shucks" demeanor belied her quick intelligence and a fiery political instinct.

Margaret listened cheerfully and said, "David, darlin', you are doing a good job. Great job." Then, lightly but seriously, "But David, please. Just get me a damn faith bill. Any bill. I don't care what kind of bill. Just get me a damn faith bill."

CHAPTER ELEVEN

This Is the White House

I had always thought of working in the White House the same way I thought about going to the moon. People went to the moon; it was surely breathtaking; it would be great to go there myself but I knew I wouldn't. I wasn't an astronaut. Yet there I was at 1600 Pennsylvania Avenue, learning the place as only a resident—or in my case a butler—can ever do in a house. The great discoveries weren't in figuring out where the bowling alley was (sort of under the front lawn) or finding Teddy Roosevelt's Nobel Peace Prize medal casually displayed on a mantel. The revelations were more intimate: seeing flame damage on uncovered bricks from when the British burned the place down, finding lantern hooks still secured to outside walls, noticing that the "ground floor" of the White House, really a basement, smelled like an ordinary basement.

Perhaps because I knew my time there was brief by design and I would be long gone by the end of summer, I also reveled in the wonder of everything going on around me. At every message meeting I listened intently to discussions about every event; at domestic policy meetings, I did the same. So when Ken Mehlman, head of White House Political Affairs, briefed Domestic Policy staff on how we were to understand the political world, I paid close attention. I figured that if I understood White House politics enough, I could figure out a way to stir passion in the White House staff for the faith-based effort.

Ken's briefing wasn't really his. It was Karl's. Ken's job as head of Political Affairs wasn't really his, either. That belonged to Karl, too. It was just that Karl couldn't meet with everyone simultaneously and therefore needed smart and able intermediaries to help.

Ken said that the country was more divided than at any point since the 1880s. No president had been elected with more than 50 percent of the vote since 1988. In congressional elections, Republicans held on to the House in '96, '98, and 2000 with about 48.5 percent of the vote. To win in early twenty-first-century politics was to steal just a percentage point, or less, from the other side.

Our focus for the 2002 midterm elections and the 2004 presidential race centered on several different demographic groups. For starters, we needed to maintain our base, defined as conservatives, farm voters, and so-called resource Republicans (a conglomeration of rural voters who produce coal, steel, tobacco, and the like). Then we needed to "grow" Latinos, Catholics, suburban women, high-tech workers, and union members. Separately, we needed to "improve" African-American voters. Finally, and most importantly, we needed to remember the single most important group for us, crosscutting all the other categories: "believers." Believers were people who opposed abortion, supported guns, opposed gay rights. Believers were evangelical Christians. And our White House political shop and therefore all the White House was obsessed with evangelical voters. Rove believed millions of them had stayed home in 2000 after the revelation of Bush's drunk driving arrest. To win in '04 they had to be brought back into the fold.

Listening to all of this I realized I had passed through to the other side. I wasn't just a Christian trying to serve God in politics. Now I was a Christian in politics looking for ways to recruit other Christians into politics so that we would have their votes. I couldn't figure out if I was suddenly playing for a different team or if I was an Amway business owner suddenly let into some elite multilevel marketing club.

More significantly, I didn't know what to do with that revelation. I had spent my years in the nation's capital as part of a Christian movement to gain power. My spiritual struggles had to do with how we were arguing and how we were treating our enemies. In my best moments I feared I wasn't representing Jesus. Now it was different. Now I had to ask if I was a corrupting force in other people's faith. Chuck Colson inspired me to tackle great moral issues. Was I doing that, or was I part of an effort to get people to support a political leader? There were enormous differences between the two possibilities. One sought to serve Jesus' concerns for people through political ends. The other sought to serve a political end by using Jesus' concerns as justification.

Unlike my first Washington go-round, I wasn't swept up by the politics or the power. I loved that I got to fight for things in which I believed. That it was on behalf of as good a man as President Bush made it better. That it was with a dear friend made it a joy.

Max Finberg, an old college friend, said that the moment he heard I was working late, working weekends, and otherwise becoming work-obsessed, he would launch a one-person intervention. But he didn't need to worry. It was just a tough but temporary job, with the long hours required to get it done. My priorities were straight. There wasn't any drifting from God, from Kim, from my two young daughters.

Mehlman highlighted our strategy for winning the targeted groups for Bush. Our priorities were reforming education, cutting taxes, strengthening the military (particularly against threats like China), modernizing Social Security, reforming Medicare, and empowering faith-based institutions. Our office made the list, but our place there seemed shaky.

Listening to Mehlman's presentation in the midst of the fight to get the House to pass the legislation we never wanted in the first place made things clearer. White House staff didn't want to have anything to do with the faith-based initiative because they didn't understand it any more than did congressional Republicans. It wasn't that midlevel staffers like the ones I regularly dealt with or senior staffers like Calio, Spellings, or Card were hostile to the initiative. They didn't lie awake at night trying to kill it. They simply didn't care. It didn't resonate with them. This was disappointing but not shocking. Compassion as policy really wasn't what Republicans did. Republicans were for tax cuts, business growth, a strong military. All of this meant that making meaningful substantive changes would be challenging. Yes, I expected more from the president. I had hoped his commitment to compassion meant creating a staff who valued it as much as he did. But maybe that many compassionate conservative Republicans didn't exist.

At the same time, it couldn't have been clearer that the White House needed the faith-based initiative because it had the potential to successfully evangelize more voters than any other. The campaign team already knew compassionate conservatism played to a broad array of voters. Now, if it was handled correctly, it could turn even more heads. Women would see that this "different kind of Republican" delivered on his promise to help the homeless, build houses for struggling families, and help people find jobs. Hispanic voters, who tended to be pro-life, pro-family, and pro-poor, would see he was a Republican who cared. The black community could even be persuaded that George W. Bush was worth trusting. They were open to it. As several African-American pastors had said during Bush's December 2000 meeting with them, "We have no expectations; surprise us." For evangelical Christians, who might not be thrilled with the initiative's details, it nevertheless reinforced their belief in President Bush's personal relationship with Jesus. That belief grounded their support of him.

While we handled the "soft" compassion issues, Rove's Public Liaison office had a religious outreach team in constant contact with evangelical and social conservative groups about every facet of the president's policy and political agenda. Leading that team was Tim Goeglein, a bow-tied friend of William Buckley. Goeglein was perpetually cheery, rosy-cheeked, seemingly able to quote Dante in virtually any situation, and proudly wore seersucker suits with white oxford loafers all summer long. One of the least ambitious people I had ever met, he found his dream job years before when he was press secretary for Senator Dan Coats. He would have been happy staying there for decades. Unfortunately for him, Coats retired. Tim ended up with Gary Bauer's presidential campaign, then moved to Austin to handle message outreach to evangelical and social conservative groups. He signed each e-mail, "Warmly, TSG."

He talked to religious conservatives about everything: judges, stem cell research, abortion, presidential appointments, health care, and anything else they wanted to discuss. As part of their outreach they held weekly—or more often, as necessary—conference calls to update that community on events and announcements while simultaneously soliciting their feedback. Regulars on the call were Tom Minnery, head of public policy for James Dobson's Focus on the Family; Ted Haggard, pastor of New Life Church in Colorado Springs and head of the National Association of Evangelicals; Deal Hudson, conservative Catholic and publisher of *Crisis* magazine; Jay Sekulow, head of Pat Robertson's American Center for Law and Justice; Ken Connor, then head of the Family Research Council; Richard Land, president of the Southern Baptist Convention's Ethics and Religious Liberty Commission; and Christian talk radio hosts Janet Parshall and Michael Reagan, among others.

This network of people covered virtually every area of evangelical Christianity. The calls began with an overview of what the president would be talking about in the coming week. If necessary, participants were asked to talk to their people about whatever issue was pending. Talking points were distributed and advice was solicited. That advice rarely went much further than the conference call. There wasn't any malice or negligence behind this. It was just that the true purpose of these calls was to keep prominent social conservatives and their groups or audiences happy. In most ways it wasn't a tough sell. Evangelicals in and out of politics were all aware of the president's explicit Christian faith. The campaign strategy had been successful.

In 2 Chronicles 7:14 of the Old Testament, God appears to Solomon. He declares that the temple Solomon built will be his place to receive sacrifices. Then, in words of advice, he tells Solomon that when he punishes the Jewish people, "if my people, who are called by my name, will humble themselves and pray and seek my face and turn from their wicked ways, then will I hear from heaven and will forgive their sin and will heal their land."

Christians like me had heard this passage for years and seen it as a prayerful strategy for God to heal America. With George Bush it seemed that the prayer had been fulfilled. There were theological questions about whether the passage, clearly referring to Israel, had anything to do with the United States. But those questions didn't matter. God had heard the prayers of his people, and in the person of George W. Bush had given us the man who was to heal our land. With that reality, Public Liaison's job of convincing Christians that President Bush was on the right side of virtually any tactic wasn't hard.

It should have been a whole lot harder because Christians should have demanded a whole lot more. But all too often, when put before power, Christian leaders wilt. Chuck Colson tells the story of his own experience with religious interest groups in the early 1970s. "I arranged special briefings in the Roosevelt Room for religious leaders, ushered wide-eyed denominational leaders into the Oval Office for private sessions with the president, and even arranged dinner cruises on the presidential yacht for key leaders who just happened to come from states we had targeted in the 1972 election." He goes on to say, "From these meetings grew very agreeable alliances. Religious leaders were able to make their points with the President—though most were so in awe that they didn't. Most important to us, we reaped handsome dividends on election day. The significance of Nixon's frequent photos with Evangelical and Fundamentalist leaders was not lost on Bible Belt voters, and, in the electoral-rich states of the Northeast, his open courting of the blue-collar Roman Catholic vote proved decisive."

Colson closes the story saying, "On the whole, of all the groups I dealt with, I found religious leaders the most naïve about politics. Maybe that is because so many come from sheltered backgrounds, or perhaps it is the result of a mistaken perception of the demands of Christian charity. . . . Or, most worrisome of all, they may simply like to be around power." Twenty-five years later, little has changed.

As I was learning, White House power was a different kind of power. It was a power that bends any knee. Every president tells a similar story. They say they love sitting behind their desk knowing that the very important person they are about to see really wants to rip their head off about something or another, and knowing that the moment that person walks into the Oval Office he or she will cower at the weight of history and the weight of the presidency and say very little.

That same glory reflects off staffers and we used it to our advantage. We learned that simply mentioning "the president" in a conversation could cool a hot temper. Having a White House operator place a call awes the person on the other end of the line. Allowing someone to come through the White House gates can make them dizzy. Some time after I started I saw John Chambers, CEO of Cisco Systems, walking through the White House gates. I happened to be in front of him as he passed through security. His eyes were wide as he nervously collected his binder, keys, and phone. He looked at me and stopped. "Ummm, is this where I'm supposed to be? I mean is it OK if I come in?" Chambers wasn't even there to see the president.

Christian conservatives seemed especially vulnerable to that power and everyone working with them knew that. There were just so many ways to make them happy. In addition to myriad White House events, phone calls, and meetings, they could be given passes to be in the crowd greeting the president when he arrived on Air Force One or tickets for a speech he was giving in their hometown. Little trinkets like cufflinks or pens or pads of paper were passed out like business cards. The White House used them all, knowing the Christian leaders could give them to their congregations or donors or friends to show just how influential they were. Making politically active Christians personally happy meant having to worry far less about the Christian political agenda.

In July, as the faith-based bill moved toward a House vote and we didn't know if we had enough votes to win, we fought to use some of that White House power to muscle some votes. We turned to our only reliable West Wing ally, John Bridgeland.

"Bridge," as everyone called him, had left a lucrative law practice because he wanted to engage in public service. A bird lover who owned a pet hawk as a boy that landed in his thick, bushy hair, Bridge was a former professional tennis player and a supreme diplomat. During the first week in office, when members of an advocacy group for rights of the disabled handcuffed themselves to the White House gate, a collective shout bounced through the West Wing: "Bridge!!! Help!!" Bridge put down what he was working on, walked out to the gates, talked the protestors down, and met with them for two hours. By the end of the meeting, they were about ready to volunteer for Bush's 2004 reelection campaign. Bridge was arguably the only indispensable person outside of the president. He single-handedly oversaw every issue from global warming to welfare, AIDS to the environment. Though he was technically Margaret Spellings's deputy, in practice she handled education and he handled everything else. His personal binder was labeled SISYPHUS. Occasionally he would shut his office door, take out a tennis racket, and launch a full serve at the door. It made him feel better.

We needed several specific things from the president, and Bridge could help. First, we needed President Bush to meet with a group of Democratic congressmen who were seriously considering voting for the bill. Second, we needed to contain a growing rebellion by two socially liberal Republicans in the House, Mark Foley of Florida and Jim Kolbe of Arizona. They hated that the bill was so tough on the hiring issue, and so clearly anti–gay rights. Third, we needed serious lobbying from White House Legislative Affairs for the first time. Bridge enlisted Rove on the first point, Rove on the second, and Rove on the third. He did it in no small part by painting a very dire picture for Karl about what would happen if the president were defeated on what the president had repeatedly labeled his biggest domestic priority. Not only would it be embarrassing, it could be portrayed as a loss of power and show that the president was not a forceful leader.

Twenty-four hours later the president hosted seven Democratic congressmen in order to talk to them about the bill. The group included Representative Danny Davis from Illinois, a member of the Congressional Black Caucus and certainly not a conservative. The president schmoozed Davis, shared his own faith, assuaged Davis's concerns, and put his arm around him. By the time the meeting was done, Davis went out to the microphones in front of the West Wing and declared his support for the bill. "We need every weapon in the arsenal if we're going to tackle these social problems," Davis declared.

What happened next was power politics. Hilary Shelton, political head of the NAACP, consulted with the Congressional Black Caucus to figure out what to do to punish Davis. They were going to support a primary challenge against him. He was only in his third term and wasn't fully established. He would be taken down unless he withdrew his support for the president's bill.

Davis was called into a meeting with the Caucus and the NAACP. The message was simple: "Back off the faith-based thing, Danny, or we're going to cut you dry."

For these men the faith-based vote wasn't the problem. The problem was its broader political significance. They knew that the initiative could inject hundreds of millions of dollars into poor, largely black communities. But that money, directed at black-run community groups and churches, had the potential to swing African-American voters to the GOP. Earlier in the year, Caucus founder Charles Rangel debated fellow congressman J. C. Watts on the faith-based initiative. When asked if he supported the president's plan to allow poorer Americans to deduct their charitable giving in hopes of spurring more charitable giving, Rangel replied, "I don't think so. I really think that's a political question . . . I'm telling you, you can pick up a vote here and there, but the president and the Republicans are walking on very thin ice by trying to give out patronage to the religious sector." Rangel and the Congressional Black Caucus couldn't afford to let the bill pass.

Rangel knew what he was talking about. For decades the Democratic Party engaged in exactly the kind of patronage he condemned. He knew something about picking up votes by distributing dollars because that is exactly what Democrats had done.

He was also worried about Republicans. In April, J. C. Watts hosted a gathering for African-American clergy at the Library of Congress. More than three hundred pastors, from mostly small Southern churches, attended. This group wasn't going to swing any states electorally. They probably couldn't have swung a school board race. But what it represented for Rangel and other Democrats was a threat to their electoral power base.

Danny Davis didn't merely abstain from the vote; he voted against the bill.

I learned details of the story slowly over the next year from Hill colleagues. It was hard to believe. How could a group as religiously oriented as the NAACP become nothing more than a tool for the most liberal elements of the Democratic Party? And how could a group that once disturbed the social order become little more than a forgotten stepchild of partisans?

Sure, Democratic candidates paraded before the NAACP and said the right things about racial equality, civil rights, and affirmative action. But neither the NAACP nor the network of mainline African-American churches exerted any real influence over the Democrats. They had been co-opted. They were taken for granted.

Though I didn't appreciate it at the time, the White House conference calls with evangelical leaders, and the absolute devotion of these Christian conservatives to the Republican Party and to George W. Bush, were the flip side of the NAACP and the Democratic Party. If Christians became captive to only one party, why would that party listen to them? The business of a political party is straightforward. Groups may get something in exchange for their support, but they are just pieces of a puzzle put together to get one more vote than the other guy has. They don't get anything on principle, only based on raw horse-trading. Who was using whom in the Christian-Republican relationship?

Ralph Reed once told me that political power both "ennobles and corrupts." For the most faithful Christian leaders in politics, the ones who regularly fall on their knees in prayer and study, the chance to inspire and lead can be ennobling. Leaders like Martin Luther King Jr. and William Wilberforce famously spent countless hours in prayer before God. They did so because their tasks were so great, and they realized that their personal strength was insufficient to tackle them. Politics made them better Christians. But for many other Christians, politics has the opposite effect. It corrupts their souls. Instead of driving them to their knees, it fills them with a sense of accomplishing "God's work" by their own means. Were we in the Bush White House encouraging that or trying to prevent it? Did we even know the difference?

Like most other conservative Christians, in all of this I took great solace from the president's own faith. I trusted his leadership and knew that he began and ended his day praying to God. It isn't that his faith gave him a free pass, although it mostly did. As a professing fellow believer in Jesus, I trusted him. He was the kind of Christian that Christians had been dreaming for decades about having in the Oval Office. There wasn't any reason not to trust him. I had heard him talk about racial, economic, and social justice. I had seen him around the addicted. He was real.

I also looked at the task set before us. Our goal was to try to radically improve how millions of hurting people received treatment for addictions or depravations or lack of privilege. That wasn't corrupting. It was ennobling.

In the end, the political and religious conflicts engendered by the faith bill didn't need Danny Davis. The bill passed the House mostly along party lines, 233–198. The president, in England, issued a statement thanking the House and looking forward to Senate passage.

I had come to understand the faith-based conundrum. It went back to the Austin strategy Karl Rove adopted leading up to the 2000 campaign. While all the other Republican candidates slogged through Iowa and New Hampshire speaking at firehouses and coffeehouses and waffle houses, Governor Bush sat in Austin and hosted lunches for everyone who wanted to see him. He had won over virtually everyone he met with his charm, enthusiasm, humor, openness, and evident integrity. There wasn't any need for him to make controversial statements about issues that could get him in trouble. In fact, the plan was that his would be a moderate face.

Accentuating the moderation was the tireless work of convincing evangelicals and other social conservatives that he was one of them. He was born again. He loved Jesus. He hated abortion and loved the family. But the message to those social conservatives was that the only way to get their issues taken care of was to get him into office. And the only way to get him into office was to not have him appear to be a radically religious man. He needed to be as stealthy to the American public as Supreme Court Justice David Souter was, except that George W. Bush was for real.

It was a strategy that worked despite glaring bumps like Bob Jones University.

Now that he was president the plan was to replicate 2000 all over again. He would present a moderate face to the American people. He had cooperated with Ted Kennedy on an education bill, and though he would push hard for tax cuts, they'd be very popular tax cuts. On issue after issue he would be very acceptable.

Social conservatives would be quietly kept in the loop and assured that, though things might appear moderate, they needn't worry. George Bush was a hardcore conservative and on things that mattered he would deliver for evangelicals.

The only thing that gummed up the works was the faith-based initiative. Advisers thought the initiative would be as innocuous as compassionate conservatism was during the campaign. Why wouldn't they? Al Gore endorsed it and said it wasn't a political thing. But it became a political thing and now the White House didn't know what to do. It couldn't kill it and it couldn't fully promote it.

The White House wanted to put the office and its agenda out of business while still receiving political benefits from religious leaders and voters. What the *New York Times* had come to label the president's "religion initiative" wasn't selling with mainstream voters. "Compassionate conservatism" had become a core tenet of Bush's 2000 campaign in no small part because of its appeal to suburban women. But now religion was turning them off even as religion excited religious conservatives. The only way to solve that problem was to minimize the office while maximizing its perception in the Christian community. At one point an idea circulated among senior staff that the office might be moved to Philadelphia—"closer to the field." That idea didn't last long.

Another effort was a possible new White House fall initiative called "Communities of Character." The effort's goal was to "unite Americans by focusing on children, quality of life and universally appreciated values." It wasn't big-picture stuff, or even terribly ambitious. It was low-cost but nice. The government would somehow help provide e-mail services to link grandparents and grandchildren, add citizenship to the curriculum in schools, increase community use of the Internet, encourage news organizations to "increase reporting of good news," and promote movies that help break down racial stereotypes. The president would also address adoption, teen pregnancy, truancy, drugs, school safety, affordable housing, mental illness, gang prevention, and prison ministries.

The political goal was to help Bush regain the mantle of "a different kind of Republican" that he had successfully used in 2000. It also would help him appear more moderate to Hispanics, Catholics, and suburban women. Because the issues were also "social" issues, conservatives would like them. But as a memo from Rove's Strategic Initiatives Office made clear, "it was not to be seen as a religious initiative."

Religion was more complicated than politics.

Meanwhile, in August, we issued *Unlevel Playing Field,* the first ever report about the federal government and faith-based groups. For John DiIulio it was the main reason he had taken the job. For six months, faith-based centers in the five biggest nonmilitary federal departments took stock of how faith-based groups were treated. While six months was admittedly not long enough to do a comprehensive analysis, it was still the most insightful work ever done.

The conclusions were mixed. Most significantly and most clearly, the report found that "a funding gap exists between the government and grassroots. Smaller groups, faith-based and secular, receive very little Federal support relative to the size and scope of the social services they provide." That finding was the true heart of the compassionate conservative message. The small groups were the local groups known by the community and trusted by the community. They were the antithesis of big government programs and they were being ignored.

A bias against faith- and community-based organizations existed. In part it was a bureaucratic bias of no particular antireligious bent. Government grants could be insanely complicated. One Justice Department program's application kit was fifty-eight pages long. But it referenced an additional thousand pages of federal statutes necessary to actually complete the application. Their rules were nonsensical. For instance, in order to get a grant, a group had to first have a grant. Much of the bias was institutional. Government officials didn't think faith-based groups were permitted and so tended to exclude them.

Nevertheless, faith-based groups did receive government grants and had done so for many years. In some programs there was actually a favoritism *for* faith-based organizations. Exactly how much funding faith-based groups received was hard to determine because the vast majority of federal funds are spent by states and cities and because even the agencies didn't know. In a particularly amusing example, the Department of Housing and Urban Development declared that no faith-based organization had received any funding for a particular program. In reality, Habitat for Humanity, a Christian organization, received more than half of the funds for that program. "With mind-bending logic, HUD officials apparently reasoned that since the government may not aid religion, and yet HUD funds Habitat, then Habitat must not be a faith-based organization."

The night the report was issued John called me. "I've just resigned."

I was back in the White House compound after a run and leaned against the nearest fence. Six months were up; he was going back to Philly and resuming his life in academia and on the streets working with social service groups. It wasn't a real surprise. Still, I would miss him. The initiative would miss him more. He knew he had made some mistakes. In hindsight it was silly for him to think he could be a member of the president's most senior staff while living in Philly. Though the president asked for greater input from him, he had resisted the battle because no one else on the senior staff wanted him to see the president. John had a way of upsetting things. Yet every positive thing the initiative accomplished was because of him. I didn't have any idea what would happen with him gone.

He asked me to stay at least through the transition, maybe a month or two. He had worked things out so I could do my dot-com book tour and stay employed through the transition to a new director. I didn't mind. It was a good place to work.

I was a Special Assistant to the President of the United States. I was a junior member of the senior staff. A car and driver were mine for any official business. Seats in the presidential box at the Kennedy Center were mine for the asking. My blue-and-white-striped badge allowed me to walk virtually anywhere in the White House unimpeded. Mail to me was addressed to "The Honorable David Kuo." I could eat any meal I chose in the White House mess.

The temptation when working there is to think that the place has something, anything, to do with you. After all, every phone call is returned. Even the people who don't really like you are generally nice. Yet nothing could be further from the truth. People genuflected not to us but to our titles and our perceived power. They would have been nice to whoever held our offices. We just filled spots for whatever time we were there. We were Post-it notes attached to job titles.

With his usual flair for casual understatement, Mike Gerson put it well: "As far as White Houses go, this one is a fairly good one. There's relatively little backstabbing or climbing over people. Character assassination is virtually unheard of and people seem to generally like each other." He was right. My frustration with people's ambivalence about the president's compassion agenda was lessened by how much I liked the people. They were, to a person, nice people. As politically pulsating as Karl Rove was, I had not only grown to respect his genius but to enjoy his prankish humor. To him, things grew funnier with repetition. If teasing someone about something once was good, teasing them about a thousand times was that much better. For as much power as he wielded, he never lorded it over people. Perhaps he didn't have to. Karen Hughes's high-wire intensity masked deep sensitivity to other people. Even the curmudgeonly vice president had a surprising jocularity.

Before the summer was done there was one last thing I wanted to do. It was actually something I had wanted to do from the moment I learned I would be working at the White House.

I invited my father for a tour.

As I showed him the Old Executive Office Building and then the West Wing, he slowly turned around, looking at every corner. He beamed. He was dazzled. "Da-wei, Da-wei," he said, calling me by my Chinese name. All he could do was say my name. He was near tears most of the time. It was my gift to him.

I pointed out the Oval Office. The president was in that morning, so a tour was impossible. We walked out onto the column-lined promenade made famous by pictures of nearly every president who had walked there. This was where JFK and RFK huddled with bowed heads during the Cuban Missile Crisis and where Reagan was seen pacing. Hard-heeled shoes clicked against the blue slate tiles and echoed into the Rose Garden that lay to our right, fully abloom.

Suddenly, my father grabbed my hand and started leading me. He wanted to go into the Rose Garden. I tried to warn him that this wasn't a good idea given the presence of Secret Service. He ignored me. He spied a black wrought-iron bench right next to Barney's water bowl, and pulled me down onto it. We were facing the Oval Office.

"Da-wei, Da-wei . . ." He was shaking. "Da-wei, Da-wei. You know what this is? You know what this is? This . . . this . . . this is the White House. We spoke of this place during the war. We knew that this White House . . . the Oval Office . . . we knew that it was going to save the world. This is the White House. It helped save the world."

CHAPTER TWELVE

Sunny Days

It was 7 A.M. on September 11, and I had been back from my book tour in the United Kingdom for two days. I parked my car on State Place, a few yards from the southwest entrance of the White House, and walked up the driveway for my last DiIulio breakfast. He was coming in from Philly to clean up paperwork and to deliver to the president a strategy for winning Senate passage of the faith-based bill.

The vice president's motorcade pulled up. Cheney got out of the car with an armful of papers. He looked like an absentminded professor, deep in thought, oblivious to the world. I was talking with some friends and he glanced our way, gave one of his patented crooked smiles, said, "Ehh," and went inside. An aide followed behind, picking up the papers Cheney dropped.

John and I relished our last White House breakfast together. We had kicked off this little adventure over dinner in April and now we were finishing it off with breakfast. He had an afternoon meeting with the president, who had written him a two-page handwritten letter thanking "my rumpled John" for his service. He would tell the president what he thought about the first six months and what needed to be done in the months ahead. The only way for things to work, John would say, was for the president to appoint someone with West Wing authority and expertise to run it. That person, John submitted, should be John Bridgeland.

The only problem with that was Bridge. Bridge liked his jack-of-all-trades policy portfolio. He loved the West Wing—except when he hated it, which was most of the time. It was kind of like eating jalapeño peppers: when the fire hits your mouth, one way to make it feel better is to eat more pepper. The problem is that you can only do that for so long. Eventually your mouth loses out. Our job was to convince him to stop eating the peppers, and make the full-time compassion plunge.

We left the mess to head up to Bridge's second-floor West Wing office. As we exited the elevator we saw him walking in our direction looking pale and sickly. For the first time in my life I saw someone who really looked like "death warmed over." Yet John and I were accustomed to seeing Bridge in various states of emotional disrepair, so we weren't shocked.

"Bridge, what's up?"

He kept walking toward us as if he were about to pass right through us. "Bridge?"

"Did you . . . did you see?"

"See what?"

"The plane. The plane. Did you see the plane hit the World Trade Center?"

We piled into Bridge's office. He tried to explain to us what was going on. A plane had flown into one of the trade center towers. Then, live, on television, he had just seen another plane fly into the other tower. We sat around his little television, stupefied.

Bridge's assistant burst in the door, "The Pentagon has been hit. A friend said the Pentagon has been hit."

"It can't be. No one has told us."

The same sequence of thoughts simultaneously occurred to all of us. They are attacking Washington. They are attacking important places. What else might they hit? The Capitol. The White House. The State . . . wait!!! *We're* in the White House. We all stood up and looked around.

We left John's office and headed down the hallway. Someone suggested we call the Sit Room. The White House Situation Room is responsible for knowing everything all the time. This is not an exaggeration. Their assignment is to be able to answer anything anyone asks of them while also providing timely information on any important topic. Calling them was a good idea.

We stopped outside General Counsel Al Gonzales's office and

had his assistant call the Sit Room. "We hear the Pentagon has been hit," she said into the phone. "No, we have no confirmation of that. It is just a rumor," came the reply.

The group paused a beat. We heard voices from the stairwell yelling. "Get out! Get out! Everyone get out. Get down to the basement. Get out! Get down!"

Secret Service agents suddenly appeared en masse, bearing all sorts of elaborate weaponry. "Get downstairs now. Get down."

We were herded down to the White House mess. All the tables had been tossed onto their sides to make room for as many people as possible. Fifty people stood there, shocked, quiet, confused.

Moments later another order. "Out, out, get out . . ."

We ran up the hall and turned left past the Secret Service station. There, more weapon-toting agents were gathered. "Get out of the building NOW. RUN. GET OUT."

We burst through the doors we'd entered two hours before and into more screaming and running. Agents were screaming, "WE HAVE AN INCOMING, WE HAVE AN INCOMING. RUN. WOMEN . . . TAKE OFF YOUR HEELS. RUN!!!" Men and women were running up and down the avenue between the White House and the OEOB crying, screaming, and holding their coffee. All the White House gates were open. For one unique moment absolutely no one wanted to go into the White House. Plainclothes and uniformed agents were all holding submachine guns and had the unmistakable look of people who wanted badly to shoot something but weren't able to find a target. The black-suited agents—we called them ninjas—from the Counter Assault Team had materialized with even more exotic weaponry. These were the really mean guys. Their job was to attack anyone attacking the president. If someone was firing they were to go straight at the shooter. They had no regard for their own lives. Their sole purpose was to destroy any attacker.

Everyone with a weapon was looking up. We did, too. Several thousand feet above us was a silver-bellied jetliner with two engines beneath each wing. It was banking to the left, directly over White House airspace. That, we assumed, was the plane that would shortly destroy the White House. In all the days and months that followed, the media never reported it. Yet we all saw it . . . or we thought we did.

John and I looked at each other and ran. I later saw some video and it looked kind of funny. We were like Laurel and Hardy. John is short and very large. I am very tall and relatively skinny. We looked like we were running from Godzilla. John was still toting the garment bag he had carried in to breakfast.

We leapt into my car and, seeing that the path out of the private drive was backed up, I hopped the curb and drove onto a secure stretch of grass outside the Old Executive Office Building. I headed down the grass stretch only to run into barriers that had been put in place to prevent car bombers from getting close to the White House. We opened the doors and started running again. Hundreds of people surrounded us. Without thinking, we both headed for open space. If they were flying jet planes into buildings, we wanted as much warning as possible so we could get out of the path of the plane. We stood in the middle of the Ellipse, where the national Christmas tree is lit every year. With one eye we watched the skies around the Washington Monument, checking for planes. With another eye we looked back at the White House, absolutely sure we would see it blown to pieces at any moment.

My cell phone rang. It was Kim. She was in San Diego at a trade show. She had seen the whole thing on television and was frantic. The television shots made it look like the Pentagon smoke was billowing from the Office Building. I assured her I was fine but I needed her to talk to all the people around me, get the names and numbers of their families, and let them know they were fine. All the lines were jammed. Person after person from the White House whom I had never met got on the phone with my wife and gave her the names and numbers of their parents, their spouses, their kids. Only later did it all seem like a movie scene.

We watched and watched and watched. Then we all looked at each other and headed toward home. I retrieved my car and left D.C. over Memorial Bridge. As I drove across, I saw the black smoke billow from the Pentagon. Everything seemed as hazy as the smoke. I dropped John off in Philly, hearing on the radio, but not believing, that the World Trade Center towers had collapsed. What seemed like moments after being in Philly, I found myself driving back into Washington, crossing the 14th Street Bridge into Virginia, passing the burning Pentagon. The roads were empty. My apartment was less than half a mile from the Pentagon. I didn't know what I was going back to, only that I had to get back. Frantic, rumor-filled phone calls were nonstop all day. The most plausible and frightening one had the planes carrying anthrax that had, in turn, spread through the smoke. Everyone survived the night, and at six the next morning I headed to work. I had wanted to go in the night before but virtually everyone had been locked out of the place. Unless you were part of the national security team or the communications team you weren't welcome.

The next morning the city was locked down. I went through four separate checkpoints on the way to work. I wasn't angry or enraged, I wasn't scared, I was just determined. I remembered my father's words and knew it was our turn to save the world. Our country had been attacked. And I worked for our country. A job needed to be done and in whatever way I could I was going to do that job. As I drove to work and went into my office I thought I now had an inkling about what my father felt when he ran off at sixteen to fight the Japanese. I didn't need some abstract concept like justice or vengeance. I just needed to fight for my country no matter what it might cost me. Five years later it all seems so melodramatic, but on that day it was just life.

We convened at eight with Bridge and Margaret Spellings. They hadn't any clue what we were supposed to be doing. We soon learned a valuable lesson about the role of the White House in the federal bureaucracy: sometimes the professionals in the executive branch didn't need the White House to tell them how to do their jobs. Bridge tried to take control and give his policy team assignments. We were told to come up with things we could tell the federal agencies to do. What kind of security features might we implement on aircraft? What could be done to help rescue survivors in New York? What charities might we enlist? They were great questions. We spent the next hour arguing about whether we needed air marshals to guard planes and when commercial airlines should fly again and what to do about any biological attacks. Then, slowly, it dawned on us that our discussion was interesting but pointless. While we Special Assistants to the President were bright and able, there was an entire federal government devoted to asking and answering strategic questions and then implementing them. They didn't need us. It was, arrogant as it may sound, a revelation: we really felt as if we ran everything. We quietly left the conference to sit at our desks and find something useful to do.

This lesson soon led to another, much bigger one, about the role of government in caring for America's soul. For years a national debate had raged over whether or not America was falling apart morally and culturally. Like so many other Christian conservatives, I knew the answer: absolutely. New policies, strategies, and political leaders were needed to help us reclaim America's greatness. On 9/12 I discovered something else.

At the time, I was put in charge of assisting "all" of America's charities and mobilizing "all" of America's religious groups, a task that both highlighted the White House–centric view of the world and showed how desperately we all wanted to help. Our office developed a massive list of ideas and plans: we planned candlelight services and telethons and moments of silence. Then we discovered the obvious. People were doing all of those things on their own. They didn't need us to do it. America didn't need anyone else to rally it. It rallied itself. The American soul wasn't sick.

That same evening we were put in charge of the National Day of Prayer and Remembrance, focused on the service to be held in two days, on Friday, at the National Cathedral. Laura Bush and Karen Hughes were working on the program. My friend Tim Goeglein was assisting them and lining up clergy. We were in charge of making sure all the right people were there—no small challenge, given that air travel was shut down.

We set about trying to contact the nation's leading pastors. We called people regardless of political orientation. Liberal pastors from the National Council of Churches were called at the same time as the head of the Southern Baptist Convention. Jesse Jackson wasn't treated any differently from Pat Robertson. Not surprisingly, everyone we talked to offered their prayers, support, love, and appreciation for what we were doing. That was a change of no small note. Some declined our invitation to attend the service because they felt they needed to attend to their flocks at home or because they were heading to New York to comfort people or because they just couldn't get to Washington.

We shared our list of invitees with people at the Office of Public Liaison. They demanded additions: leaders from the National Right to Life Committee, Family Research Council, Focus on the Family, the conservative American Center for Law and Justice, the evangelical National Association of Religious Broadcasters, and the largest conservative think tanks. Even in mourning, politics mattered.

We were all numb. We went from meetings on the church service to briefings on the disaster. The Department of Health and Human Services briefed us on what they were calling "Ground Zero." Fifteen thousand people were thought to be dead. The plague might break out. Air over Manhattan could cause cancer deaths in the years to come. If someone weaponized anthrax and released it over Washington, for instance, millions could die. Cholera and botulism were possible dangers. It went on and on.

The morning of the church service was, fittingly, cloudy and rainy. Office staff and interns stood on a street corner several blocks from the White House to hand out tickets. At first it was going smoothly. Suddenly, however, we had a Jerry Falwell problem. Someone asked if we had heard what Falwell said: The day before, Falwell had gone on Pat Robertson's *700 Club* and let loose. The attack, Falwell said, was evidence God had lifted his veil of protection from the United States. God was angry at America for its cultural immorality and we were now paying the price. Things were probably going to get worse before they got better. "The ACLU's got to take a lot of blame for this," Falwell continued, "and, I know that I'll hear from them for this. But, throwing God out successfully with the help of the federal court system, throwing God out of the public square, out of the schools. The abortionists have got to bear some burden for this because God will not be mocked. And when we destroy forty million little innocent babies, we make God mad. I really believe that the pagans, and the abortionists, and the feminists, and the gays and the lesbians who are actively trying to make that an alternative lifestyle, the ACLU, People For the American Way—all of them who have tried to secularize America—I point the finger in their face and say 'you helped this happen.' "

No one doubted Falwell's ability to make outrageous statements. This wasn't outrageous. It was immoral. It was insane.

I called Rove's office to figure out what to do. Give him the ticket or let him stand in the rain?

We had already told him to go to a different street corner than the one where we were handing out tickets. He kept calling to ask about his tickets. Most of me wanted to see him stand there in the rain for hours. He was offensive. But then I kept hearing this little voice reminding me it was the National Day of Prayer and Remembrance. This day wasn't a day to punish anyone.

Thirty minutes later, I received a call. "Just let him in," Karl's deputy said, "and make sure he avoids every camera and doesn't say a word." I told Rev. Falwell the rules. He agreed. He was contrite.

A police-escorted bus took staff up to the cathedral. The massive sanctuary was filled. The diplomatic community filled up the back half of the center section, members of Congress the front half. The religious community and a few political activists filled the side sections.

It was silent. Bob Dole, who only got a ticket at the last minute because he was inadvertently left off the invite list, sobbed quietly. I watched his shoulders heave up and down. A family seated a few rows away held each other and cried. Their quiet cries echoed through the cathedral.

Ahead, Jerry Falwell was chortling with a fellow conservative leader. As Barbara Bush entered, Jerry chirped, "Whoa, does she look frumpy."

The procession formed. I noticed a tall, graying man leaning against one of the robed clergy. I knew most everyone on the program but I didn't recognize the top of his head. The procession moved toward the rear of the cathedral down a far aisle, mostly out of view, to be in place for the formal procession down the center aisle. I still couldn't make out the hunched-over man.

The organ started playing and the procession began. Everyone in the procession stood tall and somber. Now I couldn't even see the old man. Was I imagining things? Then I saw him. He had been transformed. Billy Graham walked slowly down the aisle under his own power—God's lion in winter. He walked past the row where the mourning family still sobbed. His head turned and his eyes looked longingly. The families were too far away to touch and they didn't see him.

Jerry Falwell chortled on.

Graham was helped to his seat on the stage facing the audience. He sat with an imam, a rabbi, and a priest.

The president entered and sat alongside his immediate predecessors, Clinton and his father. He ascended to the pulpit and looked at us. "We are here in the middle hour of our grief. So many have suffered so great a loss, and today we express our nation's sorrow. We come before God to pray for the missing and the dead, and for those who love them. . . ."

They were Mike Gerson's words—ones he never imagined he would have to write. Whether George Bush had taken the mantle because it was shoved on him by events or seized the mantle with resolute leadership, for the first time in my life I was watching George W. Bush, the *President*.

Whatever would come, the challenge of the moment had been met. And the three-month tour I began with levity had become something altogether different: a time to surrender any and every schedule for the sole purpose of healing our country.

Billy Graham stood. He climbed two small steps to the foot of the spiral stairs that led to the pulpit above. He paused just a moment. No one could help him up the narrow stairs. I saw his hands grab the rails. He grimaced and he pulled and he climbed. We didn't know if he would make it. For a moment he disappeared from sight. Then we saw his hands again pulling him up, grasping the lectern. Then he stood.

A few rows ahead, not even Reverend Falwell was joking anymore. Perhaps it is as simple as the different ways we deal with grief. Maybe for Jerry the only way to process his pain was through inappropriate humor. Still, there couldn't have been a starker contrast between men than there was between Graham and Falwell. Graham stood tall, speaking slowly, humbly. He had preached to more people about Jesus than anyone in history. And he had once been in love with politics.

In Graham's early years he had combined his pro-Jesus message with a stridently anticommunist one. The bigger he got the more politically inclined he became. He wrote numerous letters to President Truman requesting a meeting and an endorsement. The meeting came in 1950. Graham's team had a short meeting with the president, ending in a prayer. As the team left the White House, reporters asked what happened. Graham gave them a detailed account, kneeling on the White House lawn as he demonstrated how he had prayed with Truman. Truman was incensed and wouldn't have anything more to do with him.

Graham was close to Eisenhower and to Nixon. In 1960 he supported Nixon, whom he called his "old Quaker friend," over John Kennedy. He hit it off with LBJ, even going skinny-dipping with the president. By the time Nixon was elected, Graham's political influence couldn't have been greater. He was a frequent visitor and intimate friend. Nixon tapped him to convince George Wallace not to run for president and helped Graham with an IRS investigation.

But the relationship also cost him. In some of Nixon's secret tapes that were later released, Graham talked about the insidious Jewish influence in the media and in the culture. Nixon counseled him not to talk about it. Graham responded, "If you get elected a second time then we might be able to do something about it."

Shortly thereafter, however, something changed. Graham got tipped off that Nixon was using him for politics. Someone, maybe even Chuck Colson (though no one knows for sure), told Graham of memos from and discussions among the president and White House staffers, describing how they were using Graham to get his people's votes. While the notes themselves weren't given to Graham, the impact was the same. And if that disclosure didn't shock

Graham out of politics, the infamous 1973 White House tapes did. He had known Nixon as a born-again Quaker. But with the release of those tapes he saw Nixon the foul-mouthed manipulator, a man who wanted only to use everyone he knew. Graham read the transcripts, wept, and reportedly threw up.

What happened next is a little-discussed journey that symbolizes the power of Christian influence away from politics. Though Graham counseled future presidents, and made his explicit affection for Governor Bush known in 2000, he established what he called a "cautious distance" between his ministry and politics. The energy he had used on politics he expended elsewhere, for example, by bridging historic divides with the Catholic Church through a Polish cardinal who later became Pope John Paul II, and traveling and preaching behind the Iron Curtain.

Falwell, and others like him, seemed to have learned the opposite lesson. During the civil rights movement Falwell remarked, "Preachers are not called upon to be politicians, but soul winners. Nowhere are we commissioned to reform externals." But a few decades later he was preaching a different message. By 1980 he was saying that Ronald Reagan and the Republicans owed their power to the religious movement that he led.

Two different men were before me. Both loved Jesus and had, in their own ways, tried to do exactly what they felt God called them to do. But sitting there, looking up at Graham and over at Falwell, I found it hard to escape a simple question—had politics corrupted Falwell and had turning away from politics saved Graham? Was the principal difference between the two men C. S. Lewis's caution never to let Christian faith become a means to an end but only an end itself?

I knew where Falwell was coming from. He loved America and wanted it to be a great, moral, godly place. He had dedicated much of his public life to making that happen. The problem was that what he desired could never occur. His Christian pursuit of morality in American life was too amorphous. It wasn't like battling to end slavery or fighting for a woman's right to vote. It was indefinable. Would a 10 percent drop in teen pregnancies be enough? Fifty percent? How about divorce? Would a drop to only 500,000 divorces a year be a success? It couldn't be. He thought the answers could come, in part, from government, but they could not. They would come only from God. Only God could change enough hearts and lives to bring a moral revolution. The problem with God is that he seems to respond very poorly to our own agendas and our own timetables. Falwell was Sisyphus.

Graham was holy. He spoke as he always does, his deep, resonant voice proclaiming truth. Now though, the voice was halting. "I've become an old man now. And I've preached all over the world. And the older I get, the more I cling to that hope that I started with many years ago, and proclaimed it in many languages to many parts of the world." Words that once slipped like quicksilver off his tongue were occasionally tangled. His brokenness felt like ours. "[O]ur nation has been attacked. Buildings destroyed. Lives lost. But now we have a choice: Whether to implode and disintegrate emotionally and spiritually as a people, and a nation, or, whether we choose to become stronger through all of the struggle to rebuild on a solid foundation. And I believe that we're in the process of starting to rebuild on that foundation. That foundation is our trust in God. That's what this service is all about. And in that faith we have the strength to endure something as difficult and horrendous as what we've experienced this week."

Whether intentional or not, Graham had come full circle. He was the nation's pastor, not a pastor influencing the nation's politicians.

I talked about the Graham/Falwell distinction with too many people. One day I was handed a note to call Karl. He had received a fax from Jerry Falwell, fuming because I had been spreading rumors about him. "David, Karl. Jerry sent a fax complaining about you." I told Karl about Jerry's behavior at the Memorial Service. "Listen, I don't know. Would you just call Jerry, apologize and make things nice? We just have to put up with him." I did as I was told and called him. He was polite and happy and accepted my apology. He wanted me to know he never made any jokes at all. James Dobson was right beside him the whole time. He was my Christian brother and if I had harmed him I was certainly wrong. But I burned. I was apologizing because it was politically correct and I was told to. It felt dirty.

Things in Washington obviously changed after 9/11. Foreign policy became urgent, and we went to war in Afghanistan. But not everything changed. Domestic policy never goes away, even in wartime.

Bridge and I naïvely thought that the nation's unity and support for the president would make it easier for us to get the noncontroversial parts of the compassion agenda through the Senate. With Joe Lieberman's and Rick Santorum's staffs we drafted a new bill that included the president's requested tax credits for charitable giving, a religious nondiscrimination provision, and an increase in funding for the popular social services block grant used by states to fund day care, adoption, foster care, and employment services. It was a policy slam dunk, we thought. We called it the Charity Aid, Recovery, and Empowerment (CARE) Act. In addition to Lieberman and Santorum, Senator Clinton supported it. Max Baucus, Democratic chairman of the Senate Finance Committee, supported it. So did Charles Grassley, his Republican counterpart.

Unfortunately, a lot of other people didn't like it. DeLay's and Hastert's offices didn't like it. We were "watering down the employment provisions." Instead of fighting the divisive battle over hiring, we added provisions prohibiting the federal government from disallowing faith-based groups to apply for grants just because they displayed religious icons, had religious names, or had clergy members on their boards. Our *Unlevel Playing Field* report showed those were somewhat problematic, or at least as problematic as hiring rights. Nevertheless, the House staffers actually tried to get some of the conservative Christian groups to oppose it. The White House, they said, had gone soft. Worse, West Wingers and the Legislative Affairs shop didn't much like it, either. "It costs an awful lot of money," Nick Calio, Legislative Affairs chief, said. "Yeah, damn expensive," Margaret Spellings remarked. Bridge and I kept hitting tennis balls against his office wall. One day we pulled down his pictures, choked up on the racquets, and tried to play racquetball against the wall he shared with Karl. We thought Karl was gone. He opened up the door, looked at us quizzically, and quietly closed the door.

We were the puzzled ones. The bill met the vast majority of the president's campaign promises. Charities would be helped. We would solve a real problem. But we weren't getting anywhere. In October and November we met with Majority Leader Daschle's staff and with Daschle himself. He had minor objections but we could get past them. We had a bill supported by everyone. All we needed was a go-ahead from Josh Bolten or Andy Card. Bridge pestered them day after day. Josh finally took him aside. "Bridge, you aren't winning any friends here. Just keep it down."

Bridge didn't keep it down. Neither did I. Our office prepared binders of documents outlining the charity crisis for Karl and everyone else in the West Wing. Charities were beginning to shut down because their donations were drying up, as donors gave to the Red Cross and other 9/11-related organizations. The West Wing folks were "impressed" by the statistics. It was a "big problem." But they couldn't deal with it.

Granted, there were probably 212 more important things they were dealing with on a daily basis. An entirely new Office of Homeland Security was coming into being. The economy needed lots of help. American security needed to be bolstered. Nevertheless, even after 9/11 the White House *was* pushing nonmilitary domestic priorities. Enormous effort was expended trying to pass a patient's bill of rights. An energy bill got a lot of attention and was passed by the House. Our bill needed nothing more than an "Okay," and it would have been done. Senator Santorum tried lobbying the White House and so did Senator Grassley. Still nothing. It was "too expensive." By mid-December as Congress was about to adjourn we had a final chance. Late one evening Daschle's office called and said they could attach the bill to another bill and get it done in hours. Would the White House support it? Bridge went to Nick, Margaret, and Karl one last time. "Not now, Bridge, not now. Maybe next year."

And that was it. The president's faith-based promises almost certainly wouldn't be met. Compassion wasn't on the agenda anymore. For the rest of his presidency Bush would be called many things: a big-government conservative, a crusader captured by neocons, among others. But he could never again be called a compassionate conservative.

For security reasons the White House permanently evacuated all the offices in the OEOB that faced 17th Street. At points it was less than twenty feet from the street to the building's façade. So five floors of offices were moved. Entire White House departments moved into private offices nearby. Others were moved to offices being built for the National Park Service. Our office was moved right outside the White House gates, to a townhouse adjoining Blair House, where foreign leaders stayed. By early the next year a new volunteer initiative went into another townhouse next to the White House AIDS office. We joked that we were now part of "Compassion Alley." It felt like a dead end.

After our charity bill died we got word that a new director was being considered. No one could get his name quite right. Bridge called one day to say that he thought it was Jim Thome. The name sounded familiar. I Googled him. He was a baseball player who had just signed a three-year $18 million contract to play first base for the Philadelphia Phillies. Wow, I thought, here is someone who was willing to give it all up to try to serve the poor.

Bridge called back later. "Not Thome. Towey." I Googled again. Jim Towey had been Mother Teresa's U.S. lawyer. He was most famous for a legal dispute with a Tennessee bakery that one day took out its batch of cinnamon rolls and discovered that one looked exactly like Mother Teresa. They started calling it the "Nun Bun" and put the image on hats and T-shirts. Towey threatened to sue them for unlicensed use of a private person's image. It was settled amicably.

We desperately needed a new director, someone who was willing to fight the West Wing powers to get the president's agenda through. Bridge and I met him and were instantly enchanted. He was short and balding, with silver hair and a high voice. I wanted to call him Puck. He called John "Mr. Bridgeland," and nearly bowed to me. He was adorable, and fond of quoting Chinese proverbs that made absolutely no sense. "If on horse, don't kill gnats," and "When yawning, don't eat fish."

I briefed him on the state of the faith-based world. I also told him I completely understood that he would want to bring in his own people for the office. I would stay a few more weeks, and then move on. My time to go was at hand. The short White House tour had turned into a slightly longer one.

The first time I gave him this speech he smiled and shook his head. "No, if I get the job, I would love you to stay." I smiled and figured he was being kind. Two days later I said the same thing. He responded the same way.

In mid-January 2002, Jim got the job. He called. "Are you staying?" I sighed, "Yes, I'll stay to help you transition in."

"Can I ask for a year?"

"A year!? No. We'll just see how it goes. I'll help you transition."

"Okay. We'll see how it goes. Now, I want you to think about one thing. How do we make this office relevant? What do we do?" He hung up.

I knew the answer. It wasn't a Chinese proverb but it was close. "If you can't beat them, join them."

CHAPTER THIRTEEN

Politics Actually

In early February 2002, in a White House conference room, one hundred religious and charity leaders sat on wooden chairs painted gold, watching President Bush introduce Jim Towey as the new head of the faith-based office. "He understands there are things more important than political parties, and one of those things more important than political parties is helping to heal the nation's soul. There is nothing more important than helping the hopeless see hope, helping the addicted see a better life."

The president regularly and proudly described his faith initiative as the ultimate nonpolitical entity, even in political situations. On the day Republicans had lost the Senate because of Senator Jeffords's defection, when the president needed to defend against accusations by Jeffords that Republicans had become "too conservative and too partisan," the president addressed a Catholic parish in Cleveland. He noted, "I have set up an office [of faith-based initiatives] at the White House, run by a man named John DiIulio. . . . He's a really interesting guy. I haven't checked his party affiliation, but I suspect it's not the same as mine, because he understands that this is not an initiative to try to 'gain political gain.' Ours is an initiative to make America a better place."

As much as the president may have meant for the initiative to be nonpolitical and as much as he may have believed it, the sentiment wasn't founded in reality. The White House exists as a political entity for the sole purpose of advancing a president's agenda through the expansion and projection of his political power. Everything about a White House is political. The White House Easter Egg Roll is political, lighting the National Christmas Tree on the

Ellipse is political, and distributing White House Christmas cards is political. Every fall, staff members receive a form allowing us to name four people to receive official White House Christmas cards. Each year the list has to be different because the White House wants to be sure that new and different people get cards. It is just politics.

Jim Towey knew about politics. When John DiIulio resigned, Jim had called his friend Governor Jeb Bush to see about his chances for the job. Jeb, in turn, called Karl to tout Mother Teresa's ex-lawyer. Karl wanted to know how connected Jim was to the hierarchy of the American Catholic Church. If he wants the job, Karl told Jeb, tell him to "get as many red hats as he knows to call on his behalf." "Red hats" were cardinals, the highest-ranking officials in the Catholic Church beneath the pope, notable for their scarlet caps. The White House was still paying for the Bob Jones University speech. Enough of them called.

I hadn't appreciated the raw politics of the White House before I arrived there. I suppose at an intellectual level it made sense. How could the White House be anything but political? How could a snowman have no snow? Seeing it play out was something else. You can't appreciate snow until you fall into it.

A very intense eight months on the job had blown away any idealistic notions that the compassion agenda and the faith-based initiative were higher-order callings. They also showed me the way in from our exile outside the White House gates. If we were to have any hope of achieving the $8 billion a year for suffering Americans the president had promised, we first needed to show the West Wing we could help them politically, and second, we needed to show that giving up on us would hurt them politically.

The second part was significantly harder than the first. By the time Jim was appointed, the office had already been demoted one step further. John Bridgeland had conceived and launched USA Freedom Corps, a New Deal–like effort in volunteerism that would mobilize a network of volunteers to respond to a crisis at home, rebuild communities in need, and serve others around the world. Bridgeland was an Assistant to the President. Jim Towey reported to him and ranked below him. The faith-based office was now technically under Freedom Corps.

The first part, proving we could help the White House politically, we could do. We were nine months away from the midterm elections. The White House desperately needed to pick up seats in the Senate to make up for Senator Jeffords's defection. Solidifying the House majority was also a huge priority. Freedom Corps wasn't going to help mobilize voters. But we could. And if we were successful, we might not just help save the office, but the president's promises, too.

A few days later, Jim and I were sitting with Ken Mehlman, head of Political Affairs. We laid out a plan whereby we would hold "roundtable events" for threatened incumbents with faith and community leaders. Our office would do the work, using the aura of our White House power to get a diverse group of faith and community leaders to a "nonpartisan" event discussing how best to help poor people in their area. Though the Republican candidate would host the roundtable, it wouldn't be a campaign event. The member of Congress was just taking time away from his or her campaign to serve the community. It would be the perfect event.

The candidate would be seen as a real leader, someone respected enough to put together a broad community coalition to tackle tough problems. In turn, the White House would win not only because it was a political benefit to threatened incumbents, but also because it showed minority communities we cared. Evangelicals would be happy, too, because we would emphasize the president's deep personal faith.

Ken loved the idea and gave us our marching orders. There were twenty targets. On the Senate side, priorities included Saxby Chambliss in Georgia, Wayne Allard in Colorado, and Tim Hutchinson in Arkansas. House priorities were Melissa Hart in Pennsylvania, Shelley Capito in West Virginia, Anne Northup in Kentucky, and John Shimkus in Illinois.

"This is good, very good, very, very good," Mehlman said. "But we want to be careful, too. We can't be requesting the events, we'll have to have the candidates request them. And it can't come from the campaigns. That would make it look too political. It needs to come from the congressional offices. We'll take care of that by having our guys call the office to request the visit." It had to look like the idea came from members of Congress, just another way incumbent representatives were serving their communities. This approach inoculated us against accusations that we were using religion and religious leaders to promote specific candidates. We would begin the effort in the summer.

Any spiritual or moral qualms I had about the events were allayed because I absolutely believed the roundtables were good in every way. The events themselves were good for the community. Since the poor didn't exactly have their own powerful lobby or media presence, they relied on others to help raise the issues around them. We were the others. I didn't much care who won the races. At least for one moment in one political campaign, homeless shelters, battered women's shelters, soup kitchens, after-school programs, and food banks would be on the agenda. It wasn't world-changing, but it was good.

More broadly, I hoped the more politically useful we were the more we would matter inside the West Wing, and the more we mattered the more we could accomplish. We planned to continue to make our policy case and lay out arguments to our White House colleagues for why the president needed to fulfill his promises. But if the policy people remained hostile to us, and the legislative liaisons weren't helpful, I hoped we could now earn the ultimate trump card by the election—that the political folks would be our principal advocates. I was well educated in Washington's ways—politics equalled power and we needed power.

Attempts to pass the charity-friendly CARE Act only reinforced our need to have someone fighting on our side.

In early 2002, donations to charities were down dramatically. The previous December we had produced a two-inch pile of news reports about the charity crisis. By April we could have produced triple that amount. But no one in the West Wing, only one or two Republicans in Congress, and a Democrat or two wanted to help.

Rick Santorum was the lone Republican senator who cared about our bill. Santorum, number three in the Republican leadership, went into meeting after meeting lobbying for action. He tried every variant on every pitch he could possibly make. During one weekly meeting with Republican senators he made a political argument: helping charities could appeal to minority communities. The next week he tried a moral argument: charities are shutting their doors, we laud charities for being better than government, how can we not help? He lobbied senators on the floor and in their offices. First his colleagues laughed. Then, as he persisted, they told him to zip it. They had heard enough. A senior leadership staff member was clearest: "Forget about the f$&^ing CARE Act." There were other priorities. The charities just weren't that important. Maybe next year.

Joe Lieberman was the lone Democratic advocate in the Senate. His problem was convincing his colleagues that this bill—unlike the House bill—was silent about hiring rights, which it was. Two senators, Jack Reed from Rhode Island and Dick Durbin from Illinois, worked hard to block the bill from coming up for a vote. Senator Daschle offered no help either, other than encouraging incumbent senators in tight races to sign on as sponsors of the bill. Doing so would make it harder for a Republican opponent to label them as being "anti-God." Still, he didn't want it actually passed because that would be a victory for the president. Daschle had once called the bill "representative of what we can accomplish in Washington when we put partisanship and politics aside and focus on what matters." But that was immediately after 9/11 and before the dawn of an election year. Apparently he didn't care about the poor during an election year.

All of these problems could have been overcome by the president. He knew how to spend political capital. In 2002 he had a lot of it and was using it to get a Republican majority in the Senate. With favorability ratings near 80 percent and job approval ratings only slightly behind that, getting the charity act passed wasn't heavy lifting.

After 9/11, President Bush initiated weekly breakfasts with Senate and House leaders. During the first few months of national unity, they had been cordial breakfasts of understanding. As life got back to normal and politics resumed in earnest, however, they became politically contentious. The president could have used those breakfasts for his antipoverty efforts, but he didn't. Our struggle was to figure out some way to get the Legislative Affairs folks, or Karl, or Andy, or *somebody* to tell the president we could get the faith-based bill passed, so he would push it at a breakfast. Some weeks we were told it was definitely on the agenda. Most weeks we didn't hear anything.

Obviously, there was a lot on the president's mind. There was a war on terror, the impending war with Iraq, daily threats to American security, and a shaky American economy. But he knew the huge problems the charitable world was facing. He talked about them. In April 2002, he laid out the problem in a speech to religious and charity leaders: "America's Second Harvest, the country's largest hunger relief charity, reports that more than 80 percent of its affiliates face increased demands for food, while 40 percent have seen a significant drop in food donations and funding. That's a problem. In Northern California the United Way is facing an unprecedented fundraising shortfall for 2001. . . . The group's leader said this, 'I don't think we've ever had a drop-off of this magnitude. It affects our ability to serve our community.' And I agree. Many people in this room, many people whose sole purpose is to help an American in need, are confronting greater needs with fewer resources. And our government must recognize the problem and deal with it in a constructive way."

A few days later, at a campaign event, he challenged the Senate "to pass the faith-based initiative for the good of America. It is compassionate to aggressively fight poverty in America. It is conservative to encourage work and community spirit and responsibility and the values that often come from faith. And with this approach, we can change lives one soul at a time, and make a real difference in the lives of our citizens."

But he didn't seem to mean it. All the public talk rested on no private works by him, and in private he could have made it happen.

Jim and I grew increasingly frustrated. In mid-May Jim fired off an e-mail to his superiors: "The references to FB [faith-based] issues in welfare speeches and education events, while welcome, do not effectively move the legislation. We have waited for a high-level call from the West Wing to [Senate Finance Committee Chairman Max] Baucus for nearly two weeks, to no avail (the request that Sec. O'Neil [*sic*] call also went on deaf ears). Senate Finance, meanwhile, schedules trade and welfare reform because that is what the West Wing is calling for. . . . I don't know what I can do more under this present system other than to say that the current path we are on is likely to leave the FB legislation lingering."

No one responded to the e-mail. Did President Bush really care about the compassion agenda? Or did he just not know that his staff wasn't on board? Those were the two questions I asked myself and Jim asked himself and everyone else in our office asked as well. We felt like teenage girls plucking daisies, saying, "He loves me, he love me not. He loves me . . ." The president talked repeatedly about how important the initiative was. I couldn't believe it was a fraud. He cared about the issue too much. I knew that. But why wasn't his passion translating into leadership? That I couldn't figure. I didn't go any deeper. I didn't want to.

Between June and the election we visited all twenty targeted races. I traveled out to Denver for a rally for the besieged Senator Wayne Allard, who was running against U.S. Attorney Tom Strickland. The polls showed Allard behind. Allard's staff worked with a pastor to fill an old Safeway store-turned-church with a thousand clergy and community leaders. The church's pastor addressed the audience, talking about the community's needs and how much Wayne Allard cared. I got up and talked about how committed the president was to compassionate conservatism and to making sure that everyone felt they were part of the American Dream. One of the most vital parts of that was having the right men and women in Congress. Wayne Allard was one of those men, I said, and he was needed. I ignored the fact that he had been absolutely silent on compassion issues until that point in his Senate career. The event was part old-fashioned revival and part political tent meeting. In November Allard surprised pollsters by winning by five points. Was it all because of the meeting? Of course not. But did those thousand people tell their congregations, Bible study groups, prayer groups, volunteer groups, service groups, and Girl Scout leaders about Wayne Allard's faith and commitment to serving all of Colorado? Yes.

Most roundtables were smaller. Jim traveled to Little Rock to campaign for Senator Tim Hutchinson. At a small meeting with thirty or so community and church leaders, he toured a local soup kitchen where both men served meals for the cameras, and met with a few of the homeless. That campaign was one of the tougher ones for us to stomach. Senator Hutchinson, running on a pro-family and pro-faith platform, had ditched his family for one of his staffers. His Democratic opponent, Mark Pryor, was a devout Christian and cancer survivor who cared about families and the poor. We should have held the roundtable event with him. Unfortunately, he was in the wrong party. Fortunately, he won.

In November we celebrated 19 out of 20 wins. Mark Pryor was the only happy blemish. The only political hiccup came in mid-September when Tom Edsall, a veteran *Washington Post* reporter, called to say he was working on a piece describing how Republicans were using the faith-based initiative to woo voters. He had figured out what was going on. We huddled with the communications shop, indignant at the report.

A funny thing happens in the White House: you acquire the passionate, uncontrolled urge to defend yourself regardless of how true or false an accusation. This same instinct exists elsewhere, including in business, but it is especially strong behind those iron gates. An almost frightening inability to admit a mistake to the outside world infects you. To publicly admit a mistake, confess a wrong, or reveal a failure is inconceivable. The problem isn't simple self-preservation, though there is plenty of that. The problem is the institution. No one wants to disgrace the place or to be seen as the person who messed up a presidency. Everyone from the lowest assistant to the highest Assistant feels the same way.

The Edsall story was a perfect example. He was absolutely correct, falling short only by not grasping the size of his story. He had only tracked down two or three of the events. Nevertheless, we were mad: it felt like he was after us. Our press shop responded with a statement: "The bottom line is that Jim [Towey] travels all over the country to talk about the president's faith-based initiative," and he visits with people regardless of political affiliation. This was true in general. It was certainly *not* true of the roundtables. Democratic candidates weren't invited. Yet no one else picked up on Edsall's piece, and our work remained covert in the final weeks of the campaign. As protection, we made an intensive effort to find a Democrat who would issue us an "invitation" for a conference in his district. No one in the office but Jim and I knew about the political strategy we had worked out with Mehlman, or that we both kept handy a copy of the political map with every state shaded to reveal its importance. Mine was taped to the pullout shelf on my desk. His was in a desk drawer. We never did anything without looking at them.

A bigger idea soon fell into our laps. John Porter, head of the faith-based office at the Department of Education, put together a conference in his hometown of Pittsburgh for schools or charities that might be interested in applying for grants from Education. He had developed the idea while he was researching for the *Unlevel Playing Field* report how the department interacted with faith-based groups. The biggest problem was that not enough faith-based groups were applying. The process intimidated them, government confused them, and most small groups didn't know where to start. He put together a binder outlining the process, giving a synopsis of grant programs, and generally making the grant world more understandable. I spoke on the first day, welcoming people in the name of the White House. When I first heard about the conference I expected maybe fifty people. There were 750.

I returned to Washington and started lobbying Jim. I wanted to help set up huge regional conferences in major cities to educate social service leaders on grant applications. What John Porter was doing for Education we needed to do for the entire government. It wasn't sexy, and the information might be boring, but showing organizations how to navigate the grant process could be the most important thing we would ever do. It was something tangible for charities.

There would be one more bonus. If we had as many people as the Department of Education had, we would be accomplishing the same thing politically on a national level that we had done locally with our roundtables. It wasn't a hard sell to anyone. Our first conference was held a few months later, at the height of the campaign season in Georgia, where an all-out but long-shot effort was under way to upset a popular Democratic governor and a respected Democratic senator.

On our staff was a former Office of Management and Budget counsel, Rebecca Beynon, now serving as our general counsel. Tall, perpetually smiling, with rosy cheeks and an affinity for gardening, she was ferociously smart. While Jim and I were busy politicking, she was almost single-handedly researching, writing, and vetting documents about how faith-based groups could and should interact with the federal government. Rebecca did more to lower the barriers to faith-based participation in government than any other person. And she wasn't terribly religious—to her, faith-based groups had a right to receive funds as a matter of justice.

To tackle some of the most common questions of small faith-based or secular community groups, she created a one-stop guide. It was full of frequently asked questions. *How could a small group apply for a grant?* There are government employees who work full-time assisting groups with their applications. *Could a faith-based group have a religious name and still be eligible for federal grants?* Probably, though they could run into problems. *Could they hire or fire based on faith?* It depended on the rule, and the underlying law.

During her research, Rebecca discovered things that encouraged us, but she also discovered some inconvenient facts. First, on the encouraging side, there *were* genuinely silly laws and regulations that prevented some faith-based (and non-faith-based) groups from getting government grants. These regulations could be eliminated. In one instance, the Metropolitan Council for Jewish Poverty was denied a grant *application* because it had a religious-sounding name. The organization was thoroughly secular. On the other hand, in the category of inconvenient facts, religious groups had encountered very few instances of actual problems with their hiring practices. Alarmed, we looked under every rock and rule and regulation and report. Finding these examples became a huge priority. Without them, the powerful political rhetoric of government discrimination against faith-based groups of religious hiring would have to disappear. We recruited people who worked on faith-based matters in the federal agencies to help us look. If President Bush was making the world a better place for faith-based groups, we had to show it was a really bad place to begin with.

But in fact, it really wasn't that bad at all. One of the reasons was that most of the faith-based groups that did contract with the federal government were large and well lawyered. They had long ago figured out how to deal with pesky rules and bureaucrats. The federal government had been contracting with faith-based social service groups for as long as it had been contracting with private organizations. Between Catholic Charities and Lutheran Social Services alone, for example, more than $1.5 billion went to faith-based groups every year. But their activity had come at a spiritual cost. They were, as organizations, largely secular.

But the compassionate-conservative goal from the movement's inception more than a decade earlier had focused on the little guys. These small faith-based organizations—usually with one or two staff members—were the life-giving forces in many urban and rural neighborhoods. They had been founded by people who saw a need, started serving, and ended up building an organization out of necessity. And they were highly spiritual. Any previous thoughts of working with the federal government had been too intimidating to them. Washington was a long way from their homes and they didn't know anyone there. They couldn't afford lobbyist, consultants, or lawyers.

We hoped the conferences would help them. But we had no idea how many, if any, were interested in a White House conference on federal grants. For a test run, we did a mailing to every church, synagogue, mosque, and social service organization within two hundred miles of Atlanta, about 20,000 invitations. Within days we saw the demand. Some 2,500 people signed up and we reached capacity within forty-eight hours. Another 1,000 were turned away. President Bush's assessment that the armies of compassion were there to be mobilized was truer than even he realized.

The early September meeting in Atlanta was more crowded

than we expected. When the doors opened, people rushed for seats. Hundreds of people without invitations showed up in hopes of getting in. We had to create instant overflow rooms. The crowd was diverse. At least half the audience was black and another sizeable chunk was Hispanic. The president sent a video greeting and Secretary of Education Rod Paige gave an address. People stayed all day long and took copious notes. Our invitation to them to a White House conference marked the first time the government had ever reached out to communities that serve the poor to *give* them something.

Minority communities like these had long been part of the Democratic party, as reliable as the public employees unions. But their support had been greeted with a certain arrogance by the Democratic powers. They were expected to vote Democratic, expected to help recruit others, and to get little attention, respect, or resources in return.

The conference itself was mind-numbingly boring. Imagine the worst conference you have ever attended, and then imagine dousing it with presentations about government regulations. We tried to make it entertaining, but there are only so many fun ways to explain how to fill out a grant application or how to avoid a legal problem.

Yet people were very hopeful. One person after another came up to me and thanked me for being part of this and for caring about groups like theirs. Some came up and said, "You know, I never thought I would have said this but thank God for George W. Bush. He cares about the poor. God *bless* him." They had every reason to be hopeful. Visions of grants danced in their eyes—not multimillion-dollar grants for a building or for expanding to five cities, but for small grants so they could start paying the single mom who volunteered at the food bank but who could really use $10 an hour. These grants could let them buy books that weren't falling apart or build a real playground.

I shared their excitement. This is what the compassion initiative was meant to be. Bush had opened the first speech of his first presidential campaign, the $8 billion compassion speech, with these words, "For many people . . . addiction and abandonment and stolen childhood [are] a distant land, another world. But it is America. And these are not strangers, they are citizens, Americans, our brothers and sisters. In their hopes, we find our duties. In their hardship, we must find our calling, to serve others, relying on the goodness of America and the boundless grace of God." In a ballroom in Atlanta, the city of my mother's disillusionment, the faith-based initiative was living up to its calling.

Yet it broke my heart. We were, in some ways, behaving exactly like those Democratic leaders who presumed support but gave nothing in return. Or maybe we did worse by raising false hopes. Billions had been promised—$8 billion in the first year alone. We were $7,969,000,000 short of that promise. This was halfway through the next year. There should have been $16 billion. All we had managed to get in the federal budget for the Compassion Capital Fund was $30 million. The difference had nothing to do with 9/11. It had everything to do with White House indifference, bipartisan Capitol Hill indifference, and interest group indifference. Maybe one out of five hundred of the people in the room in Atlanta would actually get a grant, probably fewer.

My hope was for the year to come, and political plays were going to do the trick. The congressional funding process for the next fiscal year still lay before us, and with our new relevance to the White House political affairs shop, it stood to reason that we had much to gain.

I had asked Ralph Reed to drop by the conference for lunch. He had left the Christian Coalition nearly three years before. His eight-year enterprise of building and rearranging the religious conservative movement had taken its toll. Though everyone who resigns "to spend more time with their family" usually means they have either been fired or are about to get divorced, Ralph really did leave to spend more time with his family. He left Tidewater, Virginia, and moved home to Georgia. A future political run loomed (in 2005 he would declare his candidacy for lieutenant governor in Georgia), but for now he was building a private consulting firm.

He had been invaluable to the Bush team during the 2000 campaign, raising more than $100,000, counseling the campaign on how to cultivate the religious conservative vote, and working in South Carolina to deliver the state for Bush after the crushing New Hampshire primary. He was close to the president and to Rove. I hoped he would see the conference, call Karl, and tell him what an amazing occurrence it was. The more Karl liked it, the more power we would have to get money for groups like those in the room.

Ralph surveyed the enormous ballroom with wide eyes. He looked back at me. "Do you realize what you've done here? Do you realize what this is? This is what Republicans have been trying to do for the last twenty years. For the last twenty years we've tried to find a way to get this kind of an audience into a room. Does Karl know about this?"

Ralph knew why I had invited him. He pulled out his cell phone, punched in a number, and exclaimed, "Karl, I'm down here in Atlanta at the faith-based conference. You won't believe what we've got here. You've got three thousand people, mostly minorities, applauding a stinkin' *video* of the president. This is unbelievable. *This is unbelievable!!*"

The next day in the White House mess, Karl saw Jim and me as we were eating. "Towey! Towey! Kuo! Atlanta sounded good. Kinda sounds like something we need to be doing more of, huh? Let's do more."

More than a dozen conferences with more than 20,000 faith and community leaders were held in 2003 and 2004 in every significant battleground state, including two in Florida, one in Miami ten days before the 2004 election. Their political power was incalculable. They were completely off the media's radar screen.

While the conferences were being birthed, we were also figuring out what to do with the Compassion Capital Fund. Originally promised at $200 million per year, then cut in early 2001 to $100 million, and then again to $30 million, it was the only faith-based money we had to distribute. The fund functioned as a sort of venture capital source for the best charities. Research was to be undertaken to discover the most effective and efficient social service groups. Noteworthy groups that wanted to expand their existing programs could apply, as could groups that needed guidance and help on improving their work. Our problem in the faith-based office was that we didn't actually control the money. The Department of Health and Human Services did.

Despite the White House's enormous powers, directly distributing money from grant programs isn't one of them. It is an executive body, not an administrative one. Therefore, all programs that give away money reside in such federal departments as Health and Human Services.

More than three hundred groups applied for grants from the Compassion Capital Fund. The money was earmarked for "intermediary" institutions that bridged the gap between government and small charities. These larger groups could then use the money to fund virtually any kind of group they chose, regardless of the group's religious content. The government could not give a grant to a proselytizing organization. But we could give money to a "public-private partnership" group, which in turn could give it to overtly religious groups, as long as the overall use of our money seemed to be aimed at the needy. Some people have called it a sophisticated money-laundering operation and others an innovative way to reach as many charities as possible. I believe it was the latter.

The grants process is fairly straightforward. Grants are received and then reviewed by peer groups. Grants are supposed to be reviewed "objectively," in line with the strict parameters of the grant request as published by the government. The National Science Foundation, for example, recruits peer-review panels of scientists to evaluate its grantees. The Compassion Capital Fund grants process differed slightly.

The faith-based policy world is fairly small. There are, at most, a hundred people in think tanks, foundations, major nonprofits, and the like who really work on these issues and who support the president. Virtually all of them are very compassionate and dedicated evangelical Christians who tend to be politically conservative. That meant that the group that gathered to review the applications was an overwhelmingly Christian group of wonks, ministers, and well-meaning types. They were supposed to review the application in a religiously neutral fashion, and assign each applicant a score on a range of 1–100. But their biases were transparent.

Many of the grant-winning organizations that rose to the top of this process were politically friendly to the administration. Bishop Harold Ray of Redemptive Life Fellowship Church in West Palm Beach had been one of the most vocal black voices supporting the president during the 2000 election. His newly created National Center for Faith-Based Initiatives somehow scored a 98 out of a possible 100 on the grading system used by the fund's "peer" reviewers. Pat Robertson's overseas aid organization, Operation Blessing, scored a 95.67. Nueva Esperanza, an umbrella of other Hispanic ministries, headed by President Bush's leading Hispanic ally, Luis Cortés (on *Time* magazine's list of the most influential evangelicals), received a 95.33. The Institute for Youth Development, which works to send positive messages to youth, earned a 94.67. The institute's head was a former Robertson staffer. Even more bizarre, a new organization called "We Care America" received a 99.67 on its grant review. It was the second-highest score. They called themselves a "network of networks," an "organizer of organizations." They had a staff of three, all from the world of Washington politics, and all very Republican. They were on tap to receive more than $2.5 million. To help the Department of Health and Human Services manage the program, an online National Resource Center was set up. That job was outsourced to an organization run by former Chuck Colson staffers.

All this information trickled in to our office when we requested updates on the Compassion Capital Fund. It took a while, but we finally got the list of recommended grantees. It was obvious that the ratings were a farce. National organizations like Big Brothers/Big Sisters of America scored an 85.33 while something called Jesus and Friends Ministry from California, a group with little more than a post office box, scored 89.33. Public/Private Ventures, arguably the nation's leading organization for maximizing program efficiency, scored only 78.

The more we looked at the list the more baffled we were. The numbers were not objective. Jesus and Friends doesn't score higher than Public/Private Ventures. But we couldn't do anything to change the scores. They were official. The top groups on the list were to be funded automatically, at their requested level, reaching as far down the list as the budget allowed. We had $30 million. It would cover only seventeen groups. The only thing we could do was cut the amount given to each organization so we could reach down the list a bit further.

Much of our fear about the list was political. Once the list was made public it would show once and for all that the initiative was purely about paying off political friends for their support. The irony, of course, is that in this instance the White House really did have nothing to do with the grantees. They had been selected by a federal department.

White House politicos didn't need to roll up their sleeves and dictate who got money from a paltry $30 million program. The political appointees in the federal departments knew what they were supposed to do. It was exceptional only in its efficiency. They performed as political appointees were supposed to per-form—they carried out the White House's will. Some in the press would later "expose" that we in the White House had doled out grants to friends. They were technically wrong. We didn't do it. We didn't have to. The White House influence was so great that its will was carried out by other appointees in other departments without thinking. It was perfect government. Somehow, the irony escaped me: that we feared another agency might expose us as political while we were using politics to advance our status in the White House.

Just recently, my wife Kim and I were together with a group of friends and acquaintances. Someone mentioned that I used to work at the White House in the faith-based office. A woman piped up and said, "Really? Wow, I was on the peer-review panel for the first Compassion Capital Fund." I asked her how she liked it and she said it was fun. She talked about how the government employees gave them grant review instructions—look at everything objectively against a discreet list of requirements and score accord-ingly. "But," she said with a giggle, "when I saw one of those non-

Christian groups in the set I was reviewing. I just stopped looking at them and gave them a zero."

At first I laughed. A funny joke. Not so much. She was proud and giggling and didn't get that there was a problem with that. I asked if she knew of others who'd done the same. "Oh sure, a lot of us did." She must have seen my surprise. "Was there a problem with that?"

I told her there was actually a huge problem with that. The programs were to be faith-neutral. Our goal was equal treatment for faith-based groups, not special treatment for them. This was a smart and accomplished Christian woman. She got it immediately. But what she had done comported with her understanding of what the faith initiative was supposed to do—help Christian groups—and with her faith. She wanted people to know Jesus.

These were the new problems for Christians in politics. We weren't on the outside looking in anymore. We were running programs, agencies, the country.

CHAPTER FOURTEEN

That's the Way
We Do It, Baby

On November 5, 2002, President Bush got what he didn't get after the 2000 election: affirmation. It was vindication. During the fall he'd stumped tirelessly for Republican candidates. He meant what he told me in Austin—he was going to spend his political capital on something that mattered. He used his post-9/11 strength to deliver a Republican Congress. Republicans retook the Senate, added five seats to their majority in the House, and held unquestionable political dominance.

Religious conservatives were emboldened. The Family Research Council circulated an analysis of the midterm elections showing once again how important religious conservatives were to Republican success. In Georgia, where Saxby Chambliss had managed to upset the incumbent Democratic Senator Max Cleland, for instance, 76 percent of self-identified religious conservatives in Georgia voted for Chambliss. Various pro-life groups submitted their to-do lists for the new Congress. Incoming Senate Majority Leader Trent Lott promised the morning after the election that he would introduce and pass legislation banning a brutal but rare late-term abortion procedure called "partial birth," in which the child is partially delivered before being killed. "I will call it up, we will pass it, and the president will sign it. I'm making that commitment—you can write it down."

The White House wasn't happy with Lott or with the enthusiasm. Immediately after the election, Tim Goeglein held a happy conference call with social conservative leaders and begged for patience. They knew the president's faith, he reminded them. He was a faithful believer and a faithful friend to social conservatives because he was a social conservative. But please, Goeglein implored, don't push things too quickly. Just wait a little bit and your patience will be rewarded. No one wanted a reprise of the post-'94 election exuberance. They waited.

We didn't wait. Realizing charity legislation of any type wasn't going to get passed in 2002, we found a way to bypass Congress. Presidents have broad authority to sign executive orders to accomplish things without legislation. They don't have the permanent effect of legislation, however. Another president can come in and abolish an executive order with his signature. Nevertheless, an executive order was better than nothing, and we prepared to announce a barrage of them in mid-December.

Our attempt for political power wasn't paying the dividends we had hope for. We were popular with Karl Rove, the Office of Political Affairs, and the candidates we helped elect. But when it came down to getting new compassion proposals inserted into the president's budget and State of the Union address, we came up short.

The items we proposed weren't new. They were taken directly from the president's own list of promised compassion programs. We requested more money for the compassion fund, money for mentoring prisoners' children, and money for teenage mothers. Everything was shot down.

The whole thing was getting very old. Many a morning I wondered if I was going to work to accomplish something—however small—for the poor and for God or if I was just propping up the compassion illusion for political purposes. Was I using the poor, Jesus, and my own life for a lie? At the time my answer was no. I knew what it was like to lose my heart and faith in politics. That wasn't going to happen again. Yet the questions and doubts grew every day.

Then came December 4. *Esquire* magazine published an article by Ron Suskind on Karl Rove. Unbeknownst to John DiIulio, he was the main source. Suskind and DiIulio had been talking on and off for several months. Suskind was well known as the author of a beautiful book called *A Hope in the Unseen,* about the troubled life of an inner-city teenager trying to make it in the Ivy League. It had won a Pulitzer Prize. He was also well known to us at the White House as the author of another *Esquire* article, about Karen Hughes, that contained quotes from Chief of Staff Andy Card that Card maintains he never made.

His new article was to be about the White House after Karen Hughes's departure, and Suskind promised DiIulio there were lots of sources, lots of people talking, and John's perspective would bring added flavor.

The article wasn't as advertised. DiIulio critiqued the Bush White House for its lack of a serious policy apparatus. Policy wasn't made by philosophy, John said, but by politics. "There is no precedent in any modern White House for what is going on in this one: a complete lack of a policy apparatus. What you've got is everything—and I mean everything—being run by the political arm." The article went on at length detailing Karl Rove's perceived power.

John publicly apologized for the statements and questioned some of the quotes attributed to him. In the midst of the controversy, *Esquire* released a five-page, single-spaced letter from DiIulio to Suskind outlining his critiques, which supported the quotes in the article. However, it also revealed that John had praised President Bush, beginning with these words:

> In my view, President Bush is a highly admirable person of enormous personal decency. He is a godly man and a moral leader. He is much, much smarter than some people—including some of his own supporters and advisers—seem to suppose. He inspires personal trust, loyalty, and confidence in those around him. In many ways he is all heart. Clinton talked "I feel your pain." But as Bush showed in the immediate aftermath of 9/11, he truly does feel deeply for others and loves this country with a passion.

When it came to policy, however, DiIulio launched tough critiques:

Beside the tax cut, which was cut-and-dried during the campaign, and the education bill, which was really a Ted Kennedy bill, the administration has not done much, either in absolute terms or in comparison to previous administrations at this stage, on domestic policy. There is a virtual absence as yet of any policy accomplishments that might, to a fair-minded non-partisan, count as the flesh on the bones of so-called compassionate conservatism. There is still two years, maybe six, for them to do more and better on domestic policy, and, specifically, on the compassion agenda.

It was the first time that anyone from the inside had substantively critiqued the administration. That it came from someone as learned and respected as DiIulio only amplified the story's power. And that John, heartsick that his hastily made criticisms of staff now seemed far too sweeping, and troubled that the article was unfair to Rove, publicly and privately apologized to all concerned only made the story more poignant.

In most ways his apology let the White House off the hook. But not in all ways. A West Wing friend called to say the president heard about the article as he walked from the Oval Office to the OEOB. He was angry. "Well," he yelled through the stairwell, "is he right or isn't he? Have we done compassion or haven't we? I wanna know."

An hour later we got the first and only call from the deputy chief of staff Josh Bolten's office requesting an urgent "compassion meeting." In the two years since the transition, it was the first time the president's senior staff fully engaged in the compassion agenda. Not to do so would have been politically devastating. Public perception of Bush's compassion was vital to his presidency. Having it seriously undermined so that women, minorities, clergy, and evangelicals were hearing about it raised the worst specter of all—that George W. Bush was sounding Clintonian.

The president's question first needed to be answered. He wanted to know how much we had spent on compassion programs in his first two years in office. We made some calls and did some calculations and discovered that if we applied his definition of compassion to federal social service programs, we were actually spending about $20 million a year *less* on them than before he had taken office. That number never actually made it to the president. The question was deemed, "still in process of being accounted for."

The uproar prompted my old Empower America friend Pete Wehner (also DiIulio's good friend) to send out an e-mail making his own pitch for a more serious emphasis on the compassionate-conservative agenda. Pete's White House role was evolving into thinker-in-chief. He was Gerson's speechwriting deputy, but Pete was also becoming a one-person think tank, presenting different ideas to senior staff. He would eventually take that job formally, becoming head of Karl's Office of Strategic Initiatives.

To Karl, Josh Bolten, Margaret Spellings, Karen Hughes (who had already returned to Texas), and others, he wrote, "The faith-based initiative is largely what [the president] understands compassionate conservatism to be about. Let me be specific: it doesn't have to do with providing more and better child safety seats or improving DNA analysis; it has to do with helping 'the least of these'—those whose lives have been broken, who are desperately in need of another caring, concerned human being, who are often poor and almost always facing hardships." He was exactly right.

Two hours after the Bolten call, Jim Towey, John Bridgeland, Margaret Spellings and her new deputy Jay Lefkowitz, Mike Gerson, Pete Wehner, I, and a member of the domestic policy staff in charge of compassion issues met to figure out what to do. Suddenly everything was on the table. "We gotta get some compassion stuff out there now," Margaret said. "What have we got?"

I wanted to laugh, but it was far more sad than funny.

"Well, I have an idea," the other domestic policy staffer said. "I hear chronic homelessness is a problem. I read an article where there are thirty thousand homeless people in America. Maybe we could do something to help them."

"I think it is just a few more than that actually," I volunteered. The actual figure at that time was over 750,000.

"What else have we got?" Margaret asked.

We went around the room and threw out ideas. We even talked

about some of the president's past promises. During the campaign he had made a promise to launch a program aiding the children of prisoners. There were more than 2 million people in prison. That left many millions more of their children in society, often subjected to stigma and consigned to a future life of crime. Great mentoring programs existed that made a tangible difference in the lives of kids like these. Some $100 million had once been promised. A month earlier, however, it had been rejected in a policy review with Spellings, Rove, Josh Bolten, and others.

Jim, with a background in work with the elderly, volunteered that there were numerous elderly assistance programs that could be launched for relatively little money. Spellings thought that might work. Someone else talked about the problem of prison rape—that was shot down. Even if it was as big a problem as it appeared, President Bush couldn't be heard talking about it. It didn't sound presidential.

We left with an assignment. Within twenty-four hours we needed to come up with several one-page (two, if absolutely necessary) policy proposals for the president to review for the upcoming State of the Union address. Given all the president's unfulfilled compassion promises, it was an easy list to compile. Two days later the president chose three new programs. One was to provide a million new mentors for disadvantaged youth in poor middle schools. The second would provide mentors for all the children of prisoners. Third was a new program of vouchers for drug and alcohol treatment that could be used for explicitly religious recovery groups. It had taken a media scandal to get the West Wing to mobilize on compassion. More was accomplished that week because of that one magazine article than in the rest of the first six years of the compassion initiative. (A notable exception was the White House's efforts on HIV/AIDS in Africa. Although the actual money given to Africa was far less than promised, under President Bush the United States is now the greatest supplier of assistance to the suffering in Africa, where nearly 20 million children will be orphaned by AIDS-related deaths by 2010.)

• • •

A week later, at our second White House Conference held in Philadelphia, President Bush signed executive orders to show progress with the initiative. It was mostly symbolic stuff: religious icons didn't have to be taken down if an institution received a federal grant. Members of the clergy could serve on a group's board of directors, even if it received federal money. Religious names didn't automatically disqualify a group from receiving a grant. Politically, we struck gold with our religious conservative friends. Looking for things to announce in Philadelphia, we discovered a fairly obscure federal rule prohibiting government contractors who received more than $10,000 to hire or fire based on faith. These contractors were *not* grant recipients for any federal program. They provided services for the government, ranging from plumbing to consulting. And the pool of money for contractors was minuscule—a small fraction of a percent of the nearly $3 trillion budget. So the executive order that eliminated the old restraint had virtually no real effect—but it was still symbolically powerful.

Our conservative friends were thrilled. From their perspective the president tackled religious liberty with a pen stroke. Religious groups were now safe. Baptists didn't have to hire Buddhists. Pat Robertson praised the president for his bold action. Jay Sekulow, leader of the conservative opposition to the ACLU, said, "The president is taking the kind of leadership that will ensure fair and equal treatment for religious organizations." It was straight from the White House talking points sheet I had helped a friend in communications draft.

In reality, the event was a betrayal. And it was a betrayal in our friends' faces.

Though I disagreed with religious conservatives about the timing of the fight for a religious organization to be able to preserve its religious identity by hiring only people who shared their faith, I agreed with the principle. A religious group has to be able to preserve its religious orientation. From the most progressive church to the most conservative one and from Anabaptists to Zoroastrians, religious organizations have the right to hire only those people who share their faith. I take the side of the majority in the unanimous Supreme Court case upholding the matter. But now we let our friends think we'd done something big. We had done something very, very small and allowed them to think it was very, very big.

In some ways the press only helped us in our deceit. As we expected—and as we came to count on—the press wanted to write a single story: how President Bush's faith-based initiative was brutalizing the historic wall between church and state and how it was political payment to the religious Right.

When the initiative began and John longed for the bipartisanship the president still talked about, accusations that we were too conservative or too religious were disastrous. But now it just showed Christians across the country how very religious the president was willing to be. Evangelical distrust and contempt for the "mainstream media" basically followed a simple formula: if mainstream media attacked a conservative for being too conservative or a Christian for being too Christian, then evangelicals believed both conservative and Christian were doing the right thing.

It all played out exactly as we hoped. Rather than report on how grand the president's announcement was and how little was actually done, the press took the "separation of church and state" story and ran with it: "Bush eases requirements on faith-based charities," "Bush to bypass Congress on faith-based charity grants," and "Bush moves on faith-based plan that OKs religious bias by government contractors." Editorials by such major papers as the *Washington Post* decried the orders, calling them "Faith-Based by Fiat." Liberal leaders stepped into line. Representative John Conyers: "All Americans should find abhorrent a government policy that allows for a religious or racial litmus test when hiring with taxpayer money a person to serve soup." Ira Forman, executive director of the National Jewish Democratic Council: "It is simply wrong for federal contractors to discard the résumés of people with names that sound 'too Jewish' or 'too Muslim' when hiring substance abuse counselors and other professionals with government money."

•   •   •

December's craziness subsided, and in January 2003, the president announced the new compassion programs in his State of the Union address.

> I propose a $450 million initiative to bring mentors to more than a million disadvantaged junior high students and children of prisoners. Government will support the training and recruiting of mentors; yet it is the men and women of America who will fill the need. One mentor, one person can change a life forever. And I urge you to be that one person.
>
> Another cause of hopelessness is addiction to drugs. Addiction crowds out friendship, ambition, moral conviction, and reduces all the richness of life to a single destructive desire. As a government, we are fighting illegal drugs by cutting off supplies and reducing demand through anti-drug education programs. Yet for those already addicted, the fight against drugs is a fight for their own lives. Too many Americans in search of treatment cannot get it. So tonight I propose a new $600 million program to help an additional 300,000 Americans receive treatment over the next three years.

It was exciting. *This* was what the initiative was always supposed to be about. The $6 billion per year in charity credits was going to spur billions more in private giving, and the $2 billion in spending was going to provide powerful weapons to help the suffering.

Unfortunately, the excitement was tempered by two realities. First, there wasn't really any money available. The Iraq War was eating up countless billions, and the president's tax cut, combined with a less than booming economy, meant that government revenues were through the floor. The federal deficit had reached historic levels. Our announcements were actually in jeopardy before they were made. That is why two of the items—the million mentors for disadvantaged kids in middle schools and the mentors for all 1.5 million kids with a mother or father in prison—were combined into one program.

Second, the numbers weren't what they seemed. Politicians,

regardless of party, want their announcements to sound grand: $50 million a year doesn't sound nearly as good as a $500 million, ten-year program. Both, however, are technically accurate. The big-money programs are almost always spread out over ten years. When President Bush's critics trashed his $1.7 trillion tax cut, for example, many listeners missed the fact that it was spread over ten years and even then it was more expensive in later years, commonly called the "out years." When the president announced our "$400 million program" for mentoring, it was actually a four-year program: $50 million in each of the first and second years, $100 million in the third, and $200 million in the fourth. But since budgets are set (or reset) every year, future plans don't always mean much.

Even if the program is included in the president's budget it won't necessarily get funded. It is just a proposal. It will only get funded if the House and Senate agree. And they only agree to the White House's proposed funding levels for certain things. They *never* agree to everything. The White House has to make clear, in quiet negotiations, what it *really* wants. Some presidential announcements are for things the White House already knows it will jettison at the first opportunity. Others are genuine commitments.

Within three weeks of the president's grand announcement it became clear the White House wasn't going to fight for mentoring or vouchers any harder than it had fought for compassion programs. It wasn't a big secret. Friends at the Office of Management and Budget let me know that they would try to get some money for the program but that they couldn't make any promises.

That was just how this White House worked. In some ways it was the most brilliant political maneuvering possible. In others it was the most cynical.

Our White House understood both the news cycle and America's attention span. It realized the latter was short and the former manic. The American public has a notoriously brief attention span even for major news. Within weeks even a tsunami can become old news. When it comes to politics, the vast majority of people look at headlines, watch a thirty-second story, and then move on to think about *American Idol*, dinner, or just about anything else more captivating.

The media markets make this worse, not better. The twenty-four-hour news cycle must be fed constantly with new stuff, and there are more and more outlets for it. There are Internet bloggers and news Web sites, the network news, cable news, weekly and monthly magazines, and daily newspapers—and that's just some of the categories. Each category is broken down into incomprehensible niches. For instance, our media shop produced a thirty-six-page spreadsheet of just the top Hispanic news outlets in America. The White House has similar lists for every conceivable group. If the president makes an environmental announcement about fish, there are no fewer than twelve outlets catering to the bass-fishing segment of the public. The White House knew every single outlet and made sure that every outlet was covered with regularity.

Unless a news story is a major one, the media churns through it quickly, keeping the public entertained with ever newer stories. The rush for new stories makes it harder for reporters to dig down deep on a story. So they are easily fooled.

The White House understood this. Everything it did catered to it.

For the harried public, there was the banner. During the 2000 campaign, a communications guy had come up with the idea to have short slogans placed on a screen behind the president at every appearance. It continued once he took office. For faith-based speeches, for instance, there was typically a blue screen with light blue letters spelling "Compassion in Action." Even someone with the news on mute understood what the speech was about. There was also the visual. Concern about the scenery or setting behind the president was hardly new to our press shop. What was new were the former TV news and entertainment producers who worked tirelessly on the lighting and setting to appeal equally to those who glanced at the TV and those really watching.

Keeping the media busy was easier. They were fed a constant barrage of little announcements with big ones sprinkled in. The big ones were then quickly followed by more little announcements. There wasn't any letup. Also, because the communications shop kept reporters at arm's length, the reporters didn't get the inside information or tips to give them a heads up for what was coming next. Already struggling reporters were always behind.*

This approach allowed the White House to make grand announcements and then do nothing to implement them with impunity. Nowhere was this clearer than in compassion announcements. In May 2001, for instance, the president announced a new $3 billion drug treatment initiative. By December 2003 not a dime had been spent. The 2003 State of the Union address announced our three programs—but they promptly disappeared. Two years later, the president announced yet another new program to help prevent teen violence. It was touted as a $100 million program. That "$100 million," however, was to be pulled out of the already dramatically underfunded Compassion Capital Fund. It was a mirage. (And one that continues: Whatever became of President Bush's three enormous promises after Hurricane Katrina? It is easy to remember his speech, in short sleeves in New Orleans, with that old building lit up behind him . . . but anything else?)

I had been around politics long enough not to be shocked. The announcements were smart politics because absolutely no one called them on anything (with the exception of the infamous "Mission Accomplished" banner when the president declared the Iraq War essentially over). As a Christian, however, what appalled me was that this was occurring under the aegis of both the president's faith and his heartfelt plea to "restore honor and dignity" to the White House. This strategy wasn't about honor or dignity, it was raw politics of the sort that old-time political bosses would applaud. Even sadder, the Christian community that elected George W. Bush didn't see any of this. They couldn't; they trusted their Christian brother too much.

Christians trust their Christian president. This is true of their evangelical political leadership. But of greater consequence, for Christian moms who home-school their kids and Christian dads

---

* Reporters generally understood what was happening but couldn't do anything about it. As a friend at a major network said, "They [the White House communications shop] act like we are to bow at the imperial throne. But one day they'll get what they deserve."

coaching soccer and everyone who follows the Dobsons and Robertsons and Falwells, George W. Bush can really do no wrong. They assume that since he professes Jesus that he won't do the kinds of things other politicians have done—break promises, cover up mistakes, parse words, say half truths, be a politician. They figure he has surrounded himself with a staff full of other evangelicals to provide him with fellowship and accountability. That, after all, is the image carefully conveyed to them through religious surrogates.

They would be wrong on all fronts. George W. Bush loves Jesus. He is a good man. But he is a politician; a very smart and shrewd politician. And if the faith-based initiative was teaching me anything, it was about the president's capacity to care about perception more than reality. He wanted it to look good. He cared less about it being good.

Christian leaders, Christian media, and Christian writers, however, didn't dare question or challenge him or the White House. He wasn't a political leader to them, he was a brother in Christ—precisely what the White House wanted them to believe. A friend in a major pro-family organization said that in their regular polling they wouldn't even ask other Christians if they were disappointed with the president. They didn't want to know.

What they didn't get to see was what the White House thought of them. For most of the rest of the White House staff, evangelical leaders were people to be tolerated, not people who were truly welcomed. No group was more eye-rolling about Christians than the political affairs shop. They knew "the nuts" were politically invaluable, but that was the extent of their usefulness. Sadly, the political affairs folks complained most often and most loudly about how boorish many politically involved Christians were. They didn't see much of the love of Jesus in their lives.

Political Affairs was hardly alone. There wasn't a week that went by that I didn't hear someone in middle- to senior-levels making some comment or another about how annoying the Christians were or how tiresome they were, or how "handling" them took so much time.

National Christian leaders received hugs and smiles in person and then were dismissed behind their backs and described as "ridiculous," "out of control," and just plain "goofy." The leaders spent much time lauding the president, but they were never shrewd enough to do what Billy Graham had done three decades before, to wonder whether they were just being used. They were.

Nowhere was this clearer than with the National Day of Prayer. Since 1988, when President Reagan created it, the National Day of Prayer has been held every spring across the country and at the White House. It is a time for Christians to gather and pray for the nation and its leadership, glorify God, and preserve the nation's Christian heritage. It is organized and run by Shirley Dobson, James Dobson's wife.

At this White House, it was another one of the eye-rolling Christian events fixed on the president's calendar. But it served a powerful purpose—it placated Christian leadership. Those involved in the breakfast got to go on the radio with their listeners and describe their encounter with the president and their time in the White House. The event, however, held absolutely no significance. Congressman Tony Hall was one of the people who helped pass through Congress the bill creating the breakfast in the 1980s. He thought it would be a time for bringing diverse leaders together. He eventually stopped going, seeing the breakfasts as worthless. A key staffer called the breakfast a "Jacob and Esau thing," referring to the story in which a hungry Esau sold his divine birthright to Jacob for a bowl of breakfast cereal.

I fell in love with my fusion of Christianity and politics in 1987. For years I had wondered what it would be like to work in the White House improving and influencing our culture and politics for Jesus. I thought the enemy was the prevailing anti-God cultural and political forces, that is, Democrats and secularists. I never thought to worry about Republicans using Christians for their own political ends—Republicans like me.

We held conference after conference across America in politically important states. An average of 1,500 people per conference received important information, materials, and resources. And those 1,500 people walked away stunned and amazed at how much President Bush and his staff cared about them. Those 1,500 people were all leaders of larger organizations. They went back to their churches, nonprofit organizations, or places of work and told everyone else about what they had seen and done.

The conferences were hardly cheap. Each one cost about $100,000. And because the White House didn't have any real money of its own we had to get money from other agencies. That proved easy: if we ran into problems we called Karl's office and had him make a call. We took turns hitting up every major agency: Justice, Health and Human Services, Labor, Agriculture, the Agency for International Development, Education, and Housing and Urban Development. All it took was a call to the secretary's chief of staff. They knew we had Rove's blessing.

I continued to be surprised about comments I received during the conferences, mostly from minorities. One woman came up to me after one and said, "You know, I've got a son who works in Washington." I asked her whether he liked it and if she saw him. "Yes," she said, "I see him a lot on TV. He plays for the Redskins. But you know, that's not why I came up here to talk to you. I wanted to thank you for even coming. No one really listens to the black churches anymore. People don't visit except for election time and that's to take money and tell us we shouldn't vote for Republicans because they are all racists. Thank you for coming. We may not agree on everything but thank you. It means the world."

People in every city said the same thing. The sad truth was that the African-American church had become a ward of the Democratic Party. Once powerful and revolutionary, it had been taken for granted. Our little conferences weren't likely to swing 25 percent of the black electorate, but they could swing some in the regions where we went. It was the equivalent of Bill Clinton's 1993 attempt at evangelical Christian outreach, with one difference: our approach worked.

But our approach was wrong. When I joined John DiIulio at the White House in 2001, our goals were simple—we were going to be absolutely bipartisan, fight for the $8 billion per year promised in the Indianapolis "Duty of Hope" speech, actually implement Charitable Choice, help small charities whether faith-based or secular, navigate the maze of government grants, and institute the dozen or so programs the president promised.

What tripped us up and angered us were the radical demands of a few congressional staffers who wanted to use the initiative for political purposes to undermine Democrats, focus on religious hiring, use vouchers to support evangelical programs, and allow direct funding of religious groups.

But by early 2003, we were using conferences to reach out to potential "nontraditional" Republican voters; starting to implement a voucher program; touting our change in religious hiring rights on federal contracts; and helping oversee a cut-rate version of the Compassion Capital Fund that accidentally discriminated against non-Christian organizations.

Perhaps that is why I felt it was time to leave. I was growing less and less certain that I was doing anything more than campaigning. My original tour of duty was for three months. Two years was now in sight. My heart wasn't broken.

And it wouldn't be. Politics lost its claim on my life. I could finally say that. The only claim on my life belonged to God. Thank God.

CHAPTER FIFTEEN

Seeing Dimly, Seeing Clearly

On a Saturday night in April 2003, the night before Palm Sunday, I was dancing with my wife at a 1950s-themed party in support of a teen empowerment program. Political celebrities mixed with entertainment celebrities, most dressed as characters straight out of *Rebel Without a Cause*. Everyone looked weird. Bill Bennett did the twist in a big black T-shirt and baggy, faded jeans. Alberto Gonzales was getting sweaty with his wife. He looked like someone auditioning for a baby boomer version of *West Side Story*. Bo Derek watched from her table. The secretary of the interior danced. Bill O'Reilly was there but refusing to play along: he wore a suit and tie and sipped a martini. My White House departure was imminent. Kim and I toasted each other and kept on dancing.

On the way home, we drove down one of the prettiest stretches of road in Washington: Rock Creek Parkway. Four divided lanes wind north and south for four miles, sometimes together and sometimes not, through the largest city park in America. Natural rock walls line the sides of some of the road, and man-made rock barriers guard against cars tumbling into the great old creek that meanders toward the Potomac River. It is the kind of road that should be cast in any movie showing a couple in love driving together. I love this road.

Kim snoozed against the passenger window.

Slowly, and without my permission, my left foot started sliding toward me. I tried to push my foot back to its proper place. I couldn't. I concentrated and tried harder to push it away. An electric jolt stiffened my whole left side. For an amazed second or two I couldn't move half my body. My left arm started flailing up against the car door. I yelled. But before I could say more than a few syllables, my right side went instantly rigid as well. My right leg and foot slammed down on the accelerator. My head was pressed back into the seat. I couldn't move. I couldn't breathe. I couldn't gasp. It felt like I was drowning.

I want to say that I don't remember anything else, but unfortunately I do. They are the fragments of a nightmare. I see the car heading very, very fast at a wall. Then I see us in an oncoming lane of traffic. I hear Kim screaming. My head won't turn. I fade to black, with absolutely no white light at the end of the tunnel. (This lack of the bright light would haunt me for months before I relayed it to a friend, who gently said, "David, um, that is why they call it *blacking* out.")

I ended up in the George Washington University Hospital emergency room and learned that I had had a grand mal seizure. My wife was okay. It was about 12:30 A.M. on Palm Sunday morning.

Kim told me what had happened. She had grabbed the wheel and somehow managed to jerk the SUV, which was going eighty miles an hour, to the left so we wouldn't crash through the rock barriers and into the creek below. She had dodged oncoming traffic, cried out to God for help, and jerked the car back to the right. We wound up crashing on perhaps the only safe 150 feet we could have found on the entire parkway. It was as if we had been put there. Kim was fine. Not a scratch, not a bruise. The same couldn't be said for my bloody head.

I was quickly wheeled in for a CT scan. The technician came back and said he needed to run a few more tests. He wouldn't look me in the eyes. I asked what it was. He just looked grim and told me to be quiet.

Involuntarily I started saying, "Oh my God, oh my God, oh my God . . ." over and over and over again. My head was rocking back and forth. I want to say I displayed William Wallace's courage in *Braveheart*. I fear I was more like one of those people chased by a raptor in *Jurassic Park*.

Then slowly, I felt something. I sensed God. I just knew. I didn't see any bushes that burned or fire coming down from heaven, but there was real peace amid the horror. It felt as if a big, heavy down comforter was being pulled up over me from head to toe. I felt inexplicably safe. A voice I could almost hear with my ears said to me, "You will be okay. You will be okay. This is a battle, but you will be okay."

The doctors disagreed. I had a brain tumor. I had months or maybe just weeks.

Kim disagreed with them. She called everyone she knew in the middle of the night to have them pray. We had somehow survived the crash and it was Palm Sunday, at the beginning of Holy Week. It was, we reasoned, a good week for miracles and for faith.

The next morning Karl Rove was among the first people to call. "Hey buddy, rough night huh?" I filled him in briefly. "I know what you're going through. I've spent more days and nights of my life than I can count in a cancer ward. Darby [his wife] is a breast cancer survivor. I know what you are going through. You let me know if there is anything I can do, anything I can get. You are gonna make it through and I'm going to hang up now because I know you don't really want to be talking to me right now."

If I wasn't the last person Karl needed to be calling early on a Saturday morning, I was way down on the list. But as I had come to know, that was Karl, a peerless political operative with a soft heart. During the twenty-two months I had worked at the White House I was often tempted to view some of my colleagues with less than loving eyes. Their indifference or apathy appalled me. Ultimately, however, it was policy indifference and policy apathy. They were doing what they felt needed to be done to serve the president in the political White House. I disagreed—vehemently—but I couldn't dislike them. My health ordeal affirmed that assessment. White House Counsel Harriet Miers (later a Supreme Court nominee) wrote, "My home church is in Dallas. I had the blessing of being there for Easter. I requested prayers for you. . . . It was great to be able to describe such a remarkable young person with such an abiding faith as part of the President's staff. Quite a testimony for the Administration. I know you will feel the sustaining prayers offered by so many and the love felt by so many all over. May God hold you in his arms and bless you every minute of this ordeal." God listened to her and did hold us close.

From the moment I found Jesus—or Jesus found me—in high school, it was his peace I longed for. I didn't know what it meant or what it felt like. But wanting Jesus' peace made me ache. I knew what I wanted it to do: take away the tumult, ache, barbs, and fear, and take something to make everything better. I never thought I would find it in the helplessness of a brain tumor.

It was different than I thought. Fighting cancer and thereby coming closer to God was like being a rock under one of those dripping streams that eat you away over centuries. You have to be still enough to feel God hovering, and open enough to receive love from everyone God puts in front of you. You have to love God enough to put him before anything he can give you.

On April 23, ten days after Palm Sunday, I had nine hours of surgery to remove an egg-sized tumor from my brain. The prognosis improved. Pathology reports revealed that the tumor was "low-grade" and unlikely to kill me right away. It would, the doctors agreed, probably return at some unknown point, and potentially with greater ferocity. That could be decades away, or it could be months. I would have to live by faith.

I didn't want that. I wanted the guarantee, the one I always thought I had. The one that promised me I would live to be eighty, at least, and hold Kim's hand when our saggy skin blends into one flesh; that I would see my daughters through the teen years when they would be ashamed at everything about me and into their twenties and thirties when they would hopefully realize I was a good dad and a good friend to have. Though I said the words to Kim "in sickness and in health," I was only imagining her migraines and my bad back. This was something else entirely. I was thirty-four. I ate organic. It wasn't even time for a real midlife crisis yet.

I recuperated from the surgery in the weeks that followed and returned to work quickly. I needed to, because I didn't want to be a brain tumor patient. I wanted to "live strong." Three weeks after brain surgery I went back to work. I didn't think now was the time to change jobs. The return to a place with such power after being so powerless was jarring. Six weeks of life in the "real world" had passed me by and I realized I didn't miss it. Politics was among the first things to fall away when I got sick. Walking back into the White House felt like walking back into high school years later. It, or I, felt odd. People came up to me and spoke softly and slowly. I think they assumed I might have turned into Raymond from *Rain Man*. But by the second day they spoke normally and asked me some questions about this and that. On the third day everyone acted as if I had never left. It felt good to be treated normally.

The president was no different. I saw him on my first day back. I was in the office of the White House physician, Dick Tubb, on the ground floor of the White House residence. He was my friend and informal doctor. He only had two formal patients—Mr. and Mrs. Bush. He warned me that people would treat me weirdly at first because they wouldn't know what to say. I thanked him for that advice and all his help and walked into the next room. In front of me was the president's behind.

He was bent over, talking to one of the nurses about his knee. "It hurts here if I do that."

Tubb and I stood a safe distance away. Secret Service didn't accompany the president into the doc's office. It was a private place free of any prying eyes. Bush stood up, spun around, and saw us looking at him. Before he could unloose any self-deprecating quip he exclaimed, "Kuo! You're back. You look . . . good. You look good. How you feeling?" I told him that I felt older, wiser, more reflective. "Good, good. Good to see you." He backed out of the door. Tubb said, "Mr. President, do you need something?"

"No, no, not at all, I'll come back."

We assured him we were done but he kept backing out. "Good to see you." He turned to go and then turned back. "You look good. You look good. You're not . . . you're not emaciated. You look big."

"Mr. President, are you saying I'm fat?"

"Uh, no, no not at all. I just thought, you know, brain tumor, cancer, thin, frail. You aren't frail. I got to go."

Tubby looked at me and laughed. "See, people are going to be awkward for a bit."

I stepped back into the fight over religious hiring. Jim Towey and I had argued the issue for months. He thought it was crucial to show what a big problem it was. There were lots of federal rules that differed slightly on the subject, and he strongly believed they needed to be confronted. He wanted to issue a new White House report on how faith-based groups were being discriminated against because some federal programs prohibited them from hiring as they desired. My counterargument was tactical. No one in the field cared about the issue. There were many other things we should be focusing our attention on. It was still a political gold mine.

He was preparing for the report's launch. He had commissioned our staff to come up with more examples of hiring difficulties from across the country. There was only one problem. Hundreds of calls were made and not one additional example was found. Jeremy White, our director of outreach, took me aside and told me the story of a black minister he had talked to in Detroit. He asked her if she had any problems with being forced to hire someone who held a different faith or if anyone had sued her because she asked them about their religion. *"Honey,"* she told him, "if you can't figure out someone's religion without asking them the question, well, then you just stupid." These groups had been in the business of figuring out faith-based grants for a long time before we ever showed up.

I talked to Jim about this and tried to get him off the case, but he insisted on continuing. My passion for arguing was far below his. And for his purposes, it made sense. Jim was fully engaged in West Wing politics and smart enough to know how best to tickle political fancies. The religious hiring issue was polarizing. He had seen the strong reaction after President Bush's executive order on federal contracts. More action on the same subject would mean more attention for Jim's efforts. Therefore the religious hiring issue was good.

• • •

Three days after returning I was called into a meeting of black pastors from around the country. These ministers, most of them high-ranking clergy from the Churches of God in Christ, wanted to talk about what the White House initiative had done, and what it continued to do. I mingled with about twenty pastors before being tapped on the shoulder. A colleague whispered, "The president wants to see you."

I headed over to the Oval Office with Jeremy White. He briefed me on the meeting so I could brief the president. I walked in to find the president prowling around behind the desk looking for something. "Kuo! Tell me about this meeting."

I started by telling him that the group wanted to know about the faith-based initiative and that we recommended he talk about the administrative reforms we had implemented, and the tax credits we were still fighting for—

He interrupted me. "Forget about all that. Money. All these guys care about is money. They want money. How much money have we given them?"

For two years I had bitten my tongue and toed the line. We in the faith-based office didn't speak too loudly or thunder too much. We were nice. I wasn't angry now, but I was no longer willing to lie. "Sir, we've given them virtually nothing because we have had virtually nothing new to give."

He had been looking down at some papers I had given him but his head jerked up. "Nothing? What do you mean we've given them nothing?" He glared and angrily pointed toward the window. "Don't we have new money in programs like the Compassion Fund thing?"

Karl was standing next to me in front of the president's desk. He looked stunned. I glanced at him and then looked at the president. "No, sir. In the last two years we've gotten less than eighty million dollars in new grants." I was probably being generous.

"What?! What do you mean?"

Karl looked a bit confused, too. "But what about the other money? You know, the money we've opened up to new charities."

He was remembering our own spin from the winter. Yes, I told the president, because of new regulations there was *technically* about $8 billion in existing programs that were now eligible for faith-based groups. But, I assured him, faith-based groups had been getting money from those programs for years.

"Eight billion in new dollars?"

"No sir. Eight billion in existing dollars for which groups will find it technically easier to apply. But faith-based groups have been getting that money for years."

"Eight billion. That's what we'll tell them. Eight billion in new funds for faith-based groups. Okay, let's go."

As we walked I vaguely recalled one of Jesus' parables about only being able to reap what you have sown. We had sown the symbolic seeds of compassion with our constituents. They had accepted them gratefully. We had sown them with the president, too, and he was happy with them.

We walked to the Old Executive Office Building, up the steps, and into the conference room, where the president told the group that because of the faith-based initiative, billions of dollars in new funds were now available to faith-based groups like theirs. The pastors listened respectfully. Before the president left they prayed for him.

Karl stayed behind to share some thoughts and answer questions.

"Before I get started I want to say something. This initiative isn't political. If I walked into the Oval Office and said it was going to be political the president would bash my head in. This isn't political."

The questions started shortly thereafter. "Since the president brought up money, where, exactly is that money?" "We've talked to the Cabinet secretaries and they say there isn't any new money." They peppered him with questions for several minutes. Finally he smiled at them and said, "Tell you what, I'm going to get those guys in a room and bash some heads together and get to the bottom of this. I'll be back in touch with you." He left confidently.

Some of the pastors came over and told me they knew of my recent illness. They asked if they could lay hands on me and pray for my healing. I stood and closed my eyes and felt hands rest on my head and heard passionate prayers. The spirit of Washington is arrogance, the spirit of Christ is humility. They lived in the latter and were confronting the former.

In the faith-based office, we were not arrogant at this point; we were concerned. Several of us huddled in Jim's office after the meeting. "How can we show progress?" he asked urgently. "We've got to be able to show progress with grants."

I failed to point out the irony in what he was saying. We were about to release a report showing how religious discrimination was hurting faith-based groups and preventing them from getting grants. Now he was saying we needed to show how many more groups were getting grants after all.

Desperation breeds confusion. The most fundamental basis of President Bush's compassionate conservatism was that he, unlike other Republicans, recognized that government had a big role to play in helping social service groups. He once specifically denounced conservatives who thought that charities could simply go it alone. Now, however, we were trying to cover up all that the White House *hadn't* done. President Bush's compassion office was doing the very thing Governor Bush said charities shouldn't have to do—make bricks without straw.

The next morning one of our staff members assembled everyone who worked on faith-based issues in the federal agencies. "We've got to make it look like we're doing something," he ordered them. "Stop whatever you are working on and focus on making it look like we're doing something."

For much of the next year the initiative's main focus was on collecting information about how much money the federal government gave to faith-based groups and how much that money had increased under President Bush. It was an easy thing to spin. No one had ever asked the question before, so we started looking at different programs, trying to identify religious-sounding group names. Staff did research to try to figure out if each such grant recipient was actually faith-based (we looked mainly at Web sites). A retroactive "baseline" was established for the previous year. A "new" report would be issued as soon as the "new data" was ready.

241

In practice, however, we knew that very few new groups were getting money, and we had no way to get them more money of significance. There was only one option. When the Compassion Capital Fund increased by a few million dollars in the 2004 budget, we devised something we called "mini-grants." These small grants of $50,000 or less were given to the kind of small faith-based groups who had once dreamed of millions. For any one of these groups, $50,000 could mean the difference between air conditioning or no air conditioning, or the difference between no new programs and one new one. At $50,000 per pop, we figured we could advertise fifty or sixty new groups per year. Thousands of groups applied. Most were turned away because there wasn't any financial room at the inn. But we had our new talking point.

With the exception of our political activities, our faith-based office had become exactly like one of those small charities we were originally supposed to help—understaffed and underfunded.

We were good people forced to run a sad charade, to provide political cover to a White House that needed compassion and religion as political tools.

In the weeks that followed I headed up to Capitol Hill to meet with Senate Finance Committee friends about the long-dormant CARE Act. There was nothing new under the sun. The faith-based office was still pushing it but the White House legislative and senior staff were still utterly silent on its behalf. I was told to keep pressing the case.

I tried but I couldn't. I was tired of pushing the rock up the hill.

Jim grew increasingly frustrated with me. Again and again he told me my heart wasn't in the work. I wasn't thoroughly doing this memo or that memo. My hours weren't long enough. My attitude wasn't right. One day I snapped at him and told him to screw off. He wanted to fire me on the spot. He had every right. I apologized. So did he. Then I made a decision: I told him I was leaving.

One day in December I turned in my badge and on my way out did the customary thing by delivering my resignation letter to Andy Card. He accepted it, shook my hand, thanked me for all I'd done, wished me well on my future and health, and asked me if I had any thoughts on how the White House could improve. I had been through too much not to say something. I told him everything I thought. The president had made great promises but they hadn't been delivered on. Worse than that, the White House hadn't tried. Worse than *that,* we had used people of faith to further our political agenda and hadn't given them anything in return. I went on and on for a few minutes. He sat there a bit bug-eyed. "Formality meetings" are supposed to be just that.

"And finally, sir, this thought. I don't know if you are aware of this, but your staff frequently refers to the faith-based initiative as the 'f*#$ing faith-based initiative.' That doesn't help."

He shook my hand and assured me that he would look into it and that the president was committed to the initiative. I was being spun. I was already an outsider. Kim was waiting for me in the West Wing lobby. I took her hand, left the building, looked back at the beautiful place where I had been blessed to work, gave her a kiss, and we walked through the gates and back into life.

CHAPTER SIXTEEN

Reel Life

Two days before my thirty-sixth birthday I was stalking fish on Lake Erie. It was June 2004 and day one of my new life as a professional bass fisherman. The only thing between me, the fish, the $70,000 top prize, and that birthday were 30-mph winds, pelting rain, and six- to ten-foot waves hell-bent on sinking my boat and sucking me into an early death. I could see Kim's e-mail to friends: "David survived a high-speed car crash, a brain tumor, and nine hours of surgery but died tragically in a bass fishing tournament."

A brand-new $50,000 twenty-foot bass boat, lent to me by the fine people at Skeeter Boats, makers of the world's finest bass boats, danced more than a rubber ducky at the bottom of Niagara Falls. I weebled and wobbled about, soaking wet, trying to fish. I would have braced myself against the boat's railings except for the fact that it didn't have any. The front of the boat, from where I was purportedly fishing, was flat and carpeted with a nice snag-free weave that dropped sleekly off into the water on all sides. This ingenious design made it easy for a fisherman to lean over and bring his catch into the boat. It also prevented lures from tangling or snagging on the boat. But in this weather, the boat's bow felt like a carpeted diving board.

These waves were no freak of nature. They were Erie regulars. It has something to do with Lake Erie being very big (about the size of Connecticut), very shallow (imagine a gigantic community pool), and very windy (think early moments of *The Wizard of Oz*). They were also not what I pictured when I decided that a season of pro fishing sounded like a great departure from the White House.

My visions were of still lakes with morning mist sitting on lily pads, interrupted only by the big, splashing bass I had just wrestled into my boat. What I was getting instead was a perfect storm in polluted water with dozens of abandoned industrial plants dotting the shore.

An experienced bass pro I had talked to the night before solemnly advised me that the only way to handle the big waves was "surfing" my almost flat-bottomed 225-horsepower bass boat over their backs. Otherwise water would pour into my boat and I would sink. I pursed my lips together, forced a chin-rumpling frown, nodded gravely and said, "Yeah, yeah, absolutely, without a doubt. Surf the waves. Yeah."

He looked at me seriously and said, "Boy, men *die* on Lake Erie. You understand? They sink and then they *die*."

Out on the water in the midst of the waves with few fish to land, no hot chocolate to warm me up, and dwindling chances of returning to land safely, I wondered if my fellow angler's words were prophetic. I later learned that four boats did sink, though all the anglers were fine. The waves were coming from every direction and I didn't know which way to turn the boat. I couldn't see beyond them. All in all, it felt a lot like my life.

I had had the bass-fishing revelation a few weeks before my last day at the White House. I was sitting in the mess, eating the Bush-inspired, lard-laden combo of tacos, enchiladas, refried beans, and a burrito, known as the Texas Fiesta platter. Across from me sat a friend from the Senate Finance Committee. During a pause between a bite of beans and a bite of burrito, a short burst of thoughts hit me. *David, you love to fish for bass. Leave the White House and become a professional bass fisherman. You'll love it.* There, in the basement of the West Wing, where President Kennedy celebrated his last birthday, amid the rich oak paneling, White House china, and artery-clogging food, I found my heart's pilgrimage. I was going to become a professional bass fisherman.

Seconds later, Karl Rove walked in and over to my table, and gave me a spontaneous kiss on the cheek. I didn't know if that kiss was a sign of divine affirmation or divine warning but it didn't matter much. I was going back to something I hadn't done since I was in high school. I was going fishing.

I would tour the country with a bass boat, fish in tournaments, catalog the great experiences, and write about them. That, of course, wasn't what it was really about. Thoreau got it right: *"Many men go fishing all of their lives without knowing that it is not fish they are after."* From the time I was a kid, fishing helped me make sense of the world. I needed that again. I needed to climb back underneath that fence near my parents' house, find the rocky shoreline again, look into the water, feel safe, and sort out the world.

I was confused, frustrated, and scared. No doctor could ever pronounce me cured. The kind of tumor I had almost always recurred and most of the time eventually became more malignant and more deadly. That usually happened within a decade, sometimes much faster, sometimes much slower.

On top of that I continued to have irregular seizures. They were nothing like the one that caused the car crash. They were small, isolated to my left foot and leg, and over in less than thirty seconds. But they seemed to last forever, and each one felt like a nick to my confidence. I didn't ever know when they were coming. It could happen on a bass boat, which it once did, or in an airport, which occurred once as well. I wanted to be strong and conquering, but instead I felt very small.

My dear friend Martha Williamson suggested that much like Jacob had the limp after wrestling with God, so I had these small twitches to prevent me from wandering too far. I hated the thought. I wanted everything to be okay. Jesus promised me his burden was light. This burden felt horribly heavy.

But where else could I turn if not to God? He was incomprehensibly bigger and more splendid than I could imagine. Bigger than the infinite universe. I knew from the stories about him that he also watches when the doe bears her fawn, and he counted the months till it happened. He knows each sparrow. I wasn't forgotten, even if it sometimes felt like I was.

All the strength and power I wanted could never come from me alone. It couldn't. Whatever I had would eventually run out, just as it did that night in the CT scan. There was no independence for me anymore, even though a part of me craved it—a big part of me. The only one I could lean on was Jesus. He alone was my comforter and strength and he alone could be my healer. Like everyone else, I couldn't get any life guarantees. The lesson I had to learn was the best of all clichés: know that every moment of every day is a gift, revel in it, and don't worry about tomorrow. Long ago I told God I trusted him with my life. Now I had to live with the confidence that my life was in good hands. Often, though, this seemed very hard to do.

I also had to live with my frustration at the White House. My fishing-centric world crowded out politics. But Jim invited me to the first National Faith-Based Conference in Washington several months after I left. I debated going because I didn't want to dredge up past frustrations. I had told Andy Card what I thought and what he needed to know. Fixing it, doing anything about it, was entirely up to him. My debate was picking between a Shimano baitcasting reel and a Daiwa.

Nevertheless, I went. Kim thought I might be surprised by something good the president would announce or talk about. I doubted it but went anyway. There, in front of three thousand faith and charity leaders, the president touted his initiative's success: ". . . I got a little frustrated in Washington because I couldn't get the [faith-based and charity] bill passed out of the Congress. They were arguing process. I kept saying, wait a minute, there are entrepreneurs all over our country who are making a huge difference in somebody's life; they're helping us meet a social objective. Congress wouldn't act, so I signed an executive order—that means I did it on my own." The crowd erupted in applause. I turned to Kim, who had suffered through my evening litany of compassion frustrations for two and a half years, and sighed.

History was being rewritten. The Bush White House, which did less than nothing to advance the faith-and-charity bill and which substituted symbolic executive orders for real change, claimed "Mission Accomplished" on faith-based legislation.

It did the same thing with money. "In a year, there was a $144 million increase in the amount that HUD and HHS grant dollars were granted to faith-based organizations. So from last year to this year, there's a $144 million increase; the two agencies granted $1.1 billion to faith-based groups in 2003. That's a measurable number." The number was meaningless and it had a singular purpose—to make it seem like old promises were fulfilled. It was said to a group of religious and charity leaders who trusted a Christian brother at his word.

He concluded by saying, "My job is to get the initiative going, is to stay on it, not yield, and then to ask the questions to the people responsible for getting the money out the door, how are we doing." If that was his job, he had done it very poorly.

Kim and I got up, said hi to some friends, and went home. She was right. The event did surprise me. I was surprised by the brazen deception and I was crushed by it, too. That same passion for the poor I first heard in Austin was in his voice and in his eyes. But the passion was a passion for talking about compassion, not fighting for compassion.

Aides tried to say that all the inaction was purely a result of the new post-9/11 world. Nothing new domestically was possible and all Bush's good intentions from early 2001 had been foiled by terrorism. Sadly, that wasn't true. I had been there in 2001 and had seen the exact same things happening before 9/11 as were happening in 2004. The announcements and speeches were stirring but the inaction was glaring.

I was angry. But it wasn't my fight anymore.

So I went fishing.

When I wasn't fishing in a tournament I hauled my bass boat down to the Potomac and launched into the river. Most of the great bass fishing was south of Alexandria on the wide, shallow, meandering part of the river. But that area also had lots of houses, lots of other boats, and lots of noise from surrounding roads. I went north to the more secluded waters of the river. Surrounded by sheer cliffs on one side and woods on the other, I dropped anchor, fished a bit, and lay on the boat looking up at the sky. Occasionally I saw Marine One, the president's helicopter, shuttling him to Camp David and back. I looked up and asked myself whether I missed it—the power, prestige, and perks. My answer was always no. And he certainly didn't miss me. Bill Bennett's lesson remained true: absolutely everyone in Washington is replaceable. I had long ago been replaced. Once, that would have bothered me. Being in the middle of things was once a necessity. Now being in the middle of a river was enough.

As the summer passed I paid less and less attention to politics. Elizabeth Dole did call to ask for help with her Republican National Convention speech. She was supposed to speak on "family values." We talked about it. I had no interest in writing a speech highlighting all the socially divisive issues that mobilized Republican voters. I wanted to write about compassion. It had been my political and policy interest for nearly a decade and I wasn't about to give up on it now.

The draft was good. Maybe that's because I wrote it on a laptop on my bass boat. She was ready to talk about poverty and compassion, faith-based charities, and the power of communities. But hours before she was to step onstage to deliver it, White House aides changed it. The compassion stuff was scaled back. Faith-based references were stripped out. "It might highlight what hasn't been done," they said.

The longer I was away the more I understood the White House. As much as I pretended it was just another job, it wasn't just another job. It was everything great and dangerous about politics rolled into one. The White House could be, as my father remembered it from World War II, a place that saved the world. It could certainly inspire the world. I had seen that with my own eyes as President Bush rallied the nation and the world in the days and weeks after 9/11. While we all prepared for more attacks, he was leading the charge to prevent those attacks.

But the White House was also one of the most seductive places imaginable. Not just because of the perks, which are nice, but because of the raw power of the place hidden in a true desire to save the world. It is the ring of power from Tolkien's *Lord of the Rings*.

The longer anyone holds the ring the more he loves it, the more he hates it, and the more desperate he is to hold on to it. It becomes the most precious thing in his life. Priorities, loves, interests, life are lost in it. The ring owns, it is not owned.

Over time, the White House owns a little bit more of everyone who works there. In some ways it is easiest to see in how hard it is to leave. I saw friend after friend promise he would leave after this month or that one. Traditional tenure for commissioned officers was eighteen months. Yet more than three years after the Bush administration began, virtually no one had left. They were physically exhausted and mentally drained. Marriages were in danger, and in one instance a young child literally forgot what his White House–working parent looked like. Pledges to leave were reneged on because, well, "The country needs me." One friend, among the most religious people I know, signed on knowing the place's seductive power. He had promised his wife no more than two years. He served more than five. Another friend promised his wife and young boys just two years. Even after a heart attack he could not leave. On the eve of the 2004 election his son told him he was voting for John Kerry. My friend asked his ten-year-old boy why. "So I can see you again." He still serves and serves well.

I know what it is like. At the end I knew I wanted to leave and that it was time for me to leave. Yet I pushed back my departure date two or three times to add just another few weeks. There was no way I could explain it at the time. I wanted just a little bit more.

One of the by-products of this seduction is increasing insularity. The "us against the world" mentality that helped win elections and make it through tough days becomes a sort of governing philosophy where everything the White House does it right. Those on the outside who question, critique, or oppose are equal enemies. And people make decisions they would never have made before.

As summer turned to fall, a friend in the faith-based world called me to say that a final 2004 conference had been added in mid-October. The conference was going to be in Miami two weeks before the election. At first I couldn't believe it. It was so blatantly political that I figured the White House or Jim had to see that and would pull back. They didn't. As always the information the people received was first-rate and important. But a conference recruiting predominantly Hispanic and black religious leaders just days before the presidential election in Florida? Amazingly, no one in the press picked up on it.

I heard the news and spent another day on the water. It was hard to get too vexed about politics when chasing bass.

On Election Day some of the early exit poll numbers looked awful. The president was down significantly in Ohio, Pennsylvania, Florida, Michigan, and Missouri. I called one of his senior campaign advisers to see what was going on. "Can't talk now, on the phone with Ohio pastors. They've gotta turn out, just gotta turn out and they will. Say a prayer. We'll get it done." He hung up.

Later that night Ohio turned for the president. In the days that followed, some commentators suggested it was the anti-gay marriage amendment that turned out voters. As people took a closer look, however, the real difference was in a small but significant switch in black voting patterns. In Ohio 16 percent went for President Bush, the highest any Republican had received in years. For weeks, analysts speculated on what the cause might have been. They missed the most obvious. Every church and charity in Ohio had received an invitation to at least two (some received three) faith-based conferences in surrounding states. More than a thousand pastors and religious leaders from Ohio attended the conferences. There can be little doubt that Ohio's success and the president's reelection was at least partially tied to the conferences we had launched two years before.

A few days after the election, the president laid out the agenda for his second term. He wanted to restrict legal liability in health care, provide incentives for small business, flatten the tax code, and tackle Social Security reform. He said nothing about compassion programs. No expanding or starting previously promised programs. No increasing the pittance of funding for existing programs. Toward the end of the press conference, when someone asked him about the tax code reformation, he mentioned "charitable giving" right next to "mortgage interest reform." His "signature domestic policy issue" was nowhere to be found.

In the 2005 State of the Union address he announced a new program for teen violence prevention. It wasn't big, $90 million over three years, but it was something. The next day I listened in on a conference call Jim conducted with reporters. He talked in grand terms about the "extraordinary" program and how powerfully it would impact tens of thousands of kids who would otherwise be headed for delinquency. Near the end of the call one of the reporters asked how it was going to be paid for. Jim paused. The press person on the call with him jumped in and said it was an accounted-for part of the president's budget. The reporter pushed on. How was it going to be paid for? Well, Jim finally said, the money was coming out of the Compassion Capital Fund.

There was no expansion of anything. There was only the marketing of a new program that sucked money from another already grossly underfunded program. It was Clintonian.

Throughout the 1990s we conservatives mocked President Clinton for his sleight of hand. He would announce something like his desire to "end welfare as we know it" and then work behind the scenes to keep the welfare system intact. Only after the Republican Congress passed a tougher version did he sign it and declare it a victory. Similarly, he declared that the "era of big government" was over, only to oversee an expansion of government. All of this, we concluded, showed his deep moral and ethical flaws.

Now, however, George W. Bush's White House was doing the same thing: it was deceiving the public, and in doing so it was mocking the trust of the American people. More disappointing, it was mocking the millions of faithful Christians who had put their trust and hope in the president and his administration.

In the next few days, President and Mrs. Laura Bush went to Pittsburgh to talk up their "new" program. Like all such events it was carefully scripted and perfectly done. They were surrounded by minorities—it showed how inclusive he had become. The banner behind them read "Compassion in Action," my term from two years before. No one bothered to ask the simple question made famous by Walter Mondale to Gary Hart: "Where's the beef?"

Shortly thereafter, the faith-based office had its staff cut by nearly 30 percent.

I thought about it all, about everything I saw and everything I did, and I thought about my responsibility. What was it? Concerns once passionately held about career advancement were long gone. Concerns about efforts to help millions of hurting Americans were still passionately held. My White House experience showed me there was a single thing I could do to help—say something . . . publicly.

There is much that I could have said. Instead, I wrote a short piece expressing my disappointment with the White House, and with Congress, and with both parties for failing the poor. It was for the Beliefnet Web site.

Before the piece ran I e-mailed Jim to let him know I would be writing something. The Friday before the piece ran I e-mailed White House Press Secretary Scott McClellan, Mike Gerson, Pete Wehner, and Jim, telling them about the piece and the gist of what it said. In case anyone asked, I didn't want them to be surprised. I also let my friends know I expected I would see their toughest response. It didn't concern me. They each had a job to do.

At first, when the piece went online, there was silence. I knew the White House would have seen it, however, because it was certainly included in the press clips circulated every morning. That was all I needed. I prayed I might have a small ripple of the impact John DiIulio had.

Then there was noise. The phone started ringing off the hook. NPR, ABC, NBC, the *Washington Post,* and countless others wanted to talk. Why was I writing this? What was I really saying? Was this all about Karl? Who was the person or people who blocked the initiative? Did this mean I was a liberal?

Kim sent out a prayer request to the Bible study group that had met twice a week in the evening in the faith-based office. The media response, she wrote, was a complete shock. Pray, she asked, for wisdom and guidance in what to say and what not to say.

An hour later John Bridgeland called. Bridge had left the White House six months before and was happily reorienting himself to society. That morning, however, he had been asked to deliver a message from Karl. It was short. My facts were wrong and Karl knew about Kim's e-mail to her Bible study group.

I was confused. The former wasn't true. I had no idea what the latter meant. Was it simply a power play that he could get his hands on anything? Did he just like getting Bible study e-mails? Just as confusing, why would one of Kim's trusted friends in a confidential Bible study send the e-mail to Karl? It seemed the most likely occurence. Did politics really trump Jesus?

None of this was terribly surprising. Even though I took great pains to say the failure wasn't just a "White House failure but a Washington failure," no one wanted to focus on that. Everyone wanted to focus on the White House. In every interview I described how Capitol Hill Republicans were startlingly indifferent to the poor and Democrats were just as startlingly opposed to anything faith-oriented. But since I was a former White House person, the questions were about them.

Publicly, the White House defended itself by alternating between showing how many billions it had "opened" up to faith-based groups and saying the president never made the promises I said he had made in his 1999 campaign speech.

While much of the "secular" media covered the story, the Christian media was hauntingly silent. Only Pat Robertson's *700 Club* wanted me on. But even on that taped interview, I was gently reminded by the day's hosts (not Robertson) that I shouldn't be critical of President Bush, just discuss what I thought needed to be done.

I asked a friend in the Christian media why she thought there was so little coverage of the story. "Because," she said, "the White House was going to cut off anyone who gave you coverage." Another television reporter who had interviewed me told me the White House press shop criticized him because the story included a shot of my dog. "Who can hate someone with a dog?" they asked him.

As with all things in Washington, the small tempest blew over.

Not surprisingly, a lot of Democrats called me to see if they could talk to me. I told everyone who called I was happy to talk to anyone. My sole interest was advancing the agenda.

The Democrats gave me such little hope it was discouraging. Aides for Senate Minority Leader Harry Reid met with me and asked how they could appeal to religious conservatives. I told them it was easy: talk to them, let them know you don't think they have three heads, and be open to pursuing their interests. There was much more common ground than they realized. They asked me who to talk to. I started giving them names—like Tony Perkins at the Family Research Council. "Who?" "What's that?" I mentioned the support for environmentalism at the National Association of Evangelicals and again they said, "What's that?"

Their utter ignorance about faith issues reminded me of an encounter Rick Warren had had at the National Prayer Breakfast that year. After it was over someone told him he needed to meet Terry McAuliffe, former head of the Democratic National Committee and now helping lead the DNC's faith-based outreach. Warren introduced himself. McAuliffe asked him where he was from and what he did. "Well, I'm from Orange County [California] and I pastor a church there." McAuliffe was thrilled. "Great! Great, that's just great. A pastor from Orange County who is a Democrat. Terrific. I hope to see you again." Warren laughed. That Terry McAuliffe didn't even know the author of *The Purpose Driven Life* showed a staggering ignorance. Was it any wonder evangelicals preferred hanging out with Republicans?

By early 2006, total funding going to faith-based groups had actually declined. The president's latest budget contained across-the-board cuts to social programs. They were defended in nearly Orwellian terms. "Cuts" have been renamed "improvements" and "eliminated programs" are "efficiently redesigned." My former boss Jim Towey called it "the most family-friendly budget in history."

In his first campaign speech George W. Bush had promised to be a different kind of Republican, one who would care about the poor, seek reconciliation, and ensure government funds for the faith-based groups that could transform people's lives. Was it all a joke? What, finally, is the answer to the question I first asked in Austin in 1998? Is he for real? Does he really care about racial, social, and economic justice?

After leaving I learned that all budget decisions were made by three people once a year. President Bush, Karl Rove, and Andy Card would sit in the Oval Office and the president would go over the big numbers. Unlike his wonky predecessor, Bush didn't dig down into specific programs. It wasn't his style. He was America's CEO. He wanted to dictate the big picture and leave it to others to implement. That meant that while he may not have known the details of his compassion agenda, he knew it was languishing and had no problem with that.

Did he ever care about his antipoverty agenda? Personally, I doubt he could have cared more. His empathy couldn't be faked. It was the empathy of the lost and converted. George Bush, in the rawest terms, had been a drunk. Jesus rescued him. His conversion was dramatic. And as a theologian friend reminded me recently, adult converts to faith tend to be much more evangelical.

Ultimately, what George Bush wanted was souls. In a remarkable reference in a Los Angeles speech in March 2004, he discussed what faith-based groups said they would be able to do with more money. He passionately exclaimed, "There's more souls to be saved." That was what "faith-based" was about for him. It is why, when he talked about faith-based groups with no notes, he always talked about the power of those groups to change lives "from the inside out." It was his own story.

Finally, the politician understood the benefits. One of the problems Bush's opponents always ran into was "misunderstanding" him. He loved it. In briefings or discussions, if he felt someone was treating him as if he were dense, he would say, "I did go to Yale and Harvard, you know." Yes, he did. He is a bright man. Bright enough to relish the perception of him as a simpleton and then to exceed the low expectations that came along with it.

To that end, he knew well the complicated and beneficial political gains of his compassion initiative. He knew it would differentiate him from the 2000 Republican field right away and that it would appeal to women and minorities. He knew it was, in its own way, a bit of a Sister Souljah moment. Bush could buck even economic conservatives. And he knew that it, combined with his personal evangelical faith, would buy him enormous credibility with evangelical leaders.

In the end, the compassion initiative was personally important, politically significant—and policy that wasn't ever going to be implemented.

I can live with that.

Once it would have broken my heart to see the political leader of my dreams break his promises. But that's politics. For too long I've held this secret hope that just the right guy doing just the right thing would make America better: obliterate poverty, obviate the need for abortions, eliminate loneliness, end despair, wipe out crime, and increase opportunity. But those hopes were misplaced and unreasonable, and set the bar too high.

Our political leaders, after all, are just that—political. No matter what their faith, or lack thereof, they are just plain old people doing a plain old job. They can't save America. It isn't in their job description. They can make changes at the margins by helping a bit here and there. But ultimately, the work of America is our work. And my ultimate hope is back where it should be—not with fishing, not with politics, but with God.

Fast, Let's Fast

A little over a year ago I was speaking at my favorite church in America. It is located west of St. Louis. During the great floods of 1993 it was completely swamped. Instead of running for the hills, the small congregation of three hundred never stopped working, piling sandbags, evacuating people, and then spending months cleaning up after the flood. They developed a simple motto: "Honor God, Help People." Today they have more than 18,000 members on their rolls and they send people, supplies, and love around the world. While most of the country has forgotten about the tsunami and Katrina, the folks from Chesterfield, Missouri, are building houses in Sri Lanka and New Orleans. Elsewhere, they are helping people in Kosovo and Sudan. I never thought I would love a church located in what I once arrogantly called flyover country. But while I love our wonderful church in Washington, the St. Louis Family Church is my spiritual home. My former Ashcroft colleagues, and Ashcroft himself, can't help but chuckle. I used to complain about trips to Missouri. God has set me straight.

During my sickness and every day since, people from that church have prayed for my healing and complete restoration. They have become family. First among them is Jeff Perry. For twenty years he built the church and shunned the spotlight. As best a human being can, he has lived Jesus' beatitudes. He takes the last seat at the table and counts others better than himself. Where others have actively sought recognition, he has actively sought to be as anonymous as possible. He and his wife, Patsy, raised their five children in a five-room house. About his only flaw is that he sometimes fishes for catfish instead of bass.

Kim and I get out there as often as possible, which isn't nearly often enough. During one of our visits in 2004, Jeff asked me to stand up and talk about where I was in life, what I had learned at the White House, and what God was teaching me.

I talked about learning what it means to rely on God more than anyone or anything else. How hard that is. I was a pilgrim running, walking, and sometimes barely crawling toward this goal. But it was the only goal worth having.

After the service one of the congregants came up to me and said hello. He then put a polite finger in my chest and said, with a smile, "You tell President Bush to get that Supreme Court right!"

I had heard lines like that time and again. I had a pat way of dealing with them. I would laugh, say the president wanted to appoint conservatives to the court, and that they didn't have anything to worry about.

That night, though, I threw out the old script. Instead, I said, "Maybe the problem isn't the courts, maybe the problem is us. Maybe things are so screwy because we've spent more time thinking about how to advance politically than we have about just changing our own lives."

He looked at me queerly, nodded his head, and said, "Hmmm, interesting, maybe you're right. Just make sure you give President Bush my message."

I have been thinking about that exchange ever since.

Since the mid-1970s and with ever increasing passion, Christians like me have looked to politics to save America. We thought that the right president, the right Congress, and the right judge or justice would stop abortions, strengthen marriage, create a safer country for children, and ensure that our religious faith was respected. Our motivations were good ones. We wanted to save lives, homes, and our country. We saw ourselves as heirs to the Christian political tradition that fought against slavery and for a woman's right to vote. We had every right to be in the political fight.

Now, however, it is time to take stock both politically and spiritually. Has our political focus produced the desired results? By 2008, we will have had a good, conservative Republican in the Oval Office for twenty of the past twenty-eight years. Republicans have had outright control of both houses of Congress for most of the last twelve years. Republican presidents have appointed the vast majority of American judges and seven of the nine Supreme Court justices. In short, we've had almost everything we wanted politically. But things are hardly better. Social statistics are largely unchanged. Divorces are rampant and more and more children are growing up in a home with just one parent. Nearly a million and a half abortions are performed every year. There are more children in poverty today than there were twenty years ago. A greater percentage of Americans lack health care than ever before. Educational achievement is hardly soaring. Millions of Americans live in what seems like utterly intractable poverty.

We have had great electoral success and marginal political success.

Then there is the spiritual side of things. As one prominent pastor has written, "What we've done is turn a mission field into a battlefield." What he means is that by so passionately pursuing politics, Christians have alienated everyone on the other side, many of them good people with genuine policy differences. People of goodwill of all faiths can disagree about tax cuts, health care policies, or the war in Iraq. Yet these disagreements can prevent relationships, fellowship, and the chance to share Jesus. In countless discussions I've had with people across the country and around the neighborhood, the name "Jesus" doesn't bring to mind the things he said he wanted associated with his followers— love for one another; love for the poor, sick, and imprisoned; self-denial; and devotion to God. It is associated with antiabortion activities, opposition to gay rights, the Republican Party, and tax cuts. Can anything that dilutes the name of Jesus be worth it for Christians like me?

• • •

So, what now?

Some, like James Dobson, argue that we need more Christian political engagement. Our lack of success simply shows that we need to be more passionate, strategic, and engaged. Others, such as the prominent and respected theologian and pastor John MacArthur, believe Christians need to do exactly the opposite; Christians need to flee the political arena and focus instead on telling people the truth about Jesus, that he alone is the way, the truth, and the life, and that he is the only way to God.

Both Dobson and MacArthur are good men who obviously love Jesus, and they have dedicated their lives to following him. But maybe there is another option.

Maybe Christians need to begin a fast—from politics.

Fasting was an accepted part of the spiritual life for thousands of years. The Bible records that Moses fasted for at least two recorded forty-day periods. Jesus himself fasted for forty days. He assumed it was part of the spiritual life so that when he instructed his followers, he said, "when you fast," not *if* you fast.

It was a many-purposed thing seen as a way to develop greater intimacy with God and a way to be humbled in God's sight. Perhaps most dramatically, it was seen as a way to reveal someone's true spiritual condition by stripping away a basic necessity of life leading to brokenness, repentance, and transformation.

It is also understood that fasting can be the deprivation of something other than food. As the noted evangelical theologian J. I. Packer writes, "We tend to think of fasting as going without food. But we can fast from anything. If we love music and decide to miss a concert in order to spend time with God, that is fasting. It is helpful to think of the parallel of human friendship. When friends need to be together, they will cancel all other activities in order to make that possible. There's nothing magical about fasting. It's just one way of telling God that your priority at that moment is to be alone with him, sorting out whatever is necessary, and you have cancelled the meal, party, concert, or whatever else you had planned to do in order to fulfill that priority."

We Christians need a short fast from politics.

We need to eschew politics to focus more on practicing compassion. We need to spend more time studying Jesus and less time trying to get people elected. Instead of spending hundreds of millions of dollars every year in support of conservative Christian advocacy groups such as the Family Research Council, Eagle Forum, and the panoply of similar groups, let's give that money to charities and groups that are arguably closer to Jesus' heart. And we Christians should spend less time arguing with those on the other side and more time communing with them.

I've seen what it looks like when these things happen. I attend a wonderful little church just minutes away from the White House—my other favorite church. The pastor and his wife came to Washington with the sense that God wanted them to serve the poor and facilitate reconciliation. Over time, they came to see that one of the most partisanly segregated places in Washington was in church on a Sunday morning, and even though most of the people in the church were Republicans, they kept preaching that it was Jesus' church, not any political party's church.

God honored their desire. A prominent Democratic senator started attending. Then, one Sunday morning during a tumultuous political time, our pastor preached about honoring our political leaders and praying for them. He called this senator to the front and then called some others from the church to pray for him. The people he chose included someone who worked for one of the largest Christian political organizations, another who worked to help elect Republican senators, another person from the White House, and me. So we all stood up in front, praying for this Democratic leader.

It was wonderful and awkward. It was wonderful because as we prayed we all sensed that this was the way things were meant to be in church—labels and affiliations and policy positions melting away in God's presence. It was awkward because after it was all done the conservatives chuckled nervously and said they hoped no one found out about it.

Even now, I can't mention the name of the church or the people involved for fear that the conservatives will suffer recriminations if it were known that they prayed for a Democratic senator.

The best way to start is with a fast.

Not too long ago I talked to the wife of a very prominent Republican senator who shares my Christian faith and has benefited from Christian votes. I asked her if, perhaps, we Christians had gone a bit too far in mixing our politics with our faith. "You are absolutely right!" she exclaimed. "We've gone so far afield I wonder if we can find our way back."

How far afield have we gone? Consider the following sessions from a 2006 meeting of religious conservatives attended by President Bush, Senator George Allen (a leading 2008 presidential hopeful), Lt. Governor Michael Steele (running for the Maryland senate), Senator Bill Frist (another leading 2008 presidential hopeful), and ministry leaders Chuck Colson and James Dobson: "Liberal Sisters of Doom: Are They a Thing of the Past?" "Courts Gone Wild," "Left Out: Exposing Liberal Groups."

When I look at these titles I don't see how they match up with a single part of Jesus' ministry.

The last time I checked, Jesus said we should love our enemies. He hung out with the worst elements of society, much to the dismay of the religious leaders of the day. When he came upon the adulterous woman at the well, he didn't convene a conference titled, "The Sister Is Doomed." He forgave her sins.

It is worth revisiting C. S. Lewis's *The Screwtape Letters*. "Let him begin by treating patriotism . . . as a part of his religion. Then let him, under the influence of partisan spirit, come to regard it as the most important part. Then quietly and gradually nurse him on to the stage at which the religion becomes merely a part of the 'cause,' in which Christianity is valued chiefly because of the excellent arguments it can produce. . . . [O]nce he's made the world an end, and faith a means, you have almost won your man, and it makes very little difference what kind of worldly end he is pursuing."

Today, there is no doubt that many Christians have been seduced in exactly that fashion. Patriotism—a good thing—has become part of our religion. So has partisanship. We have been quietly and gradually nursed to the point where our faith and God himself are merely part of a political cause. Invoking God's name is just a rhetorical device.

That's the bad news. Here's the good news. We have not been "won" by the world or the enemy. Most of us still understand that Christ alone is the answer and our desire.

In front of us is an opportunity. For the next twenty-four months, candidates for president, senator, representative, governor, judge, county clerk, and sheriff will be seeking the conservative Christian vote, our money, and our energy. Every politician needs evangelicals. And like a teenage boy on a date with a beautiful girl, they will say anything and everything to get what they want.

Let's not give it to them. Let's tell them we are fasting from politics for a season.

I'm not talking about a permanent fast. Fasts are, obviously, temporary. I'm not suggesting that current politicians leave office. I'm not suggesting that we stop voting. I'm just suggesting that voting be *all* we do. Let's start a two-year fast. Let's take every ounce of energy we currently expend on politics and divert it to other things. Instead of sending letters to Congress and engaging in political arguments with friends and listening to political talk radio and canvassing door to door for candidates and volunteering for campaigns, let's spend our time in different ways. We can start with the things God has commanded us to do—pray, learn, listen to him, and serve a hurting world.

There are so many other things we can and should do.

Thirty-five million Americans are at risk of hunger every day. A million people are released from prison every year with virtually no one to help them productively reenter society. Hundreds of thousands of children are in foster care and will never have a permanent home. More than a million children have a parent in prison. And those are just American snapshots. Every three seconds, a child in Africa dies of a preventable disease. There is a tsunami of death equaling the Southeast Asian tsumani in Africa every week. Christian leaders like Rick Warren, the author of *The Purpose Driven Life,* are largely eschewing politics and are mobilizing churches around the world to tackle this problem. It is more important than any judicial nomination and worthy of far more of our time.

What would the news media say if we ended our nasty partisanship, ceased making political arguments, and instead just relentlessly pursued ways to serve those who are sick, needy, hungry, and hurting? What would "enemies" at the ACLU or the gay and lesbian community or in the Democratic Party say and do? If we decided to turn off the crazy political news and spend more time with our families, what would our "opponents" have to say? I believe that it would be one of the most powerful witnesses to faith ever. Extraordinary things would happen because of it. After all, Jesus promised, "Blessed are the peacemakers for they will be called sons of God."

The fast will also give us a chance to talk. And we've got a lot to talk about. What are our priorities? Earlier this year the Family Research Council, a Christian organization, released a "2006 Conservative State of the Union." It listed the organization's priorities:

1. Marriage Protection Amendment
2. Advance Religious Liberties: Defund the ACLU
3. Defund Planned Parenthood
4. Enforce Broadcast Decency
5. Child Custody Protection Act
6. Cloning Prohibition Act
7. Unborn Child Pain Awareness Act
8. Make Family-Friendly Tax Cuts Permanent
9. Protect Private Property Rights

10. End Gambling Expansion
11. Confirm Strict-Constructionist Judges

Are these really the top priorities for Christians? What about tackling poverty? What about drugs for HIV/AIDS in Africa? If we are at the point of believing these would be Jesus' political priorities, it is pretty clear we need more time with God and less time with politicians. Some will undoubtedly read this and think it is a partisan ploy—that I somehow hope "liberal" Christians will become more powerful and liberals will be swept into power. No. I hope progressive Christians will join in the fast, leaving the Democratic party to re-examine its own priorities.

Years after I first learned about William Wilberforce, I discovered that he was more than just an abolitionist who helped change laws. In 1787 he wrote in his diary, "God Almighty has set before me two great objects, the suppression of the Slave Trade and the reformation of manners."

He worked with friends inside and outside parliament. He worked with bishops and influential people throughout British society. He worked with the poor; he worked to establish educational reform, prison reform, health care reform, and to limit the number of hours children were required to work in factories. But it was much more than a legislative effort. Wilberforce believed that he and his supporters should attempt to cure every social ill in the country, and not by governmental decree. They established organizations that would work to improve or rectify each injustice. While the effort wasn't devoid of politics, politics wasn't its driving force.

Wilberforce not only brought his faith into his public life but into his private life, too. He used his large income for good causes, donating generously to charity and cutting the rents he charged the tenants on his land.

For decades evangelical Christians have looked to Wilberforce as their patron saint of political activism. Perhaps it is time to use his life as a different model, a model of the pursuit of what he called "real Christianity."

My former boss and dear friend Bill Bennett used to talk about how we were downstream from society's problems. He likened it to standing on the shoreline and seeing drowning people go by. We stand at the shore and wade in the water and do all that we can to save as many lives as possible but inevitably people get by us and drown. We can keep doing that, he said, or we can go upstream and figure out why people are ending up in the water.

We know the answer to that question. People are ending up in the water because hopelessness drives them there. It may be the hopelessness of drugs or alcohol or joblessness or health or crime or a hundred other things. We Christians need to follow Jesus' commands and flock to soup kitchens, battered women's shelters, prison cells, and hospitals. We need to seek Jesus in "the distress and disguise of the poor." Countless millions of Christians are already doing this. Let them be our guides. The politically untainted can help wash those of us grown dirty with the filth of politics.

If we take a two-year (and just a two-year) break from politics, will America go to pot? Of course it won't. The brilliance of our Founders is that they created a system where change is very slow and very gradual. Bill Clinton's problems couldn't sink us, nearly four decades of Democratic congressional control didn't sink us, and two years of Christians retreating from politics won't sink us.

Politicians from John Kennedy to Ronald Reagan have been fond of referring to America as the "shining city on a hill." It is a beautiful metaphor, and fitting in so many ways. America has been one of the greatest forces for good in world history. But we are not the shining city on a hill. When Jesus used the words "a city set on a hill" he wasn't referring to a country, he was referring to Solomon's temple—the dwelling place of God—in Jerusalem. The ancient historian Josephus described it this way: "The outward face of the Temple in its front wanted nothing that was likely to surprise either men's minds or their eyes; for it was covered all over with plates of gold of great weight, and, at the first rising of the sun, reflected back a very fiery splendour, and made those who forced themselves to look upon it to turn away their eyes, just as they would have done at the sun's own rays. The Temple appeared to strangers, when they were at a distance, like a mountain covered with snow . . ." The shining city on a hill contained the Ark of the Covenant and the Mercy Seat of God, not the seat of government. That was sufficient for Jesus; it should be sufficient for us, too.

AFTERWORD FOR THE
PAPERBACK EDITION

I first thought about writing this book in early 2003—my second year in the Bush White House. One morning, while on vacation in Nashville, I was venting to my wife, Kim, and some friends about how horrible it was that Jesus' name was more synonymous with Republican politics than with his life, death, and resurrection. My point wasn't political. It was spiritual. Jesus was being sold out for politics. I wanted to write about it.

Kim and our friends agreed but also warned that it wasn't the right time for me to write such a book. It couldn't, they concluded, be written in anger. And I was clearly angry. It had to have a different context. It had to come from a different, better, spiritual place. The next night a seizure landed me in the emergency room with a brain tumor diagnosis. The book was promptly forgotten.

Two years later, however, the White House was in my rearview mirror. I had finished what can best be described as a "fast" from politics, having spent a lot of time in prayer, in caring for others, and for some months as a professional bass fisherman. I was in a very different place. That is when I started this book.

What resulted is the chronicle of a spiritual journey—a spiritual journey that got mixed up in the world of politics. It is not a White House tell-all or an attempt to settle political scores. Yet its initial release inevitably became a political event. Sound bites about the White House captured the media's attention, partly because politics has seduced us all; our culture is so political that we often see nothing but politics, wherever we look. The media loves political stories, but gets nervous about faith stories.

The political reaction was interesting. Many Christian conservatives were furious. Yet many Democrats were silent.

The Democrats had no idea what to say or do. A Democratic writer friend was on a conference call with Democratic strategists who advised that no one speak or write about the book because it might actually be a trap to sucker Democrats into saying something about God that would hurt them in the weeks to come.

Then there was the Christian fury. A man I used to go to church with—someone who had held a series of low-ranking political positions in the government—issued a press release saying that I was "Judas." A prominent journalist noticed the quote and wrote, "This only proves David Kuo's point—if he is Judas then the Christians really do think that George W. Bush is Jesus." Reporters started calling to warn me that the White House was preparing to "go nuclear" and that they had pulled out my old CIA records (from when I had worked there as a 22-year-old). They planned to say that I had been "let go" from the agency—funny, since after I resigned, the CIA tried to recruit me to another, more classified, position—and that I had an ax to grind. I wondered if they had already forgotten the name Valerie Plame. An old White House colleague told another friend that they "were prepared to use whatever level of attack necessary to deal with the problem."

Nothing from the White House really surprised me. It was how problems were dealt with. What was interesting to me, however, was the fact that when they attacked me, they never refuted a single one of the charges that I made . . . or their refutations were little sleights of hand. For example, I talked about how we used White House conferences for political ends, traveling to different political districts to pimp Republican candidates on the backs of the poor. One of the people they threw out to "counter" me said—with a straight face—that he had even traveled to meet with Democratic senator Tom Daschle. At least, he said that until a reporter asked him where the meeting was. He was forced to say that he had traveled all the way to Daschle's office . . . on Capitol Hill.

Evangelical Christian reaction was fierce. A columnist called me a "member of the Axis of Evil." Radio talk show hosts blared lies on their Web sites and on the air: "Kuo is telling Republicans to stay home on election day!" "Kuo is telling Christians to leave politics." "Kuo is being paid by Democrats to suppress the Christian vote." "Kuo is the proximate cause of global warming." Okay, not the last one.

That the Christians vociferously attacked my call for a "fast" from politics—not from voting, mind you—served only to intensify my belief in my message and in the need for a fast. The idea of taking even a temporary vacation from politics so as to devote time, energy, and attention to God and the poor seemed, to some, akin to saying Jesus was a communist. It was a breathtaking reaction. But it was also a politically useful one: they were using it to try to energize Christians who were otherwise disgusted by Republican political corruption.

If those were the troubling moments of the book's release, they were countered by a flood of support—often from unlikely sources. A senior campaign person from 2000 and 2004 wrote to say that he shared the same concerns, was deeply troubled, and applauded the message. E-mails from friends I knew and friends I would later make tumbled in. For every negative there was an equal and more powerful positive.

As I write this, it is Holy Week for Christians and there is, again, a lot of chatter about politics. Nothing changes, it seems; two thousand years ago the story was about politics, too, though Jesus resisted . . . to the point of his death.

This week the talk is about "the first primary" results for the 2008 presidential race, i.e., the race to collect the most funds. In order to be a legitimate presidential candidate next year, the conventional thinking goes, one has to raise buckets of dollars this year.

In the first quarter of 2007, Senator Hillary Clinton raised $26 million, Senator Barack Obama took in $25 million, and former senator John Edwards brought in $14 million. Former governor Mitt Romney took in north of $20 million, and former mayor Rudy Giuliani around $14 million. Collectively, Republicans raised a much smaller figure than Democrats. In talking to political-consultant friends, I learned the reason why: most conservative Christian donors aren't giving to anyone on the Republican side (or the Democratic side). They are voting with their dollars, and they are staying home.

Perhaps there just aren't any socially conservative candidates who have excited them. Yet two of the most religious candidates, Senator Sam Brownback and former governor Mike Huckabee, have raised a grand total of $3 million between them. Something is happening, something is changing.

That something is that Christians are fundamentally reexamining their political involvement. For whatever reason—dissatisfaction with Republicans, disillusionment with President Bush, the Iraq War—conservative Christians are doing something that hasn't happened in the last thirty years: they appear to be taking a step back from politics.

This past fall, the Reverend Joel Hunter, a mega-pastor from Orlando, turned down a job he had once wanted: leading the Christian Coalition. Why? Because the Christian Coalition leadership wanted to focus solely on abortion and homosexuality and because he didn't. "I want to expand the definition of 'pro-life,'" he told me, "because that is what Jesus did. He was always about including the outcast, protecting the vulnerable, and having compassion for the powerless."

Joel Hunter is not alone. In Florida, D. James Kennedy, a long-time religious Right leader, has shuttered the doors to his Center for Reclaiming America for Christ. The reason wasn't Kennedy's health issues. It was, the ministry said, a desire to return to its "core competency": getting Kennedy's teachings about Jesus out to more and more people.

Across the country, pastors are closing their pulpits to politicians and focusing instead on preaching Jesus and serving the poor. This fall, my favorite church in America, the St. Louis Family Church, continued sending scores of people down to Louisiana and the Gulf Coast to help rebuild lives. Some in Missouri thought those teams should go door to door for Senator Jim Talent in his ferocious race against Claire McCaskill. When I asked the pastor, Jeff Perry, if he was tempted to send people politicking, he laughed, "No way."

Then there is that most powerful pastor in America—not Jim

Dobson, not Pat Robertson, not Jerry Falwell. The most powerful pastor in America is Rick Warren, author of *The Purpose Driven Life*, the bestselling hardcover book in American history according to *Publishers Weekly*. He could have used his power to become a political kingmaker—as many encouraged him to do. Instead, he has encouraged people who listen to him to give of their time, their money, and their lives to helping the poorest of the poor. He has mobilized thousands of people from his church to help reshape the entire government at the behest of the president . . . of Rwanda. He has started a new plan to tackle what he calls the five greatest problems facing the world: Spiritual Emptiness, Egocentric Leadership, Extreme Poverty, Pandemic Diseases, and Illiteracy (lack of education). It is called the P.E.A.C.E. plan, and it plants churches, equips leaders, assists the poor, cares for the sick, and educates the next generation in Africa and elsewhere. Not too long ago, I asked him about the audacity of his vision. He smiled broadly and said, yeah, it is crazy, but that is the point. God doesn't get credit for things unless he is the only explanation for their success.

There is, of course, another side to this fight. There are still those who want to get churches *more* involved in politics. In 2005 and 2006, "Justice Sunday" and "Liberty Sunday" events were held in hundreds of churches across the country to try to mobilize Christians to support President Bush's picks for the United States Supreme Court and to support Republican candidates during the 2006 midterm elections. The organizers of those events are planning even larger ones in preparation for the 2008 presidential race. Is there anything wrong with having Christians involved in politics? No, of course not. The problem is simply one of priorities. What do Christians (like me) put first? Politics? Or God?

When Jesus arrived in Jerusalem for Passover, he did so with the broad expectation upon him that Israel's Messiah had finally come. Despite his talk about suffering and dying and living again, his disciples still saw him as the conquering political and military leader who would deliver Israel from its oppression at the hands of the Romans (among others).

Jesus *was* the Messiah—but of a different sort. He was the

Lamb of God; he was going to sacrifice himself for his people. He would conquer something greater than Rome. He was going to conquer death. And he did. In so doing, however, he disappointed many who wanted political conquest more than they wanted his spiritual conquest.

Why politics? Because then as now, politics is easy to understand. It has such clear lines. There are winners and losers. The promises are easy to understand, too: "Kick out the Romans." "Lower taxes." "Stop war." Politics is an easy religion.

It is a religion I stopped practicing for several years. It was a good and a needed break. Now, however, I have reengaged to a degree, in no small part because I want to speak out against the corruption of faith by politics. But that isn't all. I am in the process of interviewing presidential candidates for Beliefnet.com, and I write a blog that is partly political. I do believe in the power of politics to change people's lives and to be God's extended arm of justice and mercy. I want to support any leader who will alleviate poverty and fight disease. I don't see many who prioritize these issues, but then again, as I look back through history, a central truth shouts out: It takes just one, with the passion to rally everyone else.

Jesus' call is complicated, demanding, and so much harder than any political platform. Jesus calls us to say no to ourselves and to our lust for power. Jesus requires that we look at the world through a different lens—a lens of self-denying service. Jesus extends to us a love so powerful we cannot fully grasp it. And Jesus says that the best way to change lives is to give ours for others. That is the faith that should tempt us all.

ACKNOWLEDGMENTS

I am blessed with wonderful friends. I would like to keep all of them. Therefore I will not publicly thank a great many of them, presuming their endorsement for what I have written or exposing them to questions about their participation with me in this book.

There are, however, certain people who can't avoid ending up on this page—family, for instance. My family starts with Kim. I think I am supposed to save her for the end as a dramatic conclusion, but I can't wait that long. Anything I say about her will be only the dimmest shadow of who she is to me. She hasn't just saved my life during a car crash; she has made my life something far greater than I ever imagined it could be. If I am half as good to her as she is to me, I am the best husband to ever live.

God has given me three amazing daughters—Laura, Rachel, and Olivia. You are the best accomplishments of my life and the only ones that matter.

One day when you are (much!) older you will read these words (gulp!). There is a lot of raw truth in here about your dad, what he's done, what he thinks, and what he believes. In it all I hope you see God's hand shaping and molding me and making me, bit by broken bit, more like him.

I have always had a wonderful family. My parents were inspirations and still are, and my sisters Andrea and Sonya just get better and better the older I get. Their husbands have become my brothers—especially Christopher, whom I love and admire far more than he knows.

I am glad that Bob and Linda McCreery love me even after I

married their daughter, and I never get to see enough of Scott, Heather, or Micah.

Lynn Chu and Glen Hartley are really my friends, but they also happen to be my agents and therefore are stuck with me. They are smart, honest, kind, patient, and fun and provide invaluable insight and assistance.

Bruce Nichols is a wonderful editor and an even finer man. He is unfailingly honest, spectacularly bright, and endowed with great patience and mediocre taste in baseball teams.

Steve Waldman can't escape thanks either. I knew he was a great editor from past experience. But then it was his job. The help he gave me with this project went above and beyond any call of duty. Now he can get back to things he loves—diet tips, for instance.

Special thanks to members of the secret circle hill society—especially Tara and Jerry, whose friendship and love have saved me on many occasions. Nicole is a brilliant editor—she just doesn't know it yet—and her husband isn't too shabby, either. Barbara is like family and I really want to be like Mike—we all do.

Finally, to the General, thank you for showing me the way; and to Constantine, Hollywood, Viper, Jeffe, and the Archangel, you are my brothers. Strength and honor.

INDEX

279

Index

Index

O'Reilly, Bill, 233
Orthodoxy (Chesterton), 11

Packer, J. I., 262–263
Paige, Rod, 210
Parables, 60–61, 121, 240
Parents Music Resource Center, 51
Parshall, Janet, 171
Partial-birth abortion, 217
Pentagon, terrorist attack on, 184–186
People for the American Way, 190
Percy, Walker, 51
Perkins, Tony, 256
Perry, Jeff, 259–260
Perry, Patsy, 259
Philippines, 27
"Piss Christ," 118
Pitts, Joe, 73
Planned Parenthood, 266
Political Affairs Office, 158, 218, 229
Pornography, 76
Porter, John, 207
Poverty, 74–75, 82, 261, 267. *See also* Faith-based initiative
Powell, Colin, 78
Prader, Mark, 161
Presidential campaigns and elections
  1972, 11, 172
  1976, 4
  1980, 4
  1984, 4
  1988, 15, 28, 39, 112
  1992, 35, 37–38, 41–43, 51
  1996, 68, 73, 105, 118
  2000, 118, 123–133, 136, 177–178, 210–212, 227, 257
  2004, 141, 168, 177–178, 251, 252
Primary Colors (Klein), 115
Prince, Elsa, 141
Prison Fellowship, 11–12, 80
  InnerChange initiative, 128

Prison rape, 222
Privacy, right to, 33, 34
Pro-choice/Pro-life positions. *See* Abortion, 25, 26
Project for American Renewal, 82
Public Liaison Office, 158–159, 170–172, 189
Public/Private Ventures, 214, 215
Purpose Driven Life, The (Warren), 256, 266

Quayle, Dan, 98–100, 107, 124, 125, 128

Rangel, Charles, 175–176
Ray, Harold, 214
Reagan, Michael, 171
Reagan, Ronald, 4, 27, 40, 41, 64, 193, 230, 268
Red Cross, 196
Redemptive Life Fellowship Church, West Palm Beach, 214
Reed, Jack, 203
Reed, Ralph, 60, 68, 73, 76, 81, 88, 93, 105, 110, 176
  beginnings of Christian Coalition and, 28–29
  Bush, informal adviser to, 125
  Faith Factor by, 64–66
  National Press Club speech of, 66–67
  on Republican National Convention (1992), 42–43
  resignation from Christian Coalition, 106, 211
  Samaritan Project and, 105, 106, 164
  2000 campaign and, 211–212
Rehnquist, William, 33, 34
Reid, Harry, 256
Religious Equality Amendment, 76

288

Index

Index

Truman, Harry, 192
Tubb, Dick, 237–238
Tuition vouchers, 105
Turner, Tina, 7
Tutu, Desmond, 27
Tutwiler, Margaret, 155–156
2 Chronicles, 171–172

Unborn Child Pain Awareness Act,
    proposed, 266
United Church of Christ, 121
United Nations, 74
United Way, 108, 204
University of Redlands, 70
Unlevel Playing Field (Office of
    Faith-Based and Community
    Initiatives), 179, 195, 207
USA Freedom Corps, 200, 201

Value America, 122, 132
Vietnam War, 11

Wall Street Journal, 79
Wallace, George, 192
Wallis, Jim, 137
War on Poverty, 57, 86
Warren, Rick, 256, 266
Washington Post, 31, 50, 100–101,
    104–105, 107, 133, 206, 207,
    224, 254
Watergate, 95

Watts, J. C., 83, 93, 175
We Care America, 214
Wehner, Peter, 55, 56, 119, 130–131,
    221, 254
Weld, Bill, 48
Welfare, 58, 62, 63, 75, 80–82,
    86–87
Weyrich, Paul, 105–106, 121
White, Jeremy, 238, 239
White House Situation Room, 233
Whitewater, 54, 62
Wilberforce, William, 14, 18, 19, 56,
    176, 267
Will, George, 33, 56
Willett, Don, 138–141
*William L. Webster v. Reproductive
    Health Services* (1989), 15–16,
    18, 32
Williamson, Marianne, 149
Williamson, Martha, 148–149, 247
Wilson, James Q., 50
Wolf, Frank, 101
World Trade Center, terrorist attack
    on, 184, 187
World War II, 57, 70

Years of Upheaval (Kissinger), 56,
    131
Young, Ed, 125

Zogby, John, 122

291

ABOUT THE AUTHOR

David Kuo served as Special Assistant to President George W. Bush and Deputy Director of the Office of Faith-Based and Community Initiatives. He has worked for a diverse group of political leaders from William Bennett and John Ashcroft to Ted Kennedy and Gary Hart. Previously, he founded and launched The American Compass, a charitable organization designed to objectively evaluate the efficacy and efficiency of social service organizations. David has written speeches and articles for various leading political and business leaders, including Governor George W. Bush, Senator Bob Dole, Congressman J. C. Watts, and AOL founder Steve Case. He is the author of the Good Morning America Book Club selection *Dot.Bomb*. He is also a professional bass fisherman. He is married with four children and lives in Virginia. He is Washington editor for the Beliefnet Web site.